COMMUNICATION AND
CREATIVE DEMOCRACY:
Interdisciplinary Perspectives

Edited by
OMAR SWARTZ

Published 2011 by arima publishing

www.arimapublishing.com

ISBN 978 1 84549 456 8

© Omar Swartz 2011

Printed and bound in the United Kingdom

Typeset in Garamond 11/14

Abramis is an imprint of arima publishing.

arima publishing
ASK House, Northgate Avenue
Bury St Edmunds, Suffolk IP32 6BB
t: (+44) 01284 700321

www.arimapublishing.com

A democracy is more than a form of government; it is primarily a mode of associated living, of conjoint communicated experience.

--John Dewey, *Democracy and Education* (1916)

ACKNOWLEDGEMENTS

I would like to thank the participants to this volume for their hard work on their contributions. Over the past year, each chapter has been scrupulously rewritten and revised multiple times, and that takes a great deal of patience, not to mention considerable good will toward the editor. I have enjoyed working with each and everyone one of them. Indeed, I have enjoyed immensely my role as an editor.

I would also like to thank my family -- Rui Zhao, Avi Zhao Swartz, and Sue Swartz -- for their continual love and support for me and for my career. Without them beside me, I would have long ago fallen victim to what Nietzsche called the "stare of the abyss." What I am, I owe to them.

TABLE OF CONTENTS

Introduction: Expanding the Notion of Creative Democracy
Omar Swartz 1

Part I: Theorizing Creative Democracy

Chapter 1: What is Created by Creative Democracy? A Deweyan Take
    on Communication, Community, and Self-Creation
Scott R. Stroud..17

Chapter 2: Communication and the Emergence of the Public: John
    Dewey and Creative Democracy
Cynthia Gayman 41

Chapter 3: Leisure, Communication, and Politics: Cultivating Creative
    Democracy
Annette M. Holba 69

Chapter 4: En/Countering Frontiers of Moral and Physical Injustice:
    Disability Studies as Creative Democracy
Margaret Rose Torrell 99

Part II: Applying Creative Democracy

Chapter 5: Appreciating Conduct and Consequences Through
    Communication: Revisiting Community Through a Deweyan Lens
Musetta Durkee...127

Chapter 6: Reimagining Community Through Julie Laible's "Loving
    Epistemology"
Valerie Palmer-Mehta 155

Chapter 7: Click on Deweyan Democracy: John Dewey Joins the Online
     Literacy Debate
Shane J. Ralston 185

Chapter 8: Building Bridges Between Tellers and Listeners: The Role
     of Digital Storytelling in the Construction of Democratic Frameworks
Margaret Ann Clarke 209

Chapter 9: Etiquette as Common Ground: The Relevance of Rules Within
     Discourse Communities
Kirstin Ruth Bratt and *Moulay Youness Elbousty* 237

Chapter 10: Discourses that Shape Public Understanding and Use of
     Electronic Voting Technology: A Deweyan Perspective
Janet L. Evans 265

About the Editor 297

About the Contributors 299

INTRODUCTION

Expanding the Notion of Creative Democracy

Omar Swartz

University of Colorado Denver

A political community such as those found in western liberal and democratic societies can be regarded in different ways; emphasis is placed *either* on the responsibility and participation of informed citizens who comprise the core of democracy *or* on political institutions and processes, such as laws, courts, and elections. In the United States, emphasis is generally placed on the latter. Although valuable in and of themselves, such ruling bodies, procedures, and processes are often assumed *to be* democracy, ignoring more substantive expressions of democracy, such as a socially inclusive, participatory process that entails serious public deliberation for determining the public policies and laws that help society to function.

The provocative chapters making up this edited volume are intended to help scholars and activists theorize the former, ways to support the cultivation and practice of engaged citizenship. Specifically, they demonstrate that the political philosophy of John Dewey (1859-1952) remains important and heuristic for understanding and advancing contemporary discourses of participatory and deliberative democracy -- what the contributors explore collectively as a "creative democracy." The term *creative democracy* is, admittedly, vague, coming from a sentiment more implied than articulated in a short speech Dewey had written, but could not himself read, on the occasion of his 80th birthday (Dewey, 1939/1993a). At that time, Dewey expressed his concern that the mere existence of "legal guarantees of the civil liberties of free belief, free expression, and free assembly would be of little avail if in daily life freedom of communication, the give and take of ideas, facts, experiences, is choked by mutual suspicion, by abuse, by fear and hatred" (p. 234). For someone living in Dewey's time, this was no idle fear. The United States was under threat. Nazism and Soviet

Communism menaced the nation from abroad, while xenophobia, racism, and predatory capitalism threatened the nation from within.

Those days, thankfully, have receded into the distant past, and the world, in many aspects, is much brighter and better today. Dewey, however, would no doubt be disappointed to learn that, more than 70 years later, the United States -- freer in terms of constitutional protections and more socially inclusive than during his lifetime -- is still not the community he imagined. Specifically, he would be sad to find that we in the United States continue to exist in a culture "choked" by fear, suspicion, and hatred. Dewey would be angered that this fear was being stoked by our elected political leadership for political gain and that this practice was aided-and-abetted by an irresponsible mass media. He would lament the fact that such fear mongering has lead to America becoming an increasingly polarized and uncivil society, threatened economically and remarkably callous to the suffering of each other as we become a nation of "haves" and "have nots."

As I write this, I recall in my mind the iconic image of the Native American who appeared on television in public service announcements in the 1970s with tears running down his cheeks as the screen exhibited grotesque scenes of environmental degradation. This is how I picture Dewey in my mind's eye, an elderly grandfather figure watching over a citizenry which fights each other, often viciously, over class, racial, religious, and sexuality concerns. Perhaps it is time to think creatively about how we conceptualize our democracy and how we think about what it means to be a community. At the very least, we cannot take our past accomplishments for granted. We have come so far with so much promise to lose our vision now. The tremendous threats of the 21st century should not cause us to lose sight of the great promises of the age of Enlightenment which animated our nation's birth.

I have commissioned this book out of a faith in the power of creative democracy, whatever that term comes to mean. Perhaps because of its vagueness, I found, and continue to find, the idea of creative democracy powerfully compelling (see Swartz, Campbell, and Pestana, 2009), as a form of "critical theory" without the European baggage that often feels alien to an American audience. In an earlier work, *Neo-Pragmatism, Communication, and the*

Culture of Creative Democracy (2009), my co-authors and I explored how this important Deweyan notion can be cultivated and advanced through a heightened awareness of the ways in which communication shapes individuals and society.[1] Being social creatures, we exist because -- and through -- our efforts to communicate with others. Through communication we (re)invent ourselves. We conceptualized communication as an organic, constructive, and holistic form of human interaction and education, expressed in our daily struggles and joys of being-in-the-world. Communication, we argued, is existential and constitutive of our life experiences as human beings and knowledge of one-another; it is indicative of the relationship between self and others. Simply, we make sense of ourselves and our worlds through communicative action. Our profound humanism is situated here. Communication is powerful: our language enables us to construct social hierarchies and unequal relationships as well create the means by which we can challenge and subvert such relationships.

At the center of the creative democracy we envisioned is a rejection of what Dewey called the guardianship theory of democracy and "epistemarchy," which claims that knowledge and what is "good," "right," and "just" are accessible only by certain groups and not others. As a society, we will make greater gains in social justice when such thinking is recognized and resisted, and when more people are able to perceive the ways that they can use their agency for creative influence in shaping their local environments. This vision requires a communication of hope and resistance to dominating and oppressive ideologies and practices and, among other things, a questioning of normative disciplinary or legalistic thought (see Swartz, 2005). As we noted, the abolition of slavery, the attainment of women's suffrage, and the winning of the 40 hour work week were all achieved through sustained and committed *resistance* to the accepted Truths of their respective time -- that of a "natural order," a hierarchy "written" by some transcendent Authority in which, for instance, Whites were considered superior to Blacks, men were superior to women, and wealthy people were superior to the working class and the poor. These changes were also created through an alternative description of the way things can, and should, be: the way we can, collectively, *will* them. In so willing, we create the meaning we want to exist in the world.

In sum, our goal in *Neo-Pragmatism, Communication, and the Culture of Creative Democracy* was to help scholars, activists, educators, and citizens to rethink commonly accepted notions of community in order to imagine new possibilities for social, political, and economic organization -- new ways of imagining solidarity and citizenship with others, especially those who languish outside the range of our moral radar. It is through communicative action that we designate who in society is worthy of consideration and whose needs and interests are validated. Those people that exist on the margins of society, or outside the boundaries of community, are often denied fair representation, access, and adequate resources. This current book, of which I am the editor, *Communication and Creative Democracy: Interdisciplinary Perspectives*, is an extension and, in some sense, a refinement of my earlier project. All the chapter authors of this volume were given copies of my earlier work and asked to engage in it with their chapters, to take it as a starting point for their thinking to bring in divergent and multidisciplinary voices to this important topic. To various extents, each author has taken up my invitation to do so. What follows is the fruits of such labor.

Common Themes in This Volume

Before I discuss each chapter specifically, I want to review some themes common to all of them. This is important because, as the subtitle to this book stresses, this is an interdisciplinary volume, drawing on scholars in Communication Studies, Education, English, Modern Languages, and Philosophy, writing from three nations: the United States, Canada, and the United Kingdom.

First, each contributor follows Dewey in maintaining as an important axiom that "democratic ends require democratic methods for their realization" (Dewey, 1939/1993b, p. 205). Fundamentally, this means that people must be involved in the decisions that affect their lives. The revolution, so-to-speak, cannot be the product of any vanguard party, and there are no saviors waiting in the wings to miraculously intervene in our messy affairs. No magic formulas can save us; nothing, in short, can substitute for the hard work of each and every member of our community to create the worlds in which we want to live. Collectively, we need to get our house in order and no one else can do it for us. We either work together fairly and with mutual respect and understanding, or we continue to practice the same old politics with the same disastrous results for ourselves and the planet. For Dewey, the democratic methods of inquiry, deliberation, consultation, persuasion, negotiation, and cooperation, as difficult to practice as they may be, must be exercised in *all* arenas of social interaction, such as in the workplace and in schools. No administrator or benevolent bureaucrat can demand orthodoxy, allegiance, or stipulate truth. In short, Dewey argued that public involvement in deliberation must extend to all social relationships and aspects of culture, including economics, politics, education, art, and religion. Democracy, Dewey tells us time and again, is a way of thinking, being, a way of understanding what it means to interact with other people.

Second, and following from the first, the chapters all stress, along with Dewey, the *process* of democracy over any particular outcome. Dewey's (1920/1950) axiom that "growth is the only moral end" emphasized that the most critical element to democracy is an inclusive, community-oriented process of inquiry, deliberation, and experimentation, not a search for timeless truths or general theories. This point does not suggest that some outcomes, such as those that strive to ensure that all people have the ability to meet their basic needs and opportunities for personal development and civic participation, are not more desirable and better for furthering a democratic society. We are free to propose and argue for specific pre-conditions or political foundations for society. What it does mean, however, is that Dewey rejected the use of scientific or ethical deliberation to create a new authority of thought that would become a new hegemonic force (a new "epistemarchy"). To privilege a value or goal such as "social justice" is to express a social *preference*, in light of current options and current knowledge, for a way of being-in-the-world. As conditions change, we can always revise our thinking and try something different. According to the contributors to this volume, we may be at one of those junctures.

As a pragmatist thinker, Dewey was staunchly anti-foundationalist and stood against tendencies to systemize or create hierarchies which, he felt, impeded the human propensity for experimentation. Specifically, Dewey (1939/1993a) opposed quests of certainty and permanence because he recognized that "all ends and values that are cut off from the ongoing process [of education and experience] become arrests, fixations. They strive to fixate what has been gained instead of using it to open the road and point the way to new and better experiences" (p. 244). Such efforts to find certainty thwart the essential human ability to remain open, poised, and responsive to address new situations and challenges. Dewey's emphasis on a democratic process positioned society to be flexible, perceptive, agile, and able to respond to emerging challenges of the times with creative acumen.

Inquiry and deliberation are the primary aspects of the Deweyan democratic process. Dewey's notion of inquiry is modeled after a humanistic version of the scientific process that combines imagination, thorough information gathering, reasoning and consideration of implications, and a historical sensitivity to other cultures and ways of life. This process requires effective universal education for adults and children (which itself implies access to health care and nutrition, suitable clothing, as well as a safe and secure living environment), which focuses on helping people to be effective inquirers and deliberators. For Dewey, education is the most significant process for any society because it helps a society to become a *community* and provides a way for people to develop a sense for being distinctive members of their community as will an appreciation for the interrelatedness of all members of society. His view of education encompassed a pedagogy that included skills of critical inquiry, hands-on work, fostering creative problem-solving skills of students rather than providing answers, exploring one's thoughts and feelings, and being able to sustain deliberation without the security of a sense of certainty.

In Dewey's view, liberation is the self-realization of a person developed through the process of contributing to a common good. This democratic vision engages a dialectical relationship between the self and community, in which Dewey argued that people's self-realization could be achieved through the process of mutual inquiry, communication, and the moral development that accompanies such communion with others. The democratic process is one that both embraces and emerges from active dialogue among people with differing and diverse perspectives and values. To cooperate, as Dewey (1939/1993a) asserted, "by giving differences a chance to show themselves because of the belief that the expression of difference is not only a right of the other persons but is a means of enriching one's own life-experience, is inherent in the democratic personal way of life" (p. 244).

Third, the contributors all recognize that the problem (or opportunity) of the democratic society is a *moral* issue, dependent more on intelligence, education, communication, and participation than on the political machinery of a society. Democratic society starts with *us*, with the choices *we* make every day in our lives. When people are knowledgeable about the implications and consequences of their various beliefs and actions, they are better equipped to participate in developing actions and resolutions to problems. *How* something gets done, therefore, follows from *what* should be done. What should be done is developed from the deliberation that ensues from a public with the capability and opportunity to participate in this deliberation. In Dewey's words:

> The freedom which is the essence of democracy is above all the freedom to develop intelligence, intelligence consisting of judgment as to what facts are relevant to action and how they are relevant to things to be done, and a corresponding alertness in the quest for such facts. To what extent we are actually democratic will in the end be decided by the degree to which the existing totalitarian menace awakens us to deeper loyalty to intelligence, pure and undefiled, and to the intrinsic connection between it and free communication. (1941/1993c, p. 208)

From a Deweyan perspective, a fully developed participatory democracy cannot be actualized within a system that excludes effectively entire classes of people from civic engagement. For democracy to exist meaningfully in the U.S., a commitment to *substantive democracy* is crucial. This means, among other things, that we become committed as a nation to strengthening and enforcing laws against discrimination, promoting affirmative action throughout all walks of life, and developing other proactive social policies to combat de facto segregation and economic inequality among all our citizens. In this important Deweyan sense, democracy cannot be separated from substantive equality or economic democracy. Poverty, in this view, betrays democracy and, along with it, the potential of our collective humanity.

Fourth, the chapters all exemplify Dewey's vision of democracy being an expression of the commitment to utilize human creative potential to work toward a better future and to continuously improve the quality and experience of life for all members of society. Dewey's sense of democracy is an attitude and orientation toward fellow human beings that values the freedom of all people to develop their potential "in harmony" with the common good. Democracy, in this sense, is a process of claiming one's power, engaging in the project of self-creation, and participating in the continual formation of one's community. In this view, democracy is a constant state of creativity and transformation from old ideas and norms to new ones, rather than a set of social and political institutions or a specific set of values that, once created, need only be encapsulated and codified into law. In fact, such institutions are inherently conservative, having verified or mummified old ideas and values at the expense of the new.

Fifth, throughout this book, the contributors privilege communication as central for thinking about how we come to know ourselves and our society and maintain that a significant part of such knowledge derives from interaction with other human beings. This interaction includes everything from face-to-face communication to a single individual sitting down and reading a book written by another. Regardless of the medium, once we engage in symbolic co/construction and interpretation, we are inevitably recreating and affirming our interconnectedness with other human beings. It is within this recurrent symbolic practice that we develop both personal and social identities as well as entrenched -- to the point of seeming natural and given -- ideas about acceptable social stratification and allocation of resources. Symbolic interaction with others is vital because we also assume that our personal knowledge becomes richer and more profound once it is challenged in dialogue with those who might hold alternative perspectives or opinions.

Overview of Chapters

I have organized this book into two sections. In Part I (Chapters 1-4), the contributors help us to theorize Dewey's notion of creative democracy so that its usefulness as a political goal to be worked toward becomes more evident. In

Part II (Chapters 5-10) the contributors apply the concept to a range of contexts to demonstrate its practical utility in the here-and-now.

In Chapter 1, Scott R. Stroud explores how Dewey consistently and consciously designed his political and moral philosophy to take seriously the process whereby communication reflects and shapes our psychological habits. In so doing, Stroud describes how a Deweyan account of creative democracy involves notions of individuality within both an intrapersonal and interpersonal context. In light of this, the goal of a functioning society is to maximize the harmony of each of these aspects, both in regard to an agent and the system of agents as a whole, and that an important manner by which such a harmonization of community and individual occurs is through the communicative reshaping of individual orientations toward self and others. Crucially, he argues, humans create their community through their communicative habits and can *recreate* themselves by altering these habits though attention to their communication practices. An understanding of this potential highlights both Dewey's ameliorative and critical perspectives that are fundamental to his philosophy and are essential to the success of the creative democracy that we are sketching.

In Chapter 2, Cynthia Gayman explores how diverse discursive practices within a pluralistic society may function to obstruct recognition of shared problems, preventing formulation of mutually beneficial outcomes. This pheneomona compromises the emergence of what John Dewey called the *Public* -- the sphere of communicative exchange and democratic process. Threats to this sphere portend a crisis for our society which is complicated by a cacophony of pseudo exchanges disguised by spectacle and disagreement in which meaningful communication does not take place. Gayman sees allegiance to group-identified frames of meaning as part of the problem and she uses, by way of example, a portion of the 2008 interviews conducted by the Reverend Rick Warren of Saddleback Church of then-Presidential candidates Barak Obama and John McCain to show how disparate frames of meaning prevent real communication from taking place. She argues that democratic process creatively re-engaged necessitates first a Deweyan problematization of today's communicative crisis, for the real challenges and seemingly intractable disagreements facing contemporary society cannot be evaluated or addressed until factors undermining the emergence of the discursive public sphere are seen and known.

In Chapter 3, Annette M. Holba explores how, by enabling people to contemplatively play with ideas that can revision new possibilities of creative citizenry especially for those citizens who may have experienced limits or challenges in their contribution and participation in the public forum -- the engagement of philosophical leisure in the lives of individual citizens can cultivate or contribute to Dewey's notion of creative democracy. She discusses how philosophical leisure has the potential to move citizens from *spectators* to *participants* in the shaping of their own human existence and concludes with practical historical examples that offer social, political, and philosophical implications of the integration of philosophical leisure into a public sociopolitical wellness. She specifically explores how folk music, practiced as an action of leisure, cultivated the oppressed lives of African slaves during the years in which slavery was a legal and common practice in the United States, especially in the south, as well as a consideration of the music that shaped and moved the civil rights movement in the US.

In Chapter 4, Margaret Rose Torrell examines how disability studies draws from the communicative action and community spirit of Dewey's creative democracy to work toward a general vision of social justice. Cornerstones of disability studies reflect Deweyan principles, including the communication of the real lived experiences of disabled people in order to bring about equality in accessibility and provide a diversity of models of disabled experience; the linguistic work of repositioning the disabled/abled binary and re-composing disabled identity on disabled people's own, often empowered, terms; and the establishment of disability as a sub-community with a unique history, story, and culture. These revisions to hegemonic, ableist thinking challenge the constrictive thought patterns held by both dominant (nondisabled) and marginalized (disabled) groups and provide examples of the types of "human creativeness" and communicative action needed to traverse the moral and physical frontiers of social injustice for the disabled community. As part of the democratic task of creating a freer and more humane society that values and includes everyone, Torrell demonstrates how we can turn to disability studies for additional information on how to use communication to counter other frontiers of social injustice.

Part II of the book begins with Chapter 5, in which Musetta Durkee discusses the precarious balance between the positive effects of communities as inclusionary spaces and relationships that foster trust, solidarity, and democratic engagement and the negative effects of communities as exclusionary mechanisms that create boundaries of "us versus them" and that breed distrust and blind loyalties. She argues that an important method for achieving such differentiated inclusivity in democratic participation and decision-making is through emphasizing the need for communication within and between communities. Not only is communication a prerequisite for the participation in activities and sharing by which to constitute a "community" (as opposed to "society"), communication is also an essential component of the dialectical process through which moral changes in communities and the culture at large occur. She explores how communication assists in creating differentiated solidarity and how current advances in information and communications technologies have created an unprecedented opportunity and environment for Dewey's "Great Community" to be realized.

In Chapter 6, Valerie Palmer-Mehta offers a practical perspective for helping us to re-imagine our democratic community grounded in the most natural and healthy of human resources: what she calls a "loving epistemology." This concept, originally designed as a corrective for academic practices that mute the voices of non-dominant peoples in research, can be a fundamental component for re-imagining democratic community in the 21st century. A loving epistemology requires intellectually minded people to consider fully the implications of our research on others, ensuring that we are doing no harm to others. The loving epistemology also demands that our research reflects the reality of our subjects' lives, equips people to resist oppression, and moves people to take action. Finally, the loving epistemology asks scholars to consider whether our own epistemology enables us to truly understand the lived reality of those who are different from us. This radical approach is necessary to transform our democracy into a sustainable and fully participatory society (i.e., a "creative democracy") that long has been part of the American cultural mythos but which has been difficult to effectuate in political practice.

In Chapter 7, Shane Ralston provides a discussion of a crucial adult literacy in our technological age. He explores how, over the past fifteen years, a heated educational policy debate has erupted over the issue of whether electronic media contribute to youth and adult illiteracy. Ralston notes how the online literacy debate has centered on sociological surveys, neurological studies, and impressionistic evidence concerning how online reading habits affect basic literacy skills. He then reorients the debate in a more normative and historical direction, specifically focusing on how we might redesign educational environments and institutions to overcome previously entrenched and obstructive dualisms. In reconstructing a "debate" between John Dewey and conservative educational critic E. D. Hirsch, Ralston demonstrates that it is possible to bridge the divide between the debate's two sides by reframing it, not as an empirical question of what methods produce measurable improvements in literacy, but as an aspirational question of how to promote multi-literacy in a thriving democracy regardless of partisan politics.

In Chapter 8, Margaret Ann Clarke discusses ways in which the use of digital media may contribute to the culture of a creative democratic politics. In particular, she focuses on the genre and practice of "digital storytelling," whereby the life stories and personal histories of citizens are collected, archived, and disseminated within educational, social. and participatory projects linked within a broader context of a democratic and participatory community with rights to public participation. Her chapter, based on comparative case studies drawn from the United States and Latin America, focuses on the ways in which digital stories, once created and amassed, may be converted into a form of "public scaffolding," an integral part of social organization enabling multiple forms of dialogue, communication and interaction with local communities, political and social networks and other forms of media. She concludes with suggestions for how this genre can become a praxis contributing to a concept of democracy as a process of both political and cultural engagement, "recomposition" and a broadening of the "horizons of expectation" on the part of citizens.

In Chapter 9, Kirstin Ruth Bratt and Youness Elbousty expand our discussion of creative democracy through the rhetoric of etiquette proposed by Emily Post during Dewey's lifetime, problematizing taken-for-granted teaching practices and assumptions to examine a trajectory of privilege that includes the mastery of grammar, etiquette, and rhetorical devices. As they explore, the teaching of etiquette is inescapably linked to the indoctrination (i.e., education) of children into adult society. Post focuses on etiquette as an opportunity to create equality and explore democratic principles, yet the problem of social stratification still persists in her work and, thus, provides an opportunity for scholarly inquiry into the nature and practice of hegemony. Specifically, their chapter examines how the teaching of grammar as a practice of etiquette helps to maintain the social order, making a creative democracy that much more difficult to construct.

In Chapter 10, Janet L. Evans explores how voting, an act of communication, constitutes a potently symbolic cultural practice. Voting machines are one tool United States' citizens currently use to vote, a technological artifact that some consider neutral or ambivalent and others consider dangerous and controlling. As a result, the development and use of electronic voting technology forms a symbolic site of struggle among different groups attempting to establish the legitimacy and authority of their preferred narratives regarding how that technology should be designed and used. At the center of this discussion is the public, the ordinary citizen, who can be pivotal in shaping the discourse which directs the next steps of electronic voting technology development. In the struggle for control of the form and process of this rapidly changing technology, the citizen -- as Dewey envisioned -- has a voice to create change as surely as she or he has an opportunity to vote and have that vote counted in the next election.

In all, what I hope to accomplish with this book is a conceptual framework for understanding what it means to be an engaged citizen. My goal, and an important goal of the contributors to this volume, is to highlight the many possibilities open to us as human beings if we could reorient our relationships with one another and move from isolation and alienation to community and interdependence. Because the ills of our social world are human constructions, we have the ability to re-imagine and re-invent a world absent debilitating social stratifications and unjust consolidation of resources. We need simply the patience and will-power to do so.

REFERENCES

Dewey, J. (1993a). Creative democracy: The task before us. In D. Morris & I. Shapiro (Eds.), *The political writings* (pp. 240-245). Indianapolis, IN: Hackett. (Original published 1939)

---. (1993b). Democratic ends need democratic methods for their realization. In D. Morris & I. Shapiro (Eds.), *The political writings* (pp. 205-206). Indianapolis, IN: Hackett. (Original published 1939)

---. (1993c). The basic values and loyalties of democracy. In D. Morris & I. Shapiro (Eds.), *The political writings* (pp. 207-209). Indianapolis, IN: Hackett. (Original published 1941)

---. (1950). *Reconstruction in philosophy.* (Original work published in 1920)

Swartz, O. (2005). *In defense of partisan criticism: Communication studies, law, & social analysis.* New York: Peter Lang.

---, Campbell, K. and Pestana, C. (2009). *Neo-pragmatism, communication, and the culture of creative democracy.* New York: Peter Lang.

Note

[1] I would like to acknowledge the input of Katia Campbell and Christina Pestana, my co-authors on that earlier project, on some of the ideas expressed in this introduction.

Part I: Theorizing Creative Democracy

CHAPTER 1

What is Created by Creative Democracy?
A Deweyan Take on Communication, Community, and Self-Creation

Scott R. Stroud
University of Texas at Austin

On his train ride to start his new job at the University of Chicago in 1894, John Dewey witnessed something he found astonishing. While desiring to arrive at his destination on time, he nevertheless became a captive observer of the large-scale Pullman railway strike. Instead of the normal disdain a train rider might have felt toward the disruptive strike of railway workers, Dewey was enthralled by the coordinated activities of the various railway unions. Thousands of railway workers banded together for a cause that transcended their own immediate self-interest as wage-earners who lived paycheck-to-paycheck. Indeed, their actions put each at risk for losing their jobs -- or worse (Swartz, 2004). Dewey wrote to his wife, Alice, of his encounter with a labor organizer during the strike:

> I only talked with him 10 or 15 minutes but when I got through my nerves were more thrilled than they had been for years; I felt as if I had better resign my job teaching and follow him around till I got into life. One lost all sense of the right or wrong of things in admiration of his absolute, almost fanatic, sincerity and earnestness, and in admiration of the magnificent combination that was going on. Simply as an aesthetic matter, I don't believe the world has seen but few times such a spectacle of magnificent, widespread union of men about a common interest as this strike evinces. (Dewey, 2008, 1894.07.02)

Dewey was amazed at the shared interest, absorption, and engagement he witnessed in this massive organized movement of workers. Moreover, he was fascinated by what the existence of such interests *created* in terms of human actions and organization. This experience was an important moment in the formation of Dewey's later thought out of his earlier work on democracy and psychology.[1] As Robert B. Westbrook (1993) points out, "The Pullman strike was not only a radicalizing experience for Dewey, it also illustrated a key point in his democratic theory, for it opened to view the moral shortcomings of a paternalistic brand of 'welfare capitalism' which failed to cultivate workers' capacity for autonomous participation in social life" (p. 88-89). The strike was clearly important for Dewey's passionate -- but evolving -- thought on what the ideal community would look like.

Fast-forward forty-five years later to 1939. On the evening of his 80th birthday, John Dewey had a dear friend read an address he wrote titled "Creative Democracy -- The Task before Us" (1939/1988). In this late iteration of his political philosophy, we find Dewey enthralled by the same image as that offered by the Pullman strike -- a lively, engaged community centering around shared interests. The only difference, four decades later, is that he describes this type of community as a *creative democracy*. This begs the question: what exactly is created in "creative democracy?" Even in the 1939 essay bearing that title, Dewey only uses the word "creative" once in the final sentence. Thus, the meaning of this term is far from clear. We are left to provide an account of how "creative democracy" relates to central concerns in Dewey's account of community and communication. In attempting to meet this challenge, this chapter will explicate two important, but still unclear, topics in Dewey's work: *creative democracy* and *communication*. Drawing upon Dewey's early work on individuality, I will argue that creative democracy is way of interacting with others such that *selves* of a certain sort are created. Part of this argument, of course, will be in specifying what sort of self we ought to create in, and through, such community.

Further, I will explicate communication as a vital way that self-realization (or more accurately, self-creation) occurs. Many claim that communication "constitutes" one's self or community or that our selves are created by communication (e.g., Charland, 1987). Dewey's political and moral philosophy, both late and early, provide us with a powerful way of specifically explaining this point -- communication reflects our formed psychological habits, and it also shapes these habits. Certain general mental habits that I have identified in my previous work on Dewey -- what I call "orientations" -- are of particular importance, since they govern how we approach and conceptualize our self, others, and what is of value in the world (Stroud, 2006). Thus, a Deweyan account of creative democracy will be argued to involve three important characteristics: (1) a notion of individuality formed in regard to internal (intrapersonal) and external aspects (social), (2) the idea that the goal of a functioning society is to maximize the harmony of each of these aspects, both in regard to an agent and the system of agents as a whole, (3) that a key way such a harmonization of community and individual occurs is through the communicative reshaping of individual orientations toward self and others. In this way, creative democracy features communication as a primary way of creating selves of a certain desired sort. In an important sense, we create our community through our habits related to communication, and we create ourselves by altering these habits though the means of communication. This is important from what Dewey would call a meliorative or critical perspective precisely because such an understanding of creative democracy and communicative habit would give us the means to reshape and expand our present community experiences.

Morality and Creativity

When a person thinks of "creativity," his or her thoughts are naturally drawn to the realm of art. Is it not, after all, great artists who create great objects, such as wonderful works of art? If this rarefied notion of creativity is what an individual has in mind, s/he will be perplexed by Dewey's application of "creative" in regard to democracy. Dewey uses this term precisely because, for him, the aesthetic (and the creative) are not mutually exclusive from the moral; instead, moral activity at its best *is* an exercise in creativity. For instance, Dewey closely connects the aesthetic and artistic to the moral in his early work. In his *Outlines of a Critical Theory of Ethics* (1891/1969), he writes:

> If the necessary part played in conduct by artistic cultivation is not so plain, it is largely because "Art" has been made such an unreal Fetich -- a sort of superfine and extraneous polish to be acquired only by specially cultivated people. In reality, living is itself the supreme art; it requires fineness of touch; skill and thoroughness of workmanship; susceptible response and delicate adjustment to a situation apart from reflective

analysis; instinctive perception of the proper harmonies of act and act, of
man and man. (p. 316)

There is a deep sense of "art" at work here that goes beyond a notion of artistic
activity that many often connect to the aesthetic. Art has less to do with certain
institutionalized objects in museums, say, and more with how activity can be
undertaken. Life is simply a collection of activities and processes, so Dewey
implies that there is an art of undertaking all of these activities. "Art" in such
activities would not imply the habitual or mindlessly routine, of course; rather,
art would be connected to novelty, freshness of meaning, and attentiveness to
new details. These are the sort of qualities we put into the concept of
"creativity." Thus, we must expect that creativity is closely bound to this notion
of the artfully-lived life. I turn now to explore how might creativity fit into moral
activity.

In one sense, the connection of creativity to moral activity occurs through
the exercise of imagination (Fesmire, 2003). This is what tones the discussion of
deliberation in Dewey's (1932/1989) portion of his *Ethics*. Deliberation is an
imaginative process of reflecting on conflicting desires, needs, and so on. There
is yet another sense of creativity at work in Dewey. From Dewey's early
"idealist" phase to his later "instrumentalist" phase, he never stopped arguing
that we *created* our characters through our actions. For instance, a student who is
an engrained cheater would cheat on a particular exam because he or she has
built up certain habits or dispositions toward cheating through past cheating.
Additionally, each instance of cheating on tests further strengthens those habits,
making the next decision to cheat that much easier. In this way, character leads
to certain actions, and certain actions build specific kinds of character. Thus,
moral experience is fundamentally creative -- it shapes and forms who we are
now, as well as who we will be in future experiences.

In Dewey's later work, creativity in moral experience becomes read in terms
of "habits." Habits are modifications of the subject in light of some
environment (Dewey, 1922/1988). Habits are formed from past experiences and
projectively shape future experiences. They are not simply repetitive bodily
actions (such as nail biting). Instead, Dewey's notion of habit encompasses
bodily functions as well as mental dispositions. For instance, individuals have

various habits of problem solving, some good and some that need improvement (Dewey, 1933/1989). How one reacts to a problem and its potential solution *is* a habit -- it has been formed by past experience (perhaps formal schooling), and it projects activity in future experiences (searching for certain indicators or evidence, say). Indeed, Dewey claims that the "essence of habit is an acquired predisposition to *ways* or modes of response, not to particular acts" (1922/1988, p. 32). These dispositions are created by acting in certain ways, and in turn, increase the likelihood of us reacting in certain ways in future situations. As Dewey (1932/1989) states, "our actions not only lead up to other actions which follow as their effects but they also leave an enduring impress on the one who performs them, strengthening and weakening permanent tendencies to act" (p. 170). These tendencies, of course, are what we call "habits."

Thus, the key to our unraveling of Dewey's notion of creative democracy will start with the bedrock of habit -- the lived interconnection of some organism to some environment in some present situation. This is the meeting place between a subject's original or acquired impulses toward activity and the resisting or enabling environment. As the environment resists or becomes an obstacle to our impulse-driven activity, reflective thought comes in, aids our activity, and our habits affecting future impulses and activities are consequently altered. As he writes in the second section of the *Ethics*, "Now every such choice sustains a double relation to the self. It reveals the existing self and it forms the future self" (1932/1989, p. 286-287). Action is shaped by impulse and habitual patterns of discharge, and the self is, in turn, shaped (in terms of its habits) by that action. The self is not only *revealed* by its actions, it is also *created*. Creativity is a vital part of Dewey's moral theory primarily because he conceives of us as active shapers of our self-hood in, and through, experience.

The Individual and the Social

The self both expresses and creates itself through its actions. The way it specifically does this is through the embodied medium of habit. Yet, individuals live in social settings, which not only introduces an interpersonal aspect to their selfhood, but also affects the status of their future well-being. In Dewey's early work, a reader sees clearly the engagement of individual and social settings. For instance, one of Dewey's earliest writings on democracy discusses the highly valued part of individuals being "personality" (Dewey, 1888/1969). He leaves this topic relatively unanalyzed until he clarifies the notion of "individuality" in his *Outlines of a Critical Theory of Ethics* (Dewey, 1891/1969). There he points out that there are

> two factors -- or better two aspects, two sides -- in individuality. On one side, it means special disposition, temperament, gifts, bent, or inclination; on the other side, it means special station, situation, limitations, surroundings, opportunities, etc. Or, let us say, it means *specific capacity* and *specific environment*. Each of these elements, apart from the other, is a bare abstraction and without reality. Nor is it strictly correct to say that individuality is constituted by these two factors together. It is rather, as intimated above, that each is individuality looked at from a certain point of view, from within or from without. (pp. 301-302)

Dewey's later work discusses this point in more biological terms -- bringing in notions of "impulse" and "habit" -- but the same sort of equation is still present. *Who* an individual *is* comes from a mixing of *internal* aspects (desires, talents, impulses, etc.) and *external* contexts (opportunities, demands from others, etc.).

Of course, Dewey aptly notes that these notions of "specific capacity" and "specific environment" are abstractions when considered as separate from the other. As in his later discussion of habit (e.g., Dewey 1922/1988), what sense can be made of *only* considering the subject side of a habit? Breathing is a habit that takes place in the lungs *and* in regard to a specific environment (viz., the air at a certain place). But Dewey's point here in the 1890's is the same in later works -- when the mix or balance between the internal pushes of a human and the obstacles/resources of its environment is optimal and continuous, the *experience* of that individual will be of maximal quality. In his early work, Dewey calls this "progressive adjustment," whereas in his later work he refers to this as "growth." Both imply the optimal engagement of an organism with its environment in a sustainable, beneficial fashion.

Theorists must connect this notion of individuality to the previous notion of habit, as the latter term carries much weight in Dewey's later work in social/political philosophy. Experience will be toned depending on the match or mismatch between specific capacity and specific environment. In many cases, the latter denotes a social environment, including the expectations others place on an individual (due to their role or relational placement). Experience, or "function" as he calls it in the 1890's, is the melding together of individual pushes to action and social environment. Experience can go felicitously, or it could involve a jarring quality, such as when an artistically inclined individual is placed in a situation that prohibits free expression with artistic media (for instance, a gifted painter forced into the activity of accounting).[2] The mismatch between the specific capacity and the environment *creates* a less-than-desirable quality of experience. Habits of using certain talents or gifts or interests in a certain way (painting, say), are de-emphasized, and habits pertaining to the other activity (using math, say) are begrudgingly emphasized and formed. Due to the potential lack of skill or interest in such an individual, the latter habits may not be gained fully or in an efficient form. A self is still created, but perhaps not the sort we envision in the fully functioning arrangement of individual agents (viz., a society). This fully functioning arrangement is connected to a certain sort of experience -- that of "growth."

Dewey discusses this notion of "growth" in his *Art as Experience* (1934/1989). There growth is construed as an organism reaching equilibrium between its needs and impulses and the resources (both sustaining and resisting) that the environment holds. Two things must be noted about this notion of growth. First, the needs that drive the organism to further interaction with some environment are functionally equivalent to "specific capacity" -- needs, desires, talents that push for employment, and so on are all projective elements of an individual that can nurtured or stymied in present experience. Second, note that environments are seldom one-dimensional. They not only hold resources and obstacles to an individual's present project (driven by their idiosyncratic needs and desires), but they also hold similar resources and obstacles for a plethora of other ways of engaging that environment. Growth comes when a certain way of engaging the environment results in a successful equilibrium being reached. This is the full "functioning" of an individual in Dewey's early work. This optimal sort of experience not only successfully connects the individual's capacities with a certain environment; it also sets up future equilibrium reaching. Thus, there is a notion of sustainability present in Dewey's idea of growth. Individuality or optimal experience (that involved in growth) does not end with a specific success; true successes in light of a certain environment result in a present harmony *and* the increased probability of reaching future harmonies between organism and environment. As Dewey (1934/1989) explains, "growth signifies that a varied series of change enters upon intervals of pause and rest; of completions that become the initial points of new processes of development" (p. 29).

This notion of growth or adjustment does not merely involve *natural* environments -- they are mostly applicable to the *social* environments that condition most human life. Dewey talks about specific social environments as being measured against the *best* sort of experience -- democratic experience. Dewey sees the ideal society as a democracy. "Democracy," in this sense, does not simply imply a political decision-making scheme, but instead indicates a deeper way of relating to one's fellow individuals in some social setting (Pappas, 2008). This ideal will enshrine the high points of individuality or functioning -- the ideal interconnection of individual capacities and surrounding environment. Thus, in Dewey's response to Walter Lippmann's (1922/2004) concerns about the applicability of democracy to the American context, the democratic ideal is noticeably given a wider scope than one might anticipate. He argues that the "democratic ideal" can be conceived from two vantage points:

> From the standpoint of the individual, it consists in having a responsible share according to capacity in forming and directing the activities of the groups to which one belongs and in participating according to need in the values which the groups sustain. From the standpoint of the groups, it demands liberation of the potentialities of members of a group in harmony with the interests and goods which are common. Since every individual is a member of many groups, this specification cannot be fulfilled except when different groups interact flexibly and fully in connection with other groups. (Dewey, 1927/1984, p. 327-328)

In this passage, we see the issue of individuality and the sort of creative experience that lies behind the formation of individuals connected to groups in a normative fashion. The best sorts of individual experience and individuality occurs when individuals are part of groups that (1) allow them an active role and (2) allow for the possession of shared interests both inside and outside the group. Individual capacity and impulse is eventually stymied in groups that do not value that individual and her/his potential role in directing the activities of that group. Such group experience leans toward the creation of a "following self," and many individuals do not see their interests and capacities best suited by being such a self. Thus, the jarring begins between the self many want to create, and the self (and its habits) that are fostered by such "top-down" groups as those represented in caste-based or dictatorial societies. Inherent limits are put on individual action, development, and interaction in such groups, and these limits will (more likely than not, from the point of view of liberalism) lead to frustration and disharmony.

Active membership in a group, however, does not exhaust what Dewey sees in the ideal of democracy. The ideal also includes the *sort* of interests involved. In the best settings, the group involves a shared interest among its members that fosters continuing harmony and functioning in interpersonal interactions. Groups that set each member *against* each other will create certain qualities of interaction and communication, qualities that do not reach the high-point of functioning Dewey puts into his democratic ideal. Even if there is some solidarity in a group's shared interest, the flourishing of its members can be impaired by the conflicts fostered between that group and other groups in a larger social setting. Dewey gives the example of a robber band:

> [A member of this group] may express his powers in a way consonant with belonging to that group and be directed by the interest common to its members. But he does so only at the cost of repression of those of his potentialities which can be realized only through membership in other groups. The robber band cannot interact flexibly with other groups; it can act only through isolating itself. It must prevent the operation of all interests save those which circumscribe it in its separateness. (Dewey, 1927/1984, p. 328)

The robber's group affiliation sets him at variance with the interests and expectations of most other groups in his social environment, and thus would limit the sort of growth or adjustment possible to this individual. The robber would not trust these other group members, nor would he ever get too close to them. Secrecy and closed communication would be fostered, not the sort of varied, rich, and growing connections that Dewey sees as valuable among individuals in a social setting.

Where does this leave us? The reader can see that moral experience is *creative* in that it involves and shapes one's habits, the essential constituents of who we are. In an important sense, we create ourselves through the experiences we have. Optimal moral experience is that of full "functioning" or "growth," which involves harmony or equilibrium between an individual's capacities and his/her specific environment. The self we want to create is one that has a set of habits that is progressively adjustable to a variety of situations, a point Dewey emphasizes in his work on education and its connection to growth (see, for instance, Dewey, 1916/1985). The next question to ask becomes obvious -- How do we *create* such a self that is more likely to experience fulfilling present situations?

Dewey on Communication and Community

Dewey so often praised science and scientific modes of inquiry, one may be tempted to say that the way to create the sort of selves we ought to create would be through the interventions of science. Indeed, Dewey's praise of science in his corpus has led many to charge him of "scientism" or the belief that all important claims of knowledge and/or value come from the scientific community (see discussions of Dewey's relation to science in Johnston, 2006; Rorty, 1991). This answer of science, while touching on the important point of method in inquiry, misses the *communicative* part of Dewey's reading of ideal social arrangements. For instance, let us start with a vitally important passage from Dewey's answer to Lippmann -- his *The Public and its Problems* (1927/1984). While Lippmann was skeptical about achieving a true democratic community on the large scale that the U.S. posed, Dewey was eternally hopeful. The latter believed that we can turn our "Great Society" into something qualitatively distinct -- the "Great Community." In discussing this democratic endpoint, Dewey claims that it will take place when two conditions hold. He asserts that the "highest and most difficult kind of inquiry" and "a subtle, delicate, vivid and responsive art of communication" must occur in order for the farthest-reaching sense of democracy to prevail in a modern community. When these two conditions are met, democracy "will come into its own, for democracy is a name for a life of free and enriching communion. . . . It will have its consummation when free social inquiry is indissolubly wedded to the art of full and moving communication" (p. 350).

Others, such as Lary S. Belman (1977), pick up on the science/inquiry portion of these claims, but fail to account for what Dewey means by the "art of full and moving communication." Nathan Crick (2004) has examined Dewey's work for the connection of art and communication, but as I explain elsewhere (Stroud, 2008), such an account still misses the relevance of Dewey's philosophy of communication to what we can call "everyday communication." Our everyday activities such as interpersonal interaction and argument consume much of our communicative energy, and these consequently shape the sort of social person we are. In other words, communication with others is a vital part of self-creation, and Dewey's democratic ideal is an attempt to specify what *type* or *quality* of communication we ought to encourage.

What does Dewey mean by "artful" communication? We first need to see what he believes "communication" denotes. In his most extensive discussion of communication, Dewey (1925/1988) points out that communication is "of all affairs . . . the most wonderful thing" (p. 132). Communication is important as it involves three main features. First, it involves the participation of multiple parties. This participation is also important because communication involves some level of imaginative thinking. For instance, a person's utterance has a meaning, and part of the employment of this utterance is thinking about how that meaning will be perceived by another person(s). Thus, communication involves perspective taking. Second, communication also involves shared meanings. Here is where much of the socializing power of communication lies -- individuals become acculturated to certain environments through their shared experiences, a point noted by both Dewey (e.g., 1916/1985) and his more sympathetic commentators (e.g., Alexander, 1995; Carey, 1992). Communication involves some sense of community, on Dewey's reading of meaning and interaction. Third, communication shapes and affects the behavior of others. This may seem like a minor point, but its implications are deep and varied.

"Communication" can be conceived of in two senses. One can see it as *instrumental*, as a tool that achieves certain effects, or one can see it as *consummatory*, as an immediate enjoyment of experience (Dewey, 1925/1988). A standard way is to take it *solely* in the first sense (see the critiques of Carey, 1992; Jensen, 2002). Communication on this account is merely a means to affect certain states of affairs (including social states). While this is not incorrect, such a view presents a limited reading of communication. Communication occurs in a present situation and can be connected to *immediately* enjoyed states or experiences. What Dewey is doing here (as he does elsewhere) is to critique the means/ends split. Ends are not radically separate in status or value from means. Communication is both an *instance* of some sort of end-state as well as a means to future states.

Communication obviously coordinates action in future states of affairs, but what is missed is that it *creates* shared experience *now*. In a long but important passage, Dewey (1925/1988) argues that communication "is uniquely instrumental and uniquely final. It is instrumental as liberating us from the otherwise overwhelming pressure of events and enabling us to live in a world of things that have meaning" (p. 158). In other words, communication

> is final as a sharing in the objects and arts precious to a community, a sharing whereby meanings are enhanced, deepened and solidified in the sense of communion. Because of its characteristic agency and finality, communication and its congenial objects are objects ultimately worthy of awe, admiration, and loyal appreciation. They are worthy as means, because they are the only means that make life rich and varied in meanings. They are worthy as ends, because in such ends man is lifted from his immediate isolation and shares in a communion of meanings. Here, as in so many other things, the great evil lies in separating instrumental and final functions. (p. 159)

The act of communication is not only a way to create community, it is an *instance* of shared meaning and community. When an individual envisions the sort of experience s/he wants to create more of in a social situation, that person will inevitably engage in communication with others to achieve what s/he wants. Dewey, along with many other thinkers, is incredibly hesitant to postulate the optimal state of affairs for an individual as solitary. One need not be surprised that Dewey places "full and moving" communication at the heart of the "Great Community."

There is more to this story, however, or all social situations would be already ideal by the mere fact that they are instances of communication. In fact, *harmful* practices of communication do exist that do not lend themselves to the rich, varied, and growing experiences I discussed in the previous section. So the mystery deepens -- what role does communication *optimally* play in a creative democracy? The answer I have provided elsewhere in regard to the qualitative distinctions in Dewey's moral and communicative theories involves what I call subjective "orientations" (Stroud, 2006, 2008). Orientations are wide-ranging mental habits that govern (1) what we think *is* in the world, (2) what we think *is of value* in the world, and (3) the various action strategies that emerge out of these two commitments. Thus, orientations fit Dewey's notion of habit in that they are dispositions to action and are created by past experience. Like all habits, orientations are important insofar as they allow for *melioration* -- the improvement of lived experience.[3]

Orientations, the wide habits that govern our view of the world and our ways of action in regard to it, are of such importance primarily because they make the difference between artful and non-artful experience (Stroud, 2009), and they are the key to growth (Stroud, 2006). This is a claim with which others have taken issue (e.g., Alexander, 2009), so I must provide my reasoning. Let us start with the example Dewey (1934/1989) takes from his student, Max Eastman. He postulates different individuals crossing the Hudson River on their way to New York City for work. One individual sees "landmarks by which to judge progress toward his destination" (p. 140). The other person sees "the scene formed by the buildings . . . as colored and lighted volumes in relation to one another, to the sky and to the river. He is now seeing esthetically" (p. 140). The latter person sees an interconnected scene, a "perceptual whole, constituted by related parts. No one single figure, aspect, or quality is picked out as a means to some further external result which is desired, nor as a sign of an inference that may be drawn" (pp. 140-141). This latter person's experience is noted as being aesthetic in nature. Both people see the same *objective* things (the skyline) differently. Their experiences, however, have differing qualities. The second person has the sort of unity and wholeness and build in the present as the aesthetic in Dewey's writings. I am not stretching the point to say that this experience, while not involving traditional art objects, *is* an aesthetic experience. To say otherwise would be to fall into the trap of conceptualizing the aesthetic as *only* represented by the institution of museums and professionalized artists (Shusterman, 2000).

Yet another example in Dewey's book on aesthetics comes when he discusses mechanized, habitual activity and aesthetic, integrated activity. Two student test-takers are illustrated, each said to have a different attitude toward the activity of taking a test in a course: "One student studies to pass an examination, to get promotion. To another, the means, the activity of learning, is completely one with what results from it. The consequence, instruction, illumination, is one with the process" (1934/1989, p. 201). The second test-taker's experience mirrors the kind of unity and integration among past, present, and future that Dewey postulates as aesthetic experience. As both this example and the previous one feature the same objective settings for the divergent qualities of experience, the crucial variable must be the subjective orientation. From both of these examples, one can see the sort of orientation involved in aesthetic experience is one that (1) sees the present activity as connected to future and past states of affairs, and (2) sees the present activity as of equal value to remote states of affairs (such as future goals). When these two conditions are not present in a person's orientation, he or she has the tendency to rush through the goal-oriented actions, since these actions are valuable as *mere* means -- if one could get the end or goal without trudging through the means, then they would (Sartwell, 1995).

Thus, it is possible to see that creative democracy is both an instance of, and a means to, a certain sort of community -- that of individuals valuing present communication and community through their interactions. This is radically different from a state of affairs animated by non-artful communication. Creative democracy is not merely in the realm of solitary action, so one more element must be added to this notion of orientation in the ideal community. As already discussed, groups are collections of individuals with a variety of interests available to drive their activities. Groups *can* have shared interests, though. This is part of Dewey's notion of the "democratic ideal" -- individuals take part in the activities and direction of the group, *and* share a variety of interests with other members of the group. As he notes in his work on education (Dewey, 1916/1985), some groups noticeably fail because they lack shared interests and individual agency (e.g., a band of robbers), whereas other groups flourish (e.g., family units).

Here we see a social-political employment of orientation. In Dewey's (1927/1984) discussion of community, he makes the distinction between *association* and *community*. *Association* is physical, and involves a force originating outside of the acting agents. Planets act in association with each other -- their motions are affected by the motions of other planets. Humans often are in association with each other -- their action is *joint* in that individual A does act P in light of what she thinks individual B is going to do. Thus, one person makes an utterance because he or she wants something from someone else. Perhaps s/he says something strategic to elicit a desired action from another individual. This could be a manipulative action or the telling of a lie. Action occurs in reference to other persons, but the action is not *shared* or *conjoint* in a rich sense of the interest of others being part of one's interest scheme. Such associated action is not coordinated in the sense implied by Dewey's notion of democracy. *Community* involves internal, often moral, forces that drive individuals. The perspectives and interests of others are taken as *part of one's interest*. Association in human communication would involve orientations that focus on *my interests* and on the "I"; community in human communication would instead involve a focus on *our interests* and on the "we." Action is coordinated in the second occasion, but it is conditioned by the orientation of the individuals toward that activity. The fundamental orientation is one that takes the interests of others to be part of my interests. This is the best sense of community for Dewey, and this is the sort of interaction that will occur in the "Great Community." This is also the kind of communication that will help *create* that sort of community.

Crea*tive* Democracy, Crea*ting* Democracy

Thus, we return once again to the starting points of this inquiry: What is creative democracy? What exactly does it create? Through the preceding exploration of vital themes in Dewey -- habits, self-creation, aesthetic experience, group activity -- we are in a position to fully understand Dewey's enigmatic short essay on creative democracy (1939/1988). There he claims that democracy is a *"personal* way of individual life . . . it signifies the possession and continual use of certain attitudes, forming personal character and determining desire and purpose in all the relations of life," and that anti-democratic forces can be combated "only by the creation of personal attitudes in individual human beings" (p. 226). Here we clearly see the notions of habit and orientation entering into his equation for the ideal society. Only individuals who *see* interaction with others as involving shared goals and meanings truly reach the level of "community," and thus communication at the highest normative level. Communication that is focused on externalized goals that are often attached to the individual qua individual ruin the communal experience and render it a mere association of agents acting while observing each other. Instead of a vibrant, participatory web of communicative relationships, an association features individuals acting out of regard for personal interests, and not from any sense of shared interests. Why is this a problem? When I try to think of human flourishing without rich relationships, I am at a loss. Human good does seem tied to relationality, and the experience of such relationships can be infused with a supportive quality, or a constant hostility. This is the point of Dewey's distinction between association and community, and the consequent reliance on orientation that such a distinction entails. The key distinction is in how each individual *orients* herself to others and the interests involved.

Communication practices reflect and shape orientation: Orientations are habits, and these habits are shaped in, and through, behavior. The most prevalent type of behavior in human life is arguably communication. All of our relationships exist in, and through, communicative interaction or else they suffer from the lack of communicative interaction. The sort of communication that goes on in Dewey's creative democracy -- or community -- is communication that is situationally engaged *and* open to the other interactants as valuable persons. Think of lies, manipulation, or even aggressive communication. All of these are uses of language animated by a certain orientation -- namely, that individuals are ultimately separate, and that "I" am the individual that matters. Too much of political or social discourse gets trapped in an orientation that sees things as black and white, right and wrong, and as yielding winners and losers. What Dewey's notion of creative democracy emphasizes is that all should be oriented toward communicative activity in a certain way. They ought to value others as equal to themselves, and to be open to their perspectives and arguments.

Dewey (1939/1988) referred to the above type of orientation as the "habit of amicable cooperation." This is the same theme as that enshrined in the distinction between association and community, as well as in his examples concerning the aesthetic experience of everyday activities. The key variable is a person's orientation -- it both shapes activity and is strengthened by such activity. In the case of communication, if we can orient ourselves in a way that values the activity of communicating with others, values others as equals to ourselves, and that foregrounds shared interests, we will be creating the sorts of selves we ought to create. The second criterion just mentioned is often violated when we assume others have less reason than us, non-privileged access to some truths we often visit, and so on. The point is to be friendly, constructive, and open in communicating with others. Focusing on a remote personal goal at the expense of listening to the other person not only decreases the effectiveness of that interaction, it renders the interaction's quality as less-than-desirable. Indeed, we are oriented toward the interaction as something to get through, the other person as an obstacle to overcome. Dewey offers this putative orientation as a "priceless addition to life," pointing out that to

> take as far as possible every conflict which arises -- and they are bound to arise -- out of the atmosphere and medium of force, of violence as a means of settlement into that of discussion and of intelligence is to treat those who disagree -- even profoundly -- with us as those from whom we may learn, and in so far, as friends. A genuinely democratic faith in peace is faith in the possibility of conducting disputes, controversies and conflicts as cooperative undertakings in which both parties learn by giving

the other a chance to express itself, instead of having one party conquer by forceful suppression of the other. (p. 228)

This use of force and coercion worries Dewey. Such force need not be physical, as illustrated in Swartz, Campbell, and Pestana's (2009) analysis of corporate influences on the media and its effect on democratic functioning (pp. 35-38). The use of force is a standard move by heavy-handed regimes and individuals to achieve their ends, no matter how grand or base. Dewey's never-ending criticism of this way of achieving ends is that it concretizes ends and means as separate, and divides them in value (Dewey, 1888/1969). This is the same way activity on individual levels is rendered as non-aesthetic. Even if our chosen activity is verbal communication, Dewey (1939/1988) warns of

suppression which is none the less one of violence when it takes place by psychological means of ridicule, abuse, intimidation, instead of by overt imprisonment or in concentration camps. To cooperate by giving differences a chance to show themselves because of the belief that the expression of difference is not only a right of the other persons but is a means of enriching one's own life-experience, is inherent in the democratic personal way of life. (p. 228)

Such a pluralism is difficult for many to instantiate, yet we must try. This is the sort of tolerance and openness that pragmatists such as William James and John Dewey exemplify in their dealings with various intellectual movements (Danisch, 2007), and it is the sort of orientation that individuals must try to create and instantiate in their communicative activity. In this way can we create a democratic community, and allow it to create us in an important sense.

Communicative experience matters for individual character: Another important lesson of this analysis of creative democracy is the power of experience. Experience *is* the end of our activity, and our activities occupy some present experience. This is fundamentally important when we grasp the sort of *end-instantiating* logic I see evident in Dewey -- to get to certain states in the *future*, we ought to instantiate such states *now*. To be a good father in the future, do what a good father would do *now*. Do not put off this activity thinking that a remote end will be achieved in some future state. The same sort of logic holds for our communicative experiences. The sort of communicator that we want to be in the *future* requires the instantiation of those sorts of habits in lived experience *now*. This applies to the association/community distinction: if we want to create a real community (versus an association) in the future, the surest way to do this is to instantiate that type of community now. This is why Dewey was so concerned in his educational writings to create certain types of group interaction in school settings -- those instances of communal experience translate to future experiences of community when those students are full grown citizens (see Dewey, 1916/1985).

Beyond matters of education and interpersonal interaction, we must give some thought to the sort of communicative experience that is created by mass media and new technology. Others have discussed Deweyan critiques of communication technology and how such technology sometimes adversely affects our experience (e.g., Hickman, 1992). Indeed, media homogeneity and ownership are important concerns to a Deweyan sense of creative democracy (Swartz, Campbell, and Pestana, 2009). Additionally, attention must be paid to how communication practices shape us, even in those cases where no evident human interactant is present. Computer-mediated communication, television, video games, and so on all affect the quality of our experience. We must continue to study these technologies and how they prepare us or fail to prepare us for community life. Solitarily playing video games may prepare us for association, whereas communal gaming may inculcate orientations amenable to true community in real life. Like all things in life, pragmatism will find good aspects and bad aspects to such communicative experiences. The point of pragmatism's *meliorism* is to intelligently engage one's communicative experience to maximize the beneficial characteristics and to mitigate the harmful aspects (Mackin, 1990; Stroud, 2010).

The most important point I feel Dewey is trying to convey with his notion of the aesthetic is that it matters *how* we shape and focus our attention. Too much focus on remote goals and an individual may mishandle the present and reduce lived experience to drudgery. Too much focus on a simple present, and an individual's projects may become unguided failures. The same sort of concern holds for our communicative practices. Shaping our habits of attention to communication, our communicative partners, and how we interact with communication technology are all vital steps in creating the sort of democracy envisioned in this chapter.

This goal of community, taken here in the normative sense, is what Dewey's philosophy has aimed for in the varied analyses of the normative endpoint to human activities that he provides in his work on education, politics, ethics, and psychology. Adjusting self to community, and communities to self, is often a matter of focusing attention in the right way and on the right things. Attending to others, messages, and our goals with the right orientation can make all the difference in the world. We also must attend to the sorts of orientations that our social structures seem poised to inculcate in us, and consider if they are in need of melioration. For instance, look at how Dewey (1930/1984) ends his collection of essays on the "Lost Individual":

> To gain an integrated individuality, each of us needs to cultivate his own garden. But there is no fence about this garden: it is no sharply marked-off enclosure. Our garden is the world, in the angle at which it touches our own manner of being. By accepting the corporate and industrial world in which we live, and by thus fulfilling the precondition for interaction with it, we, who are also parts of the moving present, create ourselves as we create an unknown future. (pp. 122-123)

Individuality is tied to community membership, and affecting one affects the other aspect to our being. Improving the ways we interact with others *is* a way to create or recreate a specific type of community.

Conclusion

We reach the end of this inquiry into what Dewey meant by "creative democracy" with the preceding enunciation of how communication creates selves and communities. As Dewey suggests, not only must we question the sorts of habits our culture often takes for granted, we must also attend to matters of our moral improvement. In the sketch I have given in this chapter, this moral improvement comes from instantiating certain ways of attending and thinking about communication in such a way that certain habits are formed and created. Cultivating the individual is an improvement of the group, and improvement of the group will assist the individual. Habits, interests, and communicative activity all play a vital role in this account of creative democracy. Each group of individuals, however, must find the optimal way to maximize the quality of communicative experience. Such examinations occur in the realm of scholarly discussions as those contained in this book, as well as in the hustle and bustle of everyday life as represented by the Pullman strike that Dewey found so captivating. The important point is that we should attend to the sort of community we are instantiating in the present, as this will be reflected in the sort of self and community we create for tomorrow. This sort of attention is important because such societies create us as much as we create them.

REFERENCES

Alexander, T. (1995). John Dewey and the roots of democratic imagination. In L. Langsdorf and A. R. Smith (Eds.), *Recovering pragmatism's voice* (pp. 131-154). Albany: State University of New York Press.

Alexander, T. (2009). The music in the heart, the way of water, and the light of a thousand suns: A response to Richard Shusterman, Crispin Sartwell, and Scott Stroud. *Journal of Aesthetic Education, 43(1)*, 41-58.

Belman, L. (1977). John Dewey's concept of communication, *Journal of Communication, 27(1)*, 29-37.

Carey, J. W. (1992). *Communication as culture.* Baltimore: Johns Hopkins University Press.

Charland, M. (1987). Constitutive rhetoric: The case of the *peuple Quebecois. Quarterly Journal of Speech, 73(2)*, 133-150.

Crick, N. (2004). John Dewey's aesthetics of communication. *Southern Communication Journal, 69(4)*, 303-319.

Danisch, R. (2007). *Pragmatism, democracy, and the necessity of rhetoric.* Columbia: University of South Carolina Press.

Dewey, J. (1888/1969). The ethics of democracy. In J. A. Boydston, (Ed.), *The early works of John Dewey* (Vol. 1) (pp. 227-252). Carbondale: Southern Illinois University Press.

---. (1891/1969). Outlines of a critical theory of ethics. In J. A. Boydston, (Ed.), *The early works of John Dewey* (Vol. 3) (pp. 239-388). Carbondale: Southern Illinois University Press.

---. (1916/1985). Democracy and education. In J. A. Boydston, (Ed.), *The middle works of John Dewey* (Vol. 9). Carbondale: Southern Illinois University Press.

---. (1922/1988). Human nature and conduct. In J. A. Boydston, (Ed.), *The middle works of John Dewey* (Vol. 14). Carbondale: Southern Illinois University Press.

---. (1925/1988). Experience and nature. In J. A. Boydston, (Ed.), *The later works of John Dewey* (Vol. 1). Carbondale: Southern Illinois University Press.

---. (1927/1984). The public and its problems. In J. A. Boydston, (Ed.), *The later works of John Dewey* (Vol. 2) (pp. 235-372). Carbondale: Southern Illinois University Press.

---. (1930/1984). Individuality in our day. In J. A. Boydston, (Ed.), *The later works of John Dewey* (Vol. 5) (pp. 111-124). Carbondale: Southern Illinois University Press.

---. (1932/1989). Ethics. In J. A. Boydston, (Ed.), *The later works of John Dewey* (Vol. 7). Carbondale: Southern Illinois University Press.

---. (1933/1989). How we think. In J. A. Boydston, (Ed.), *The later works of John Dewey* (Vol. 8) (pp. 105-352). Carbondale: Southern Illinois University Press.

---. (1934/1989). Art as experience. In J. A. Boydston, (Ed.), *The later works of John Dewey* (Vol. 10). Carbondale: Southern Illinois University Press.

---. (1939/1988). Creative democracy -- The task before us. In J. A. Boydston, (Ed.), *The later works of John Dewey* (Vol. 14) (pp. 224-230). Carbondale: Southern Illinois University Press.

---. (2008). John Dewey to Alice Chipman Dewey. In L. A. Hickman, (Ed.), *The correspondence of John Dewey, 1871-1952* (1894.07.02). Carbondale: Southern Illinois University Press.

Fesmire, S. (2003). *John Dewey and moral imagination: Pragmatism in ethics.* Bloomington: Indiana University Press.

Jensen, J. (2002). *Is art good for us? Beliefs about high culture in American life.* New York: Rowman & Littlefield.

Johnston, J. S. (2006). *Inquiry and education: John Dewey and the quest for democracy.* Albany: State University of New York Press.

Lippmann, W. (2004). *Public opinion.* New York: Dover Publications. (Original published in 1922)

Mackin, Jr., J. A. (1990). Rhetoric, pragmatism, and practical wisdom. In R. A. Cherwitz (Ed.). *Rhetoric and philosophy* (pp. 275-302). Hillsdale, NJ: Lawrence Erlbaum Associates.

McDermott, J. J. (1989). The pragmatists. In G. F. McLean, (Ed.), *Reading Philosophy for the 21ˢᵗ Century* (pp. 245-263). New York: University Press of America.

Pappas, G. F. (2008). *John Dewey's ethics: Democracy as experience*. Bloomington: Indiana University Press.

Rorty, R. (1991). *Objectivity, relativism, and truth*. New York: Cambridge University Press.

Sartwell, C. (1995). *The art of living: Aesthetics of the ordinary in world spiritual traditions*. Albany: State University of New York University Press.

Shusterman, R. (2000). *Pragmatist aesthetics: Living beauty, rethinking art* (2ⁿᵈ ed.). New York: Rowman & Littlefield.

Stroud, S. R. (2006). Pragmatism and orientation. *Journal of Speculative Philosophy, 20(4)*, 287–307.

---. (2008). John Dewey and the question of artful communication. *Philosophy and Rhetoric 41(2)*, 153-183.

---. (2009). Orientational meliorism, pragmatist aesthetics, and the *Bhagavad Gita, Journal of Aesthetic Education, 43(1)*, 1-17.

---. (2010). What does pragmatic meliorism mean for rhetoric? *Western Journal of Communication, 74(1)*, 43-60.

Swartz, O. (2004). On power and equity: Toward a working-class rhetoric. *Reconstruction: Studies in Contemporary Culture, 4(2)*. Retrieved from http://www.reconstruction. ws/042/ swartz.htm

---. (2005). *In defense of partisan criticism: Communication studies, law, & social analysis*. New York: Peter Lang.

Swartz, O., Campbell, K. and Pestana, C. (2009). *Neo-pragmatism, communication, and the culture of creative democracy*. New York: Peter Lang.

Westbrook, R. B. (1993). *John Dewey and American democracy*. Ithaca: Cornell University Press.

Notes

[1] Dewey's work is commonly divided into a period where he was clearly influenced by the German philosopher G. W. Hegel, and the period in which his work broke from this influence. More on the timing and content of this change can be found in Westbrook (1993). An important claim in this chapter is that the vital core of his thoughts on creative democracy can be found in *all* major periods of his work.

[2] For a connection of this observation to politics, see Swartz (2005, pp. 258-258).

[3] For more on pragmatism and meliorism, see McDermott (1989) and Stroud (2010).

CHAPTER 2

Communication and the Emergence of the Public:
John Dewey and Creative Democracy

Cynthia Gayman
Murray State University

Writing in *The Public and its Problems* (1927/1954), John Dewey warned against the disappearance of the public sphere and the crisis this would portend for democracy in the United States. This crisis, which he defined as a breakdown in shared meaning necessary to underpin community life, is, fundamentally, one of communication and association. For Dewey, if "signs and symbols, language, are the means of communication by which a fraternally shared experience is ushered in and sustained," the absence of shared meanings vitiates recognition of what ever might be held in common, and makes impossible the simple "face-to-face" interchange that is a "precondition of the creation of a true public" (Dewey, 1927/1954, p. 218). Access to information is not necessarily the problem today; rather, the intellectual means by which to make sense of it is lacking. Familiar terms and phrases convey "facts" in the abbreviated space of a sound-bite, and "slant" directs opinion before the next wave of "news" necessitates further elucidation of any subject matter by pundits. Codification disguises value commitments that underlie even ordinary conversation: those who have ears to hear listen for key words and map worldviews onto new experiences. Viewpoints coalesce along lines of pre-existent affinities; shared alliances find common bonds with those who "speak our language." People with whom we disagree are simply "wrong."

This state of affairs is not what Dewey meant by the "discursive exchange" he thought to be fundamentally constitutive of the public sphere. As Dewey understood community, the catalyst for emergence of the public sphere is not forged by social bonds, but, rather, by recognition of a commonly shared world.

According to Dewey, the "public consists of all those who are affected by the indirect consequences of transactions to such an extent that it is deemed necessary to have those consequences systematically care for" (1927/1954, p. 16). Dewey's "public" is constituted by those whose concern for a shared world provokes communal engagement, and who together recognize that "the ever-expanding and intricately ramifying consequences of associated activities shall be known in the full sense of that word" (Dewey, 1927/1954, p. 184). Public engagement, that is, the activities of speaking and acting purposively together, presumes that speech and action are efficacious, meaningful, and thus, in Dewey's sense, "known" (1927/1954, p. 184). *How* problems are defined, evaluated and resolved determines, or at least might influence outcomes, and so it matters profoundly that persons recognize they have "a common interest in controlling consequences" (Dewey, 1927/1954, p. 126; Green, 1995; McAffee, 2008; Hildebrand, 2008).

Arguably, we today are at so far removed from each other that we are deaf to common interests or concerns and blind to the possibility of conceiving shared goals. Perhaps to speak of "ties that bind men together in action" (Dewey, 1927/1954, p. 142) is merely to wax nostalgic for a world that was never as homogeneous as some imagine it to have been. Still, we can look back on the vital beginnings of an "American democratic polity developed out of genuine community life" (1927/1954, p. 111) and acknowledge that subsequent growth and change have vastly altered the nation's landscape and social organization. Our increasing reliance upon "impersonal and mechanical modes" (Dewey, 1927/1954, p. 114) of communication has altered both the means and content of our interactions. While it may border on the banal to write that contemporary American society has become increasingly fractured and factious, the differences that divide us today seem increasingly intractable. As Chris Hedges describes in his book, *Empire of Illusion: The End of Literacy and the Triumph of the Spectacle*, "More than the divides of race, class, or gender, more than rural or urban, believer or non-believer, red state or blue state, our culture has been carved up into radically distinct, unbridgeable, and antagonistic entities that no longer speak the same language and cannot communicate" (2009, p. 190).[1]

In his 1939 essay, "Creative Democracy -- The Task Before Us," Dewey argued that American democracy as an organization of government and as "a way of life" is not merely of historical moment and, thereafter, self-sustaining, but, instead, must serve as an *ideal* that orients attitudes and actions if it is to remain vital (1939a/1991, p. 226). Even the public institutions built for the protection of democracy do not, in-and-of themselves, constitute a tangible reality sufficient to orient public and democratic interchange. In other words, no "matter how uniform and constant human nature is in the abstract, the conditions within which and upon which it operates have changed so greatly since political democracy was established among us, that democracy cannot now depend upon or be expressed in political institutions alone" (Dewey, 1939b/2008, p. 151).

A creative revision of democracy demands that we "get rid of the habit of thinking of democracy as something institutional," Dewey wrote, and instead "acquire the habit of treating it as a way of personal life" -- that is, as a "moral ideal" (1939a/1991, p. 228) informing our attitudes and interactions, our values and goals. Democracy as an ideal should create conditions conducive to creating *more* democracy (Dewey, 1927/1954; Green, 1995), and would lead to "a freer and more humane experience in which all share and to which all contribute" (1939a/1991, p. 230). If this vision is not actually realizable, it may nonetheless orient attitude and action, or so Dewey thought, for he believed that as a vision it grows from the shared moral ideal of "democracy as a personal way of life" signified by "the possession and continual use of certain attitudes, forming personal character and determining desire and purpose in all the relations of life" (1939a/1991, p. 226). I find such a view edifying.

Meanwhile, today, in the United States, wide divides of social/ideological differences manifest as persons align with unitary discursive frames, and democratic discourse becomes compromised. As Hedges argues, democracy today "is not ascendant. It is not dominant. It is beleaguered" (Hedges, 2009, p. 149). Whether or not this is hyperbole, the communicative crisis in contemporary American society shows itself not by an absence of speech -- we are subject to an endless stream of talk, cross-talk, harangues, vitriol, chat, blather, etc. -- but by an absence of the fruitful communication that occurs with reference to a common world. For philosophers and communication scholars, this raises a serious professional concern, one that we can and should address. This problem of incommunicability in our *polis* and the loss of the public sphere is the subject matter of this chapter, but I also wish to consider conditions or even "pre-conditions" necessary for the emergence of this site of democratic engagement, and whether, or in what sense, ideality -- the ideal of democracy -- functions as one of these conditions (Dewey, 1939a/1991; 1927/1954, p. 218).

Specifically, in the first part of this chapter I suggest ways of distinguishing speaking within a democratic public sphere from the cacophony of "cross-talk," resulting in an incommunicability we have become so familiar with that the absence of communication sees to be increasingly unrecognized, or at least unacknowledged. To illustrate, I use, as an example, a portion of the 2008 Presidential candidate interviews conducted by the Reverend Rick Warren at his Saddleback Church, in Lake Forest, California. In the second portion of this chapter, I look more closely at the criteria for public, democratic process and at Dewey's notion of ideality as it might inform possibilities for actual communication.

The Ties That Bind: Frames For and Transactions of Experience

The "eclipse" of the public sphere warned by Dewey (1927/1954, p. 42) entails the loss of a certain kind of communication, as well as a loss of commitment to a way of comportment in the world, but it does not end human interaction; rather, it personalizes communication. Or, to use a phrase coined by Hannah Arendt, it relegates talk strictly to the "social realm," that is, to a type of exchange remaining when the public sphere disappears (Arendt, 1977, p. 149). Hannah Arendt distinguishes the social realm from the political or public sphere in such a way that might be useful in considering the contemporary communicative crisis. She distinguished what she saw as the individual interrelatedness of persons within the public sphere from "the social realm," where "the bonds among a people are formed only with reference to and in relation to each other, and not to the world each bears witness to" (1955, p. 149). Arendt, like Dewey, was concerned about the loss or disappearance of the public sphere (i.e., Arendt's *polis*, which she defines as "the organization of the people as it arises out of their acting and speaking together," 1958, p. 196). Thus, the loss of the public sphere signifies a dislocation of our relationship to the world, and, therefore, Dewey's warning of the "crisis" facing democracy portends the loss of a shared world.

Dewey did not make a distinction between the public and the social realms, and in fact, as John Stuhr (1997) argues, Dewey rejected and "ceaselessly criticized dualisms such as private/public, fact/value, and self/society" (p. 122). But Arendt's distinction between the realms of the social and political or public is not metaphysical but descriptive -- and descriptive in such a way as to be of benefit to the inquiry here on the crisis of communication facing our society in the United States today. Because the modality of interaction in what Arendt calls the social realm is different from that in the public, democratic sphere, then, *pace* Stuhr, it seems worthwhile to look at how or whether these differences make a difference.

The difference is one of orientation. The social realm links persons together by the bonds they share with each other, and these "are formed *only* with reference to and in relation to each other, and not to the world each bears witness to" (Arendt, 1955, p. 149, emphasis added). Like-mindedness informs these bonds, and indeed, "belonging together" (Arendt, 1977, p. 149), is the fundamental feeling of the social milieu. No doubt, "the warmth of human relationships" and "brotherly attachment to other human beings" (Arendt, 1977, p. 149), are deeply enjoyable and meaningful, but their value can become restrictive, and serve to bind people together in such a way as to mark boundaries between those who belong and those who do not.

In contrast, in Arendt's words: "Under the condition of a common world, reality is not guaranteed primarily by the 'common nature' of all men who constitute it, but rather by the fact that, difference of position and the resulting variety of perspectives notwithstanding, everybody is always concerned with the same object" (1958, p. 50). This is the reality shared by those in the public sphere, where the links binding persons together are bound to a common world. As Arendt described by analogy, to "live together in the world means essentially that a world of things is between those who have it in common, as a table is located between those who sit around it; the world, like every in-between, relates and separates men at the same time" (1958, p. 52).

But if the bonds among persons are merely social, similarity of perspective or belief informs discursive exchange; thus *our* church, our values, our club, our way of doing things -- *and not theirs* -- can be signified through a short-hand use of terms or tropes marking differences between *our* group and another. These shared symbols might even coalesce to inform an entire discursive "frame" (Goffman, 1974; Lakoff, 2004, Sorrells and Nakagawa, 2008, p. 28), through which an ideological schema is signified. In this sense, frames are, as Omar Swartz (2009) describes, "norm-building and prescriptive; they provide a singular interpretation of a particular situation and then indicate appropriate behavior for that context" (p. 278). Thus, framing can be used as an intentional means to situate what "our" view might be, which is to "fix meanings and organize experience for an audience" (p. 278). These frames function as "conceptual 'boundaries' that are constructed for us by a persuader and from within which we form our understandings of the world . . . . *It is the frame or context that situates meaning*" (p. 278, emphasis added).

Of course, the context *of* experience always situates meaning, and if context cannot be said to completely determine experience, context, in a very broad and rich sense, is that through which experience *can be* experienced (Rosenthal, 2005). Thus perspective is inextricably bound to the particular trajectories of our lives, making all that we do experience a kind of "transaction" between the activity *of* experiencing and that which *is* experienced (Dewey, 1925/1988b; Stuhr, 2003; Rosenthal, 2005). This is an important Deweyan point, for as he held, the primary feature of human life is the "primary, irreducible transactional character of experience, and the irreducible connections between meaning and existence" (Stuhr, 1997, p. 128). This means that everything we perceive, discern, realize, find disappointing, or believe is co-constituted through the activity of experiencing itself (Stuhr, 1997). Or, as Stuhr explains, experience "is understood as a transaction, as 'double-barreled,' as the irreducible unity of subject and object, organism and environment, foreground and background" (1997, p. 128). The point here is that we are not only socially situated in a world we *experience* as reality, our experience *is constitutive of this reality*: "Experience constitutes reality" (Stuhr, 1997, p. 128).

What follows from this is that there is no view from "nowhere." There is no non-perspectival point of reference or such a thing as a de-contextualized experience; instead *all* experience is, in a fundamental sense, enframed (Stuhr, 2003; Rosenthal, 2005; McAffee, 2008). But it does not then follow that we are nothing but prisoners to our own histories and contexts. As transactional, experience is also constituted by what we bring to it, that is, what we think, discover, value, analyze, and argue about in order that we might, according to Dewey, "construct freer and more secure goods, turning assent and assertion into free communication of shareable meanings" (1925/1988b, p. 325). This is why Dewey sees criticism and critical evaluation as fundamental for living and, further, why he views critical activity as the fundamental activity of philosophy itself (1925/1988b, p. 312). Dewey's vision of philosophy "intellectualizes practice" (Eldridge, 1998, p. 5), which makes experience the fecund source for ongoing evaluation and critique, in order that we live better lives. When perspective becomes rigidified through ideological discursive frames, experiential "transactions" are in a sense pre-determined. Meanings are "mapped on to experience" without thought or critique of the ways in which perspective alters experience and subsequent understanding. This not only "short-changes" our experience; it makes us susceptible to manipulation through persuasion and propaganda.

Absence of Communication and the Loss of the Public Sphere

Dewey's concern over the loss of the public sphere is expressed in his warning of the "crisis" facing democracy, which portends the loss of a common world and shared reality. While no one can live within the public sphere, "all the time," as Arendt noted, "to be deprived of it means to be deprived of reality" (1958, p. 196). Today, along with the eclipse of the public sphere, reality itself seems to have disappeared (Hedges, 2009).

Increasingly, the arena of private interests intervenes on social consciousness in a society directed by "the need for intimacy in a world governed by the impersonal dynamics of the market" (Lasch, 1991, p. 165). Since the market functions within the realm of the social world, in Arendt's sense, the framing of meanings occurs on several levels of social organization. Social groups conform to discursive meaning frames, according to which those belonging to a group might recognize members with whom they have social and/or ideological affinities (Swartz, 2009, p. 278). But on a much broader scale -- and at a much deeper level -- what John Berger calls "publicity" or the "publicity image" (Berger, 1977, p. 6) informs or manipulates meanings vis-à-vis the persuasive powers of corporate capitalism (Boorstin, 1961/1987; Berger, 1977; Klein, 2007; Swartz, 2008; Hedges, 2009).

The market functions within the realm of the personal by the use of "publicity images" (Berger, 1977, p. 130) so pervasive that, despite competing messages or products, they serve to relay one message, operating as a "language in itself, which is always being used to make the same general proposal" (Berger, 1977, p. 131). This proposal is that "we can transform ourselves" (p. 131) -- of course, by buying more -- but, and this is the central message, by desiring that which we cannot have and cannot be, which is the selling of an illusion (Berger, 1977; Hedges, 2009). On the mass scale of American society, the "image" (Boorstin, 1961/1987, p. 6) orients, yearning for the unreal, the illusory, yet, such publicity "is effective precisely because it feeds upon the real" (p. 132).

But the real disappears. Hedges states that we have become as a nation "unmoored from reality," uprooted by fantasy and illusion, and have "retreated into a world of magic" (2009, p. 50). We have exchanged "the confusion of reality" (Hedges, 2009, p. 14) for fantasy, fabrication, and entertainment, so that we might follow "the squalid dramas" (p. 16) of the latest celebrity scandal or the newest storyline of reality television. The projection of images over ideas, the replacement of "pseudo-events" for complex situations that cannot be captured in a sound-bite or compel the attention of an already distracted audience, distracts us further from a reality we do not, and, it seems, cannot share (Boorstin, 1961/1987; Lasch, 1995; Putnam, 2000; Hedges, 2009).[2]

The fact that our national discourse has arguably become dominated by manufactured events speaks to the gravity of the crisis we are experiencing currently. This crisis is signified by three factors: First, by the reduction and threatened disappearance of the public sphere, where the reference for discourse is the common world. Second, by the consequent ubiquity of the social realm, where meanings are framed through disparate group identifications. Third, by the manipulative power of market publicity which frames meanings at the broadest reaches of social consciousness by undermining reality through the relentless enticements to desire for the illusory, the unreal (Boorstin, 1961/1987; Berger, 1977; Hedges, 2009). The magnitude of this crisis threatens the heart of democratic process and thus demands immediate critical attention from scholars, journalists, and activists.

The Problem of Incommunicability

If the great project of American democracy is based upon communication and the free exchange of ideas (Dewey, 1925/1988b; 1927/1988; Green, 1995), it is today deeply compromised by the cacophony of depthless opinion, sloganeering, and manipulative speech (i.e., what James Boyd White, 2007, calls "dead speech"). This condition is blatantly illustrated by the image on the front cover of the September 28, 2009 issue of *New York Magazine* showing President Obama's face overlaid with the thought-numbing slander that passes these days for "discussion" and "debate." Here, Obama is labeled as *Parasite-in-Chief, Hitler, Liar, Imposter, Stalin, Nazi, Socialist, Muslim, and Kenya-born.* This image references ideological partisanship and the words, albeit contradictory, drop like coinage tithed to a particular discursive frame, where value is correlative with pre-designated and manipulative meanings. The projection of an image such as this evokes immediate emotional response; it serves as a form of "publicity" that taps into sentiments so deep they are "beyond conflict" -- that is, without traction for discussion or critique or debate (Berger, 1977, p. 150). Communication, in the sense that excited Dewey, is not the point.

The "world of the image" or the "pseudo-event" replaces reality with an illusion that seems, if not more real, more compelling (Hedges, 2009; Boorstin, 1961/1987). The illusionary tale is more exciting, more dramatic, and it may interweave facts with falsehoods -- such as a purportedly missing Obama birth certificate -- into a complex fabrication, altering and intensifying ordinary experience, thus making up for "the world's deficiency" (Boorstin, 1961/1987, p. 9; Lasch, 1991, p. 30). Likewise, the mere mention of healthcare reform gave rise to scare tactics used by groups that shifted the possibility of engaged inquiry to the threat of "death panels" -- made all the more compelling, since, "what the healthcare bill actually says is much less exciting than the fantasy of Grandma's last gurgle as she is tossed into the tumbrel" (Williams, 2009, p. 9). Perhaps "the members of an inchoate public have too many ways of enjoyment" (Dewey, 1927/1954, p. 188).

The partisan Right is not alone guilty of uncivil discourse. The unreflective Left, provoked by disappointment over the United States Senate-approved healthcare bill, spewed the following epithets against Obama across the blogosphere. Among other things, they called him a "sellout," "liar," "Judas," "fraud," "corrupt," "foolish," a "Liebermanite," and an "Uncle Tom," someone "groveling before the demands of the corporations that are running our country" (Hertsberg, 2010, p. 24). Hugh Dalziel Duncan, a pragmatist communication theorist who was an adherent of Kenneth Burke's (1945) view that "social reality is constituted by symbolic forms" (Hardt, 1992, p. 125), stated, "*How we communicate determines how we relate*, just as how we relate determines how we communicate" (1967, p. 261). In other words, a danger of the social realm, where the discursive frame is self-referentially meaningful, whether with respect to the relations among persons or in view of adherence to an ideological frame, is that it repetitively perpetuates meanings. While social ties bring emotional satisfaction these relations are delimited by their insularity; they are profoundly non-inclusive, unless inclusion is based on conformity.

What might disrupt conforming social bonds and lead to the kind of inquiries signifying public and democratic engagement? What would inspire us to model in our communication the civil society we wish to construct? Can a change in discursive practices lead to a more democratic exchange? If speech habits were to become more egalitarian and inclusive can this be utilized as a discursive frame for a more democratic world? Communication theorist Hanno Hardt (1992) critiques this view, stating that what he calls the "liberal-pluralist analysis of communication" is too optimistic about the capacity for human beings to speak together as equal participants in a shared world (1992, p. 230). He attributes to Dewey the view that, when pragmatist "and reformist writers define the social idea of democracy in terms of communication as a binding force in society, they rely on assumptions about the potential ability of individuals to participate in society and the quality of discourse that reflect an almost mythical belief in the spirit of community" (Hardt, 1992, p. 230). But this is not Dewey's view, except as communication might be informed by ideality -- democracy as a "moral ideal" (1939a/ 1988, p. 229) -- a distinction I will address later in this chapter. This assumption is, however, a view insinuated by neo-pragmatists who think that language is the source for meaning construction and, therefore, that the use of democratic rhetorical tropes would serve to change social attitudes and set the stage for a more democratic world (Danisch, 2007). This would infer that all social meanings are constituted through discursive frames, and so the point would be to get the most perspective-inclusive frame in place. But this begs the question as to how a democratic meaning frame is better or, if that seems obvious, then *why* it is better (Stuhr, 1997). In other words, a critique must be articulated as to why a unifying discursive meaning frame is inadequate to fully describe experience *as* pluralistic, multivalent, and complex, and why plurality, inclusion, and more fluid discursive practices are essential to democratic process -- and the achievement of freer, more meaningful experience (Dewey, 1925/1988b).

Stuhr (1997) critiques Richard Rorty's appropriation of Dewey along these lines, that is, over the fact that Rorty misses, in his view, the Deweyan understanding of philosophy as critical inquiry, and that "there is a constructive moral, educational task for philosophy" (p. 126). For Stuhr, Rorty merely invokes Dewey's central commitments *ad hoc* -- "for example, growth, communication, liberal individualism, democratic community, and human solidarity" (p. 122) -- by telling us "*what* he thinks we should do" (p. 123). The problem, Stuhr suggests, is that Rorty "is not able to tell us *why* to do it or *how* to do it" (p. 123). This takes us back to Hardt's criticism of "the liberal-pluralist view of communication" (1992, p. 230). As Stuhr remarks, referring to Rorty's assertion that we should not be cruel (1992, p 230), this demands that we ask "liberals *why* we shouldn't be cruel" -- and "this need not be to ask for any transcendental proof" (1997, p. 125). Instead:

> It is a request for liberals to support intelligently their commitments. It is a
> request for criticism -- what Dewey calls "criticism of criticism." This

request may not be important to like-minded liberal[s]… but it has been and continues to be important in real struggles and larger cultures. (1997, pp. 125-126)

In any case, we do not relate, and this is not a matter reducible to the adequacy of our communication skills. As Dewey noted, our Babel "is not one of tongues but of the signs and symbols without which shared experience is impossible" (1927/1954, p. 142). We do not share signs and symbols because, through the divides of group-identified frames of meaning, we are not sharing experience; we seem not to share a common world (Burke, 1950; Hardt, 1992; Hedges, 2009). Problems that could conceivably be viewed as shared concerns -- such as inadequate access to healthcare or pervasive unemployment -- are instead framed by ideological loyalties, and the ensuing "debates" are disguised as civic engagement and marketed as meaningful social discourse. But words used to communicate agreement or disagreement must find reference in common experience, and this, like the public, is, arguably, in eclipse.

Across contemporary divides of politics and culture -- represented by the town meeting or Tea Party, the Drudge Report or Fox News, the religious Right or the liberal Left (to name but a few of the more publicized divisions), -- viewpoints align and are signified according to the symbols of a discursive frame. Terms such as *value, choice, life, honor, good, bad,* and *evil* evoke entire meaning-schemas. We glue ourselves to mediums of favored messages, the spin of our choice, where words find foothold in our opinions and beliefs, traction in the foundations of our worldview. Hedges states, correctly I believe, that, in this world, "all that matters is the consistency of our belief systems" (2009, p. 49).

Democracy as a Publicity Event, The Reverend Rick Warren Interviews with Barak Obama and John McCain

Changes in social organization today call to mind Dewey's concern, early in the twentieth century, that the disappearance of community life entails both a loss of a shared world and the disappearance of a "democratic public" (1927/1954, p. 109). While "communication is the way in which [people] come to possess things in common" (Dewey, 1916/1944, p. 4), the complications of communicating across social differences today indicate something more than stubborn refusal to compromise. We have lost the capacity to share experience and to speak to each other because we have lost a common reference. Thus, the "eclipse" of the public sphere signifies the "eclipse" of democracy itself (Dewey, 1927/1954, p. 142; Hedges, 2009).

During the 2008 Presidential campaign, Reverend Rick Warren, evangelical pastor of Saddleback Church in Lake Forest, California, conducted interviews with then candidates Barak Obama and John McCain. This was not a debate; Reverend Warren prepared a set of questions that he asked both candidates, and each interview was conducted separately. These questions were Warren's own -- that is, they were questions he wanted both candidates to answer. This was an invited event, public in that it was widely publicized, but private in the sense that the interviews took place in a non-public venue, in the space of Reverend Warren's own evangelical Christian church.

In this section, I will examine a very brief segment of this "interview event" that I think conveys an important facet of the contemporary crisis of communication. Specifically, my examination will show how adherence to a group-identified meaning "frame" compromises the possibility of communication about shared concerns when the discursive reference is not shared. Such a frame not only orients perspective, it filters and codifies experience through a conforming belief pattern. This is not to say that these interviews took place as an intentional language game where some knew the rules and others did not; if that is the case, then the crisis of incommunicability is no crisis, it is a mere child's game of refusal to work together. That is not the case. Group-identified frames are closed systems in that they are self-informing, self-referential, prescriptive; they are, thus, constitutive of an illusory "reality."

Reverend Warren's questions about evil infer a scope of meaning that was not directly referenced by the content of the questions. Specially, Warren asked if evil existed and that, if it did, how should we deal with it? Should we, as a nation, ignore the existence of evil? Should we fight it? How should we defeat it.[3] These questions are not open-ended; they seem already to refer *to* something, a set of meanings or a cosmology, without saying what that is. The referent is hidden, assumed. What is the "it" whose existence is in question? What is being asked? What would be a "right" or "good" answer? Is a particular way of answering implicitly indicated or expected?

In our post-9/11 world, the word "evil" evokes, at the least, the threat of terrorism (Swartz, 2008; McAffee, 2008). But this threat raises another problem of reference, as Swartz points out, since there is "no consensus on the definition of 'terrorism,' and many, even most countries simply call their political opponents 'terrorists,' making the label overly inclusive and draining the term of categorical meaning" (2008, p. 266). "Terror" is also a term that was used conterminously with "evil," especially to convene American support for what Swartz called "the imperialistic ambitions" of the Bush administration (p. 267). To show how this is indeed a politically or ideologically weighted reference, Swartz points out that "terror" is not a term applied to, for example, Israeli attacks on the Palestinian territory of Gaza or to the Russian destruction of Chechnya in 2008.

In the immediate aftermath of the events on September 11, 2001, the seemingly endless replay of the crashes set in motion a level of news and information management that made credible a story about terrorism as evil that would grant "a semblance of reality" (Hedges, 2009, p. 52) to the possible existence of weapons of mass destruction and garner support for the U. S. invasion of Afghanistan and Iraq in the spring of 2002 (Swartz, 2008; MacAffee, 2008). The declaration of war against terrorism diffused "public comprehension of what [was] in fact occurring" (Swartz, 2008, p. 267). Now the word "terrorism" is also diffused in meaning, and has become a word so ambiguous it has become "meaningless in our public discourse" (Swartz, 2008, p. 267). But not so meaningless as to become devoid of affect or drama; "terrorism," like "evil," terrorizes us by its threat (Klein, 2007).

In that precipitous year of 1939, Dewey wrote that history "shows that more than once social unity has been promoted by the presence, real or alleged, of some hostile group. It has long been a part of the technique of politicians who wish to maintain themselves in power to foster the idea that the alternative is the danger of being conquered by an enemy" (1939b/2008, p. 89). Propaganda is an effective means for convincing persons to cohere against a common enemy, for example, the designated enemies of the *Reichstag* (Dewey, 1939b/2008). Dewey observed that propaganda is increasingly easy to disseminate due to advancements in communication technologies (1939b/2008, p. 90).

Using the language of "dramaticism," Kenneth Burke (1966) described the creative aspect of language as a symbolic act (Pestana and Swartz, 2008, p. 96). A term used to name something might highlight a certain meaning or deflect another (p. 96). "Partial and selective assignment of meaning to a situation or object always is related to assumptions and existing meanings held by the individual or group doing the defining" (in Swartz, 2008, p. 96). The word "evil" is a good example of this. In the context of Reverend Warren's interview questions, then, what meaning is highlighted? Who is doing the defining? What drama does "evil" symbolize? If "different definitions invoke different attitudes and imply that certain types of actions and responses are appropriate and others are inappropriate" (Pestana and Swartz, 2008, p. 97), what are the attitudes, responses, and actions "evil" this context invokes? What assumptions are in play? More specifically, are Reverend Warren's questions aimed at the alliance between the Christian Right and the Republican Party, making "evil" a symbol of patriotism and American support for the wars in Iraq and Afghanistan (Hedges, 2006)? Or does "evil" trace a theological theme? If so, "evil" is perhaps directed towards meaning on a wholly "other" scale (Hedges, 2006; Pestana and Swartz, in Swartz, 2008). These latter two meanings are not mutually exclusive, of course.

Dewey recognized over seven decades ago that exclusive focus on "the enemy" diverts our attention from critical examination of ourselves.[4] He saw that the crisis facing American democracy could not be solely blamed on events occurring outside the nation's borders, even as the United States stood precipitously on the brink of entering the Second World War. He warned against the dangers of a too complacent citizenry believing that "the democratic way of life" would simply continue uninterrupted, as if democracy "were something that perpetuated itself automatically . . . a perpetual motion [machine] in politics" (Dewey, 1939a/1991, p. 228).

Today, there exists no concomitant trust in government, and complacency has been replaced by persistent anxiety or outright fear (Klein, 2007; McAffee, 2008). Noelle McAffee warns that arenas of discourse can "become the semiotic space in which society's anxieties, sentiments, opinions, and prejudice appear" (2008, p. 19). Even if diminished trust in the corporate oligarchy should be perceived as a "wake-up" call from the "totalizing narratives" of corporate culture and elected officialdom (Swartz, 2008, p. 250; Hedges, 2009, p. 52), no such shift seems to have taken place. New narratives have proven fruitful for those not banking on the common bonds of shared interests but on the marketplace of fears, some real, many manufactured by the "image-makers" in our "culture of illusion" (Hedges, 2009, p. 45; Boorstin, 1961/1987). Legitimate fears prompted by threats to the nation, economic instability, job loss, lack of access to healthcare, global warming are used as plot-lines revised to lethal affect by "incendiary media," such as "Fox News and AM radio" -- persuasive, no matter how alien to "common notions of reality" (Williams, 2009, p. 9).

We are, notes Hedges, "fed words and phrases like *war on terror* or *pro-life* or *change*" (2009, p. 49), and the incessant repetition of these tropes vitiates critical thought and questioning, an outcome perhaps unintended by the plethora of demagogues that populate every discursive arena. The problem of incommensurability is rooted in the loss of shared meanings, but this loss disguises the loss of shared reality; manufactured events, illusions, narrative content without context, uproot us from the ground of experiential life, the only source for intelligent reflection and critique on "things as they are" and as they might "point the way to new and better experiences" (Dewey, 1939a/1991, p. 229). But unspecified meanings allow words to condition perspectives in such a way as to convince listeners of the "truth" of a particular line of thought, even when little is said.

Jaques Ellul (1965) describes a "conditioning phenomenon" as form of "sociological propaganda" because it operates diffusively within a given social context through value acceptance and conformity (p. 64). Sociological propaganda thereby "conditions" what people believe and feel. If "one hesitates to call this propaganda . . . [because] such influences, which mold behavior, seem a far cry from Hitler's great propaganda setup," its influence may be all the more pervasive (Ellul, 1965, p. 64). People tend to believe their conforming opinions and group-identified outrage to be their own. For example, strong feelings of nationalism, shown by the "America: Love it or Leave it" bumper sticker during a previous war or the "if you're not for us you're against us" proclamation after 9/11, are indicative of this "softer" handed propaganda. As Swartz et al suggest, after the attack on the Twin Towers it was easy to believe in the image of the United States as "an innocent, pure, and just player in this war that was thrust upon it by a vicious and greedy enemy" (2009, p. 25). But who was this enemy? Was it, perhaps, the same as that evoked by the Reverend Warren a few years later? Deputy Undersecretary of Defense Lt. Gen. William Boykin named it; the enemy, he said, "is a guy named Satan" (quoted in Swartz, et al, 2009, p. 25).

Obama's response to Reverend Warren's questions did not properly conform to the lexical map. Instead, Obama spoke of the "evil of social ills," not likely to be reducible to a causal "it" -- that is, the "it" indicated by the Reverend Warren's questions. One might even think that such evils would provoke intelligent inquiries into patterns of social organization. Social evils, indeed extant, are not life forms to be destroyed or defeated, ignored, or negotiated with; "containment" in this context might even lead to an exacerbation of the problem.

Obama then spoke of the evil of "political violence," another multivalent evil likely to necessitate prudent and careful interrogation of related social and political factors, as well as inquiry into extenuating contexts and meaning frames. Here again, "it" seems an inadequate or even dangerous response to reduce political violence to univalent agency that can be defeated once and for all. Indeed, as Obama also noted, "Actions taken in the name of confronting evil might serve to perpetuate it," thereby challenging, at least by inference, the delimiting scope set by the lexical frame of Reverend Warren's questions with respect to its critical and moral myopia. But in the setting where the interviews took place, Obama's answers sounded off-message, to judge by the lukewarm response from those seated in the pews of Saddleback Church. In contrast, when McCain responded to the same questions, the discursive meaning schema was laid bare, exposing, as it were, the devil in the details: Evil? "Defeat it," McCain answered, and the audience cheered.[5]

In using a portion of the Saddleback Church interviews to illustrate how a group-identified discursive frame, a coded lexicon, is problematic for communication *as* democratic process and the emergence of a public sphere, in no way should this point be taken as a rejection of religious belief or understood to infer that religion and democracy are incompatible. Dewey remarked in *Freedom and Culture* (1939b/2008), that it "used to be said that democracy is a by-product of Christianity, since the latter teaches the infinite worth of the individual human soul" (p. 152). He deliberately used the word "faith" to describe in his own belief "in the capacity of human beings for intelligent judgment and action if proper conditions are furnished" (Dewey, 1939a/1991, p. 227). These conditions must be democratic, making democracy a lived ideal. Holding beliefs is not the problem, then. The question is whether and in what ways do our beliefs and values inform how we live *and* how our lives and experience inform our beliefs and values. As Dewey puts this, "the *ways* in which we believe and expect have a tremendous effect upon *what* we believe and expect" (1925/1988b, p. 23).

Democracy as a Personal Way of Life

In 1939, Dewey wrote that assuming ourselves "immune from the disease to which others have given way, so long as the evil things [seen] in totalitarianism are not known to be developing among us" (1939b/2008, p.88) is serious self-delusion. While it is tempting today to believe that democratic freedoms are safeguarded simply because overt signs of totalitarianism are absent -- for example, signs that the world witnessed in the years prior to the Second World War such as, "purges, executions, concentrations camps, deprivation of property and means of livelihood" (Dewey, 1939b/2008, p. 88), this "absence of evidence" should not keep us "from being on our guard against the causes that may be at work undermining the values we nominally prize" (Dewey, 1939b/2008, p. 88).

Without making mention of the numerous signs that the values we nominally prize have been seriously undermined after the attacks on September 11, 2001 (see especially Swartz, 2008; Klein, 2007; Swartz, et al., 2009), it is perhaps more useful here to note, as Dewey did in 1939, that the *causes* that undermine democracy are rooted in the loss of the public sphere. The primacy of the social realm usurps the more difficult course of life constituted by democratic conduct.

Indeed, choosing instead the more tangible "satisfaction that comes from a sense of union with others, a feeling capable of being intensified till it becomes a mystical sense of fusion with others and being mistaken for love on a high level of manifestation" (Dewey, 1939b/2008, p. 89) remains a significant temptation. Today, this temptation is satisfied on a much smaller and more multitudinous scale than was the case for those who chose the unifying embrace of the Third Reich, in which the frame of meaning operated according the values put forth by the Nazi Party.

Democracy as a personal way of life is both "a moral ideal" and a self-reflective way of living, shown "in our daily walk and conversation" and in what Dewey describes as "democratic faith" in human worth, potentiality, equality, intelligence, and "the capacity of human beings for intelligent judgment and action if proper conditions are furnished" (1939a/1991, pp. 227-228). These conditions are democratic/moral, as well, and they are the conditions that inform the emergence of the public sphere as both *means* and *context* for communication. Specifically, inclusiveness and respect for the diversity of persons and viewpoints, cultivation of a "habit of amiable cooperation" (Dewey, 1939a/1991, p. 227), and intolerance of bigotry of any kind and anything that stands as barrier to "freedom and fullness of communication" (p. 227) serve as fundamental conditions. In sum, the values underlying our interactions inform our discursive practices. Dewey argued that the future of democracy demands moving beyond the provinces of special interests, divisive politics, and social bigotries in order to engage more deeply with what democracy means, both as an ideal orienting action and as means through which a more democratic society might be realized; this is a challenge, he writes, that "places a heavier demand on human creativeness" (1939a/1991, p. 225).

In such a light, Omar Swartz, Katia Campbell, and Christina Pestana (2009) offer a sustained analysis of these constitutive moral grounds for communicative engagement and develop a fertile notion of democracy that is generative of "more democracy." Specifically, by "creative democracy" the authors mean "a society that continues dynamically to evolve in its ability to be inclusive, fair, and just through the active participation of all its citizens, a society without what Marx (1852/1963) called a *lumpenproletariat* (i.e., a dejected underclass or 'surplus' population of unusable or dispensable people" (2009, p. 12). Here, too, democracy must be taken on as a personal and moral responsibility. But what are the dynamics of inclusion and communication and how do they become exemplified? McAffee (2008) helps answer this question by describing communicative/public sphere as the space of discussion, disagreement, and inquiry, informing democratic practice. She writes, without "people engaged in talking, writing, expressing, demonstrating, signifying, performing in a world with and for others, there would be no public sphere . . . This is where democracy takes place" (2008, p. 17).

But today we are failing to create conditions that foster "democratic consciousness" (Hedges, 2009, p. 148), much less those that might renew "faith in the capacity of human beings for intelligent judgment and action" (Dewey, 1939a/1991, p. 227). I argue that this is because we have lost common ground for discursive interaction. Instead, ready availability of "consumer goods, and a comfortable standard of living, along with a vast entertainment industry that provides spectacles and appealing diversions, keep the citizenry politically passive" (Hedges, 2009, p. 148; Postman, 1985). But because economic stability is increasingly under siege this creates a climate of "inverted totalitarianism" (Hedges, 2009, p. 148), rendered passive, dulled by the illusions of corporate American, and vulnerable to the rant of populist demagogues promising social and national salvation (Hedges, 2009, pp. 148-149).

Dewey believed "fraternally shared experience" to be a "precondition" for democratic process and "the creation of a true public" (1927/1954, p. 218). Shared experience finds its reference in a common world of diverse perspectives, not within a unitary group-identified discursive frame where belonging is signified by agreement and iteration of the right signs. In other words, communication for democratic life is not just "talk," but is an interchange among individuals whose bonds are forged by shared experience, not coded lexicon or conforming systems of belief. As is the case for those whose frame *for* experience is group-identified, individual frames can become rigidified, compromising the possibility of communicative exchange (Sorrells and Nakagawa, 2008). Language *as* communication, however, is transactional and therefore generative of the ways we shape and make meaning, describe problems, interpretate, understand, reflect, and criticize (Dewey, 1925/1988b; Stuhr, 1997). "Language is a tool" for this process, in fact, it is "the tool of tools" (Dewey, 1925/1988b, p. 146), "the cherishing mother of all significance" (p.146), chiseling shared experience vis-à-vis inquiry, analysis, criticism, debate, and imaginative re-visioning (Dewey, 1925/1988b; Stuhr, 1997; McAffee, 2008; Swartz, et al, 2009).

Plurality and Multiplicities

Perhaps there is a way to approach the problem of the communicative crisis and analyze American society differently. For, while Dewey believed the "responsive art" of communication to be fundamental for democracy and requisite for the emergence of the public, perhaps it is the case that the idea of "public" is better served by "publics" in the plural. The emergence of small and local "publics" still carries the possibility of the face-to-face communication that Dewey saw as a "precondition" for democratic interchange. Within the local community it is still possible to see how our own input and actions might change the course of outcomes, for example such as those we endeavor to influence when it is a matter of a school referendum, a neighborhood re-zoning, a proposal for a bus-line, or the institution of leash laws for pets. (Green, 1995; McAffee, 2008). If we were invested in a situation, we would no doubt find "semiotic modes to participate with others, to coordinate action and produce outcomes" (McAffee, 2008, p. 16). David Hildebrand (2008), following James Gouinlock (1988), suggests that this idea of "publics" in the plural is Dewey's own: "while we may habitually think of 'the public' as singular; on Dewey's account, there can be many 'publics'" (p. 115). The issues that engage public, democratic process might be controversial. The point is not that democracy begins on the side of moral rectitude and justice, but that recognition of a shared problem informs inquiry and binds "the ties which hold men together in action" (Dewey, 1927/1954, p. 142). While from the outside it may appear that a social group is engaged in shared action, inquiries and solutions are likely to align with the meaning frame of the associated group. In contrast, the democratic discursive arena is replete with diversity -- that is plurality.

Both Dewey and Arendt viewed human plurality as a fundamental feature of the public sphere, in that pluralism conveys both the separateness of persons in their perspectival uniqueness and the interrelatedness of persons as they speak and act together. Within the public sphere common bonds are forged with respect to the "common world" (Arendt, 1977, p. 50) or, for Dewey, a shared "problematic situation" (1927/1954). Human plurality is one reason democratic process is so fraught with *agon*, but the multiplicity of perspectives shared vis-à-vis the public sphere is why the "process of experience is . . . educative" (Dewey, 1939/1991, p. 229). Ideologically enframed group process is more agreeable, but meanings are transferred not generated. These groups reflect social polarizations or disengagement rather than exemplify genuine "democratic polity" (Dewey, 1927/1954, p. 111; Putnam, 2000). Bonds of association forged by shared reality are not unified through a discursive meaning schema, but multiplied through interactive and engaged communication. Unification of views is not the goal of communication, but rather, as democratic process, growth (Dewey 1916/1944; Hildebrand, 2008). Dewey emphasized the moral core of democracy as necessitating self-reflective intelligence and a social generosity -- again, a "faith" in the possibilities of human cooperation, inclusivity, civility, and peace. Pluralism lies at the heart of communication, and is a feature of experience.

"Publics" on a small and admittedly vital scale are specific-issue or problem oriented, and are temporary or relatively so, depending on the problem at hand and on the level of commitment towards finding the best solution. These small-scale publics are necessary for democratic process. But at a deeper level, Dewey's concern about the disappearance of the public sphere is of a different order than that which can be addressed or answered by local, albeit meaningful, instantiations of public action. As he writes in *The Public and its Problems*:

> [T]here are too many publics, for conjoint actions which have indirect, serious and enduring consequences are multitudinous beyond comparison, and each one of them crosses the others and generates its own group of persons especially affected with little to hold these different publics together in an integrated whole. (Dewey, 1927/1954, p. 137)

It is this loss of the "integrated whole" (Dewey, 1927/1954, p. 137) that informs Dewey's warning in 1927 about the eclipse of the public sphere and in

1939 about the potential loss of democracy itself; it is the reason he argued that democracy must become "a personal way of life" and operative as "a moral ideal" (1939a/1991, p. 226).

It may be the case that problem or interest-specific publics will increasingly represent instantiations of democratic process in the United States today. If so, the question haunts: at the end of the first decade of the 21st century, what are the ties that bind America as a nation? As Dewey warned in 1939, the "merely legal guarantees of civil liberties, of free belief, free expression, free assembly are of little avail if in daily life freedom of communication, the give and take of ideas, facts, and experiences, is choked by mutual suspicion, by abuse, by fear, and hatred" (1939a/1991, p. 228).

Conclusion

In this chapter I have taken John Dewey's warning about the eclipse of the public -- understood as the discursive arena of democratic engagement and action -- as a point of departure for evaluating the disappearance of this discursive sphere in our own contemporary era. The loss of communicative interchange curtails democratic process, resulting in the "crisis" Dewey examined in his 1939 essay. The crisis was attitudinal, in part signified by a facile sense of certainty about the future of American democracy, as if the country's heritage and institutions of governance were both self-perpetuating and adequate to withstand the dangers of fascism then engulfing the countries of Europe. But Dewey saw the real danger to democracy as lying within our country's borders. As he wrote, "Intolerance, abuse, calling of names because of differences of opinion about religion or politics or business, as well as because of differences of race, color, wealth or degree of culture are treason to the democratic way of life" (1939a/19991, p. 227). Today, this "treason" seems to have become a new moral order, for discussion and debate, and what counts for social/political commentary, align according to ideological meaning-frames, designated by tropes or conjured by an image; communication is not the point, identification is. This is why Hedges warns, in a not-so-faint echo of Dewey: "At no period in American history has our democracy been in such peril or the possibility of totalitarianism as real" (2009, p. 145).

A rigid group-identified meaning frame rejects the possibility that experience could inform and enrich belief, but it also rejects the possibility that belief might inform and enrich experience. Instead, there is an intrinsic rigidity to viewpoints tightly held, as if the world would disappoint us if we were forced to face reality (Boorstin, 1961/1987; Berger, 1972; Hedges, 2009). Dewey's answer to the crisis of democracy was to urge reassessment of detrimental and habituated attitudes, in order to re-create democratic practice as moral ideal, practiced as "a way of life controlled by a working faith in the possibilities of human nature," that is, "faith in the capacity of human beings for intelligent judgment and action if proper conditions are furnished" (1939a/1991, pp. 226-227).

Creating proper conditions for the emergence of the public sphere today would necessitate challenging the manipulative power of pseudo-events so that the possibility of working together would begin by interrogation of reality, as opposed to honing the "proper" reaction in view of how an issue, problem, or experience must be viewed, read, understood, and disseminated. But this would demand from us a "working faith" in the possibilities of communication and in democratic process -- shown by renewed commitment to "working together" according to the ideals of democracy, such as equality, justice, inclusion, fairness, and "the free play of facts and ideas which are secured by effective guarantees of free inquiry, free assembly and free communication" (Dewey, 1939a/1991, p. 227). Such work would demand recognizing that democracy is not natural or self-perpetuating, and that "no matter how uniform and constant human nature is in the abstract, the conditions within which and upon which it operates have changed so greatly since political democracy was established among us, that democracy cannot now depend upon or be expressed in political institutions alone" (Dewey, 1939b/2008, p. 151).

Democracy "expressed in the attitudes of human beings" would require an internalization of values that would make democracy a personal moral way of life. This view is not anodyne but moral; it is motivated by a genuine "love of neighbor" demanding of us respect for the diversity of persons and opinions, which is to take the very hard road of democratic process, "the road which places the greatest burden of responsibility on the greatest number of human beings" (Dewey, 1939b/2008, p. 154).

Today, the idea that "democracy is a moral ideal" seems to be lost among the voices bitterly descrying the loss of the "American dream," which lately means little more than the realization of pecuniary fantasies or momentary celebrity (Hedges, 2009). Such is the incoherence of discourse across disagreement and difference that marks a significant shift in the circumstances of our country today, and I have argued here that contemporary social/political differences cannot be evaluated solely on the basis of disagreement but rather must first address and problematize the conditions that vitiate emergence of the discursive public sphere, and the practice of democratic life.

REFERENCES

Arendt, H. (1958). *The human condition.* Chicago: University of Chicago Press.

---. (1954). *Men in dark times.* Orlando: Harcourt, Brace, Jovanovich.

Berger, J. (1977). *Ways of seeing.* New York: Penguin.

Boorstin, D. (1992). *The image: A guide to pseudo-events in America.* New York: Vintage. (Original published 1961)

Burke, K. (1945). *A grammar of motives.* New York: Prentice-Hall.

Danisch, R. (2007). *Pragmatism, democracy, and the necessity of rhetoric.* Columbia: University of South Carolina Press.

Dewey, J. (1944). *Democracy and education: An introduction to the philosophy of education.* New York: Free Press. (Original published in 1914)

---. (1988a). *The middle works, v. 14: Human nature and conduct.* Carbondale: Southern Illinois University Press: Carbondale. (Original published in 1922)

---. (1988b). *The later works, v. 1: Experience and nature.* Carbondale, IL: Southern Illinois University Press. (Original published in 1925)

---. (1954). *The public and its problems.* Athens, OH: Swallow Press. (Original published in 1927)

---. (1984). *The later works, v. 3: Meaning and Existence.* Carbondale, IL: Southern Illinois University Press. (Original published in 1928)

---. (2008). *The later works, v. 13: 1938-1939: Freedom and culture.* Carbondale, IL: Southern Illinois University Press. (Original published in 1939)

---. (1991). *The later works, v. 14: 1939-1941: Essays, reviews, and siscellany* ("Creative Democracy"). Carbondale, IL: Southern Illinois University Press. (Original published in 1939)

Duncan, H. D. (1967). The Search for a social theory of communication in American sociology. In F. E X. Dance (Ed.), *Human communication theory: Original essays* (pp. 236-263). New York: Holt, Rinehart and Winston.

Eldridge, M. (1998). *Transforming experience: John Dewey's cultural instrumentalism.* Nashville: Vanderbilt University Press.

Ellul, J. (1973). *Propaganda: The formation of men's attitudes.* New York: Vintage Books. (Original published in 1965)

Gilbert, G. (1947). *Nuremberg diary.* New York: Farrar, Straus & Co.

Goffman, E. (1959). *The presentation of self in everyday life.* Garden City, N.Y.: Doubleday.

Gouinlock, J. (1972). *John Dewey's philosophy of value.* New York: Humanities Press.

Green, J. M. (1999). *Deep democracy.* Lanham, MD: Roman & Littlefield.

Hardt, H. (1992). *Critical communication Studies: Community, history and theory in America.* New York: Routledge.

Hedges, C. (2009). *Empire of illusion: The end of literacy and the triumph of spectacle.* New York: Nation Books.

---. (2006). *American fascists: The Christian right and the war on America.* New York: Free Press.

Hertzberg, H. (2010, Jan. 11). The talk of the town. *The New Yorker,* pp. 23-24.

Hildebrand, D. (2008). *Dewey: A beginner's guide.* Oxford: One World Books.

Klein, N. (2007). *The shock doctrine: The rise of disaster capitalism.* New York: Metropolitan Books.

McAfee, N. (2008). *Democracy and the political unconscious.* New York: Columbia University Press.

Pappas, G. (2008). *John Dewey's ethics: Democracy as experience.* Indianapolis: Indiana University Press.

Postman, N. (1985). *Amusing ourselves to death: Public discourse in the age of show business.* New York: Penguin.

Putnam, R. (2000). *Bowling alone: The collapse and revival of American community.* New York: Simon Schuster.

Rosenthal, S. (2005). The ontological grounding of diversity: A pragmatic overview. *The Journal of Speculative Philosophy, 9(2)*, 107-119.

Sandel, M. (1982). *Liberalism and the limits of justice*. Cambridge: Cambridge University Press.

Sorrells, K. and Nakagawa, G. (2008). Intercultural communication praxis and the struggle for social responsibly and social justice. In O. Swartz (Ed.), *Transformative communication studies: Culture, hierarchy and the human condition* (pp. 17-43). Leicester, UK: Troubador Publishing.

Stuhr, J. (1997). *Genealogical pragmatism: Philosophy, experience, and community*. Albany, NY: SUNY Press.

---. (2003). *Pragmatism, post-modernism, and the future of philosophy*. New York: Routledge.

Swartz, O. (2009). *Persuasion as a critical activity* 2nd ed. Dubuque, IO: Kendall/Hunt.

---. (2008). Hierarchy, values and political identities in the imperial practices of the United States. In O. Swartz (Ed.), *Transformative communication studies: Culture, hierarchy and the human condition* (pp. 249-280). Leicester, UK: Troubador Publishing.

---, and Pestana, C. (2008). Communication, social justice, and creative democracy. In O. Swartz (Ed.), *Transformative communication studies: Culture, hierarchy and the human condition* (pp. 91-113). Leicester, UK: Troubador.

---, Campbell, K., and Pestana, C. (2009). *Neo-Pragmatism, communication, and the culture of creative democracy*. New York: Peter Lang.

White, J. B. (2007). *Living speech: Resisting the empire of force*. Princeton, NJ: Princeton University Press.

Williams, P. (2009). "Voice of America?" in *The Nation*. October 12 2009, p. 9.

Notes

[1] The vision some still hold out for the United States as a communal, pluralistic network of interconnecting, interrelating individuals sounds utopian (i.e., Green, 1995; Danisch, 2007; Swartz, et al., 2009). But discursive dissonance between and among a multitude of "antagonistic entities" is only one part of the communicative crisis. A related issue is the fragmentation of social space and increasing divisiveness in the absence of a public sphere.

[2] "Pseudo-events" compel attention through contrivance, enhancement of the real -- or replacement of reality -- giving us, as Daniel Boorstin describes, a "new kind of synthetic novelty," that floods our senses and replaces "the world's deficiency" by intensifying everyday experience (Boorstin, 1961/1987, p. 9; Lasch, 1991, p. 30; Hedges, 2009, p. 15).

[3] The August 2008 transcripts of the Saddleback Interviews were found on Eric Rasmusen's Weblog at http://rasmusen.org/t/2008/08/obama-and-mccain-on-evil.html. Comments within quotation marks belong to the speakers.

[4] Dewey was not the only one. Hermann Goering, Hitler's second in command, showed great acumen in utilizing this principle. In an interview shortly before he was to be tried for war crimes at the Nuremberg Trials, he remarked:

> Voice or no voice, the people can always be brought to do the bidding of the leaders. That is easy. All you have to do is tell them they are being attacked, and denounce the peacemakers for lack of patriotism and exposing the country to danger. It is the same in any country. (Quoted in Gilbert, 1947, pp. 278-279)

[5] See Swartz et al (2009), Chapter 2, for an analysis of this reference to Satan in contemporary political discourse.

CHAPTER 3

Leisure, Communication, and Politics: Cultivating Creative Democracy

Annette M. Holba
Plymouth State University

The engagement of philosophical leisure in the lives of individual citizens can help cultivate John Dewey's (1939/1991) notion of "creative democracy" by enabling people to engage thoughtfully ideas that can revision new possibilities inherent in creative citizenry. The ability for people to engage in citizenship practices, duties, and responsibilities is especially helpful for those citizens who may have previously experienced limits or challenges in their contribution and participation in the public forum. Some examples include women winning the right to vote, African Americans the right to attend the same schools as whites, and the growing public discourse regarding sexual orientation and gay marriage. Dewey's notion of creative democracy is constituted through *poiesis*, or through a creative *making*, in the public domain. As I will argue in this chapter, a healthy communicative environment where *poiesis* exists emerges from the individual participant's private domain through a habituated engagement of philosophical leisure that involves contemplative practice and an innerplay with ideas about something. This interplay is an intellectual activity that involves hard work and a disciplined focus of attention. The ability to engage ideas thoughtfully, even when ideas involve complexities, is essential in a creative democracy because intellectual acuity, agility, and perseverance are often a necessary element of democratic practices. Philosophical leisure cultivates one's mental and physical acuity so that participation in public democratic processes is productive and meaningful.

This chapter opens with a discussion of philosophical leisure through a diverse examination of theoretical and philosophical perspectives ranging from ancient to modern. Through this discussion, a rhetorical eclipse of leisure is identified whereby I describe how the distinction between *leisure* and *recreation* became lost in public discourse and in the practical doing of leisure. This overview identifies a distinction between leisure and recreation that is not widely acknowledged in contemporary public practices. Second, as philosophical leisure has the potential to move citizens from *spectators* to *participants* in the shaping of their human communicative behavior, I discuss John Dewey's notion of a creative democracy and demonstrate how citizens benefit from genuinely integrating leisure into their lives. Third, I provide a practical example that offers social, political, and philosophical implications of the integration of philosophical leisure into a public sociopolitical wellness manifested through Dewey's creative democracy. My example considers how folk music, practiced as an action of leisure, provided an escape for African slaves that would come to transform their oppressed existence during the years in which slavery was common practice in the United States, especially in the south. Philosophical leisure cultivates the ground upon which creative democracy can be embraced by citizens to forge social/political change and transform their own interiority.

Philosophical Leisure

Leisure, in this philosophical sense, has been long considered the basis of culture (Pieper, 1948/1998; Katz and Gurevitch, 1976; Sennett, 1974; and Goodale and Godbey, 1988). Philosophical leisure has the power to recuperate the human spirit, rekindle the desire to have a healthy communicative relationship with others, and enable communication competence in public settings. As Josef Pieper (1948/1998) writes, leisure "is a form of stillness that is a necessary preparation for accepting reality; only the person who is still can hear, and whoever is not still, cannot hear" (p. 31). The ability to hear enables the actor to perceive and understand the world differently so that she or he can fully engage others competently. Moreover, he notes, "the power to be at leisure is the power to step beyond the working world and win contact with those superhuman, life-giving forces that can send us, renewed and alive again, into the busy world of work" (p. 36). Pieper described leisure as a philosophical act that is internal and nourishes "the ability to have a real relationship, a relation to the external" (p. 81), which means a relationship with other human beings. In a social scientific study of leisure, Elihu Katz and Michael Gurevitch (1976) state that, in Israel, leisure activities are "devoted to 'social life'" (p. 49) and cultivating human connectedness. Finally, Ronald C. Arnett (2007) reminds us that the doing of philosophical leisure "helps us regain a communicative pulse in a dejected world" (p. 11).

Leisure in the above sense is not synonymous with recreation; but to most, this distinction is not obvious. One of the reasons that this distinction is not widely known can be traced back to precursors of the protestant work ethic described by Max Weber who suggested people are called to embrace worldly obligations to earn a living, which required people to be immersed in working in the world. The focus of attention in this case involves attending to an obligation for a particular worldly purpose rather than to engage the activity for the sake of itself. In other words, Weber described a loss of the aesthetic in human actions. This differs slightly from John Calvin's doctrine of predestination which advocated that one had to earn one's way into heaven (Weber, 1958/2003). Even earlier, Petrarch (1345-47/2002) noted that a group of monks argued that a quantifiable or profitable outcome of a given activity is necessary to be deemed worthy of entering into heaven. These monks suggested that if something tangible was not earned from a sacred and contemplative practice, then the activity was not worthy of doing. Their preference was to see a tangible outcome from any kind of work for the activity to be valuable work. The shift toward a material outcome indicates that the aesthetic notion connected to leisure was lost. The monks focused more on worldly *exteriority* than on moral excellence of one's *interiority* which was the ancient Greek ideal. This mindset pervaded popular culture as the reformation grew and the eclipse of leisure settled in the public mind which marked the beginning of the public blurring between leisure and recreation as both focused on the outcome (Holba, 2007).

A look at the western tradition of leisure can be helpful as we recall the original meaning of leisure. Aristotle (1941/2001) described leisure as the first principle of all action. Cicero (1902) claimed that a person is never busier than when at leisure. Seneca (2003) advocated that a contemplative life of leisure *was* a life of action. Petrarch (1345-47/2002) described two kinds of leisure, one as an "evil leisure" that represented a misunderstanding from the original Greek notion of leisure by having a focus on material outcomes, and the other as "true leisure" since it was action initiated within a contemplative framework. Rousseau (1755/1984) considered the metaphors of leisure and luxury and described people as being greedy in the pursuit of comforts that generally created idleness and laziness in human beings and would ultimately impoverish the human race. To the contrary, Thomas Hobbes (1651/1996) referred to leisure as the "mother" of philosophy. While other philosophers continued to have their own views on leisure, there came an early critique of leisure through the aesthetic sensibility of Immanuel Kant (1930/1963). Kant wrote about freedoms that came from our scientific advancements and provided daily luxury and argued that they came with a responsibility to use them wisely. This wisdom includes knowing how to be efficient and expeditious with one's use of time. However, Kant also suggested, many people allowed those advancements to cultivate their individual laziness, which meant that people failed to accept this newly found responsibility. According to Kant, "[m]an must, therefore, discipline his mind in regard to the necessities of life [because. . .] man becomes dependent upon a multitude of pseudo-necessities" (p. 173). Additionally, Kant suggested that the "prevalence of luxury limits the range of our welfare; the prevalence of effeminacy completely saps our human strength" (p. 173). Kant's critique of these new luxuries suggests that his observations pointed toward what Thorstein Veblen (1899/1953) would later mark as a central element of his (Veblen) economic theory and critique of America.

One of the most significant critiques on the use of leisure time in individual lives came from economic theorist Thorstein Veblen (1899/1953) who critiqued people that moved mindlessly from one consumptive experience to another just to show others that they are possessed of the power to waste. This is referred to as "conspicuous consumption" (p. 60) and "pecuniary emulation" (p. 33), which is ultimately a public fraud contributing to pervasiveness of distrust and suspicion in public society. Prior to Veblen's public distain of leisure, Adam Smith (1776/1976) voiced a similar concern and argued that the doing of leisure in a public fashion was a sign of social status, yet such status failed to contribute to life satisfaction. Other Enlightenment philosophers believed leisure equated to the attainment of happiness with the caveat that the more leisure could be experienced the more happiness could be achieved (Bentham, 1876/2005; Mill, 1848/1965).

The Industrial Revolution, followed by innovations in transportation and communication, began to take shape resulting in a mechanistic world paradigm that replaced the natural world paradigm; soon after, people began to change what they did with their non-work time. The steamboat, railroads, steel manufacturers, telegraph, telephone, and advancements in manufacturing all aided in the development of time saving amenities for the consumer. This lead to the rise of the "cult of efficiency," as emerged from the ideas of Frederick Taylor who, in 1899, created a company that provided advice on how to make business more efficient (Goodale and Godbey, 1988, p. 94). Taylor's argument addressed the labor problem in the early-to-middle stages of the industrialization period by reducing the work hours in a day through the "piece-rote" system. In such system, "scientific management and human engineering were means to increase efficiency and thus productivity. Hours of work could be reduced in this way and, coupled with movements by labor and by those promoting sanitation, safety, health, and welfare, legislation, and negotiation led to significant reduction in average hours per week" (Goodale and Godbey, 1998, p. 94-95). Additionally, a significant consequence from the "piece-rote system" increased the pace of work and also further alienated the worker from the product of his labor" (Goodale and Godbey, 198, p. 94-95). The cult of efficiency and productivity propelled the changes that people experienced with their work day, but these changes created unrest in the worker-consumer. The experience of unrest was propelled by the rapid changes people were experiencing in society. Capitalism, urbanization, and industrialization all brought about divisions of labor in society and changes in the way people spent their time away from the workday of previous years (Goodale and Godbey, 1988). These changes led to accumulations of wealth and the emergence of a leisure class.

Veblen (1899/1953) was concerned with the way people used things and money in their lives. He critiqued how people wasted time doing things for the sake of a public reputation or buying things to "keep up with the Joneses" because all of these activities, to Veblen, were mindless activities that created a public facade. Veblen (1899/1953) explained that with "the growth of settled industry, therefore, possession of wealth gains in relative importance and effectiveness as a customary basis of repute and esteem" (p. 37). In a discussion on conspicuous consumption, Veblen added that members of this emerging leisure class "consumes freely and of the best food, drink, narcotics, shelter, services, ornaments, apparel, weapons, and accoutrements, amusements, amulets, and idols or divinities . . . [s]ince the consumption of these more excellent goods is an evidence of wealth, it becomes honorific; and conversely, the failure to consume in due quantity and quality becomes a mark of inferiority and demerit" (p. 64). In other words, Veblen found that members of the emerging leisure class were ostentatious and frivolous because they consumed in order to assert their high social and or economic status. Furthermore, failure to consume in what Veblen would deem "absurd" quantities and qualities might actually reduce social and or economic status rendering the idea of moderation detrimental to a person's reputation.

John Stuart Mill's early utilitarian philosophy, in opposition, suggested that leisure would bring about some kind of benefit or observable/tangible outcome. Veblen's observations and Mill's tangible benefits of leisure contributed to the development of an early leisure industry that would become intertwined in capitalistic philosophy, as Karl Marx would come to acknowledge the abuses and exploitation of those who work and have little time and less means than the capitalist who benefited from the labor of others. Therefore, a discussion of leisure and consumption from a Marxian perspective is helpful to fully understand the implications of leisure to society.

In *Capital*, Marx (1976/1990) analyzed capital as a mode of production. For him, capital involved "a *social relation between men* and things" (p. 54), and he suggested that the capitalist had exploitive power over other beings. Marx stated that "the labour process, therefore, man's activity, *via* the instruments of labour, effects an alteration in the object of labor which was intended from the outset. The process is extinguished in the product" (1976/1990, p. 287). This means the outcome of labor alienates the worker's process of labor because the worker does not own her or his product of labor, the capitalist owned the labor and the product of the labor.

Marx (1843/1971) critiqued capitalism and drew the popular conclusion about religion being the opiate of people. He also argued that people created God in their own image as a response to an alienation of human beings that emerged from a material life. Marx (1843/1971) further suggested that, until the material aspect of life is removed from human experience, people will continue in this "social alienation" (Wilkie, 1976, p. 232). Relative to the leisure-recreation illusion, a purging of materialistic recreation creates another problem because both leisure and recreation, in balance, are needed for human existence. However, understanding the difference of the two concepts would permit the emancipation and dissolve the opiate effect. Opiates have the potential to confuse and mislead people because of their ability to alter one's state of mind physiologically. In this condition, there can be a lack of awareness of one's own reality and the inability to make good decisions. Opiates deceive and hide the truths that are necessary for a healthy private and public life. While religion was the opiate of the people, according to Marx, the merging of leisure and recreation in public consciousness and public actions had a similar opiate effect on the masses. Failure to recognize or understand the distinction between leisure and recreation would then become what Marx referred to as a "fetishism," that is, a "constitutive form of social life and 'embodied' inherently in political and economical activity we referred to as consumption" (Bartels, 1999, p. 123). This condition would be akin to a recreative fetishism that leads to more alienation from, and between, the interior self and the human community. For this reason, the leisure-recreation distinction must be acknowledged in order to bring awareness of this essential condition of human experience.

Contemporary media ecologists share concerns over the mass production of televisions, computers, cinematic offerings, video games, and now, other digital new media technologies for the purpose of overconsumption (Postman, 1985; Winter, 2002; Strate, 2006). Experiencing the technological advancements of the early and mid twentieth century, George Lukács (1972), argued that the pervasiveness of technologies deeply resonate with capitalistic ideology that continue to exploit the common person, and by doing so, create a "false" consciousness that interferes with interpretation and the ability of fully apprehending a full comprehension of things (p. 54). Lukács describes a false consciousness as "self-deceiving" that propels class struggles and continued disillusionment (p. 69). Applied to the leisure-recreation opiate, a false consciousness can be best understood when people have the opportunity to engage in recreative activities to an excess while thinking they are doing leisure. The confusion between the terms creates disillusionment in that people do not realize that they are not doing *leisure* and, in reality, they are engaging *recreation*. An example of this phenomenon happens when people claim they need a vacation after returning home from a week's vacation from their everyday routine. The vacation was a recreative vacation, a time away from the daily work-a-day living toil, but it was not hard intellectual work as much as it was a reprieve from their ordinary day. This is the self-deception of a false consciousness.

Recreation is, in some ways, like a coffee break that offers short term relief which enables a return to the completion of a task. Leisure, if approached with a philosophical spirit, offers long term cultivation, and perhaps, transformative outcomes. Leisure and recreation are necessary experiences that cultivate the human condition, yet, both are experienced differently. The underlying philosophical assumptions, methods, *telos*, and experience of time are characteristically opposing (Holba, 2007). While both aspects of leisure and recreation are needed to nurture and satisfy human experiences (Nippold, Duthie, and Larsen, 2005), the philosophical assumption inherent in recreation is *epistemological* while the philosophical assumption inherent in philosophical leisure is *ontological*. For example, recreation begins with the acquisition of knowledge that teaches how to do something and that something often turns into a social activity because we either like to do things with others or we become competitive with others and, subsequently, we focus on the outcome of the action. Often this engagement is based only on the acquisition of knowledge and the outcome of the activity. But the ontological assumption in philosophical leisure moves beyond the acquisition of knowledge and becomes concerned with one's phenomenological focus of attention on the play itself and not on the outcome. Therefore, the focus is wholly engaged within the action and experience free of expectation and ultimately open to serendipitous emergences.

Telos in recreation moves toward the completion of an activity, but in philosophical leisure, *telos* focuses on *the-thing-itself*, as a processual movement and at once always already in motion. The important aspect of philosophical leisure is the experience itself, not the outcome.

The last conceptual difference is the experience of *time*. Recreation is based on a *chronos* sense of time where there is an emphasis on the where, when, why, and how of an activity. In this mindset, the activity within a particular time of day is related to a particular sequence of events. Philosophical leisure engages time much differently as it is based upon "being" (Holba, 2007, p. 106). Experience in philosophical leisure is ontologically eternal and oppositional to any sense of *chronos* because the concern is with the experience itself through intraplay and interplay of all of the aspects of the activity. The experience of time in philosophical leisure is more aptly associated with *kairos*. According to Omar Swartz (1998), "the principle behind *kairos* is the notion of *kosmos*, or structure within the social community" (p. 77). In *kairos*, the significance is not found through a measured framework but rather emerges from the structure of living with others in a particular context responsive to the interaction with others. *Kairos* reflects the imperative nature of philosophical leisure in that through effective engagement with the "other," community can be built and negotiated in a constructive and healthy manner. The explicit difference between the experience of time in recreation and leisure is that in recreation, time provides a measure by counting and organizing the experience; in philosophical leisure, time provides meaningful experiences that contribute to the larger sense of community. In a sense, time related to *kairos* suggests a focus on the other instead of chronos (*kronos*) in which time is counted and organizes the experience.

In philosophical leisure, a person's phenomenological focus of attention is on *the-thing-itself* and there is no sense of chronological time that governs the experience. The focus of attention is on the action in play and the making that emerges within the experience. This way of engaging philosophical leisure has no attention toward a particular outcome; rather, the focus is on the experience for the sake of the experience. As Josef Pieper (1948/1998) noted, "leisure is not there for the sake of work, no matter how much new strength the one who resumes working may gain from it; leisure in our sense is not justified by providing bodily renewal or even mental refreshment to lend new vigor to further work -- although it does indeed bring such things!" (p. 34). So, what happens as a result of engaging philosophical leisure is interesting in that, at some point, there becomes something new, perhaps a transformation of a spirit, one's interiority, or something else. Nevertheless, the serendipitous outcome that occurs is not planned. This outcome is organic and emerges from the *poiesis*. In some sense, the outcome is a becoming of something that may not have been expected by the player. This kind of becoming does not occur in a recreative experience because one's focus of attention is situated on some kind of outcome, whereas, in philosophical leisure, an individual's focus of attention enters into the experience itself being removed from an expectation of outcomes. The experience of philosophical leisure transcends the mundane, whereas, recreation remains in the mundane. Understanding the difference between leisure and recreation through these differing positions can be helpful to the creation and cultivation of John Dewey's notion of a creative democracy.

Creative Democracy

John Dewey (1859-1952), a prolific philosopher and educational theorist, wrote an essay in 1939 entitled "Creative Democracy -- The Task Before Us" in which he stated that historical and current social and political circumstances had much influence in the shaping of the democracy in which he lived. In his essay, Dewey described his present time as morally contentious:

> The period of free lands that seemed boundless in extent has vanished. Unused resources are now human rather than material. They are found in the waste of grown men and women who are without the chance to work, and in the young men and women who find doors closed where there was once opportunity. The crisis that one hundred and fifty years ago called out social and political inventiveness is with us in a form which puts heavier demand on human creativeness. (p. 228)

Dewey is suggesting that freedoms had been bound, pervasive unemployment represented the wasting of human lives, and hope for future growth was stunted. The conditions that Dewey pointed out provide an ethical imperative pointing to the idea that as social beings we are responsible for the lives of others and the future of the world. For Dewey, the responsibility would need to involve a re-creation by a deliberate democratic practice from people who have had more fortunate circumstances than the Founding Fathers of our country. Dewey called forth people of his time to act as the Founding Fathers and not remain shrouded underneath the veil of entitlement. This creative process that Dewey called for would be hard work, unprecedented, and creative by thinking outside of what is already known while being willing to take a risk in developing ideas. Dewey's critique indicated that people had become complacent and they lost their ability for inventiveness as they negotiate the world. In this sense, Dewey's critique resonates with Richard Sennett's (1974) understanding of a *spectator*, in which he describes a public farce of people looking as if they are actively engaged, while really being passive spectators, unable to think for themselves and unable to take action that has not already been taken. Sennett describes spectators as having "profound self-doubt" (p. 205) and the lack of action taken is really a "defense against the experience of social relations. Observation and turning things over in your mind take the place of discourse" (p. 213). As Sennett describes society, he suggests that "sources of creativity and imagination which existed in the arts were no longer available to nourish everyday life" (p. 218).

Dewey described democracy as a "way of life controlled by a working faith in the possibilities of human nature" (1939/1991, p. 229). The nature in which he describes includes "every human being irrespective of race, color, sex, birth, and family" (1939/1991, p. 229). The notion of equality is essential in Dewey's democracy in that he believed that every person, separate from her or his personal endowment, had equal rights to develop whatever gifts with which they were endowed. Additionally, the idea of a democratic leadership was universal for Dewey as he argued for every person to have the right to lead his or her own life and to be free from imposition from others. A creative democracy was a personal way of life and a faith of human nature. According to Dewey, "Democracy as a personal, an individual, way of life involves nothing fundamentally new . . . Democracy is a way of life controlled by a working faith in the possibilities of human nature (p. 229). Dewey argued that this faith is cultivated by one's environment and by one's experience in it. This faith of democracy is *a priori* for Dewey and functions as a corrective when human beings have the ability and free range to have *free play* with ideas. This aspect, free play of ideas, which is inherent in Dewey's creative democracy, is the central connection that links philosophical leisure to Dewey's creative democracy in our society today. The caveat in this claim is consistent with Dewey's criticism of his historical moment:

> Merely legal guarantees of the civil liberties of free belief, free expression, free assembly are of little avail if in daily life freedom of communication, the give and take of ideas, facts, experiences, is choked by mutual suspicion, by abuse, by fear and hatred. These things destroy the essential condition of the democratic way of living even more effectually than open coercion which -- as the example of totalitarian states proves -- is effective only when it succeeds in breeding hate, suspicion, intolerance in the minds of individual human beings. (1939/1991, p. 230-231)

Dewey was suggesting that limits in adaptabilities create fear, negative judgment, and intolerance, which ultimately cripples the growth and ideas that constitute a creative democracy. This type of crippling creates imposters, propels unequal public power and oppression, and limits human beings to a spectator status in their own government and their own lives. Dewey's concern for complacency of human beings and their preference for spectatorship is an ethical concern tied to politics, economics, and basic social conditions of living with others. Complacency and spectatorship hampered people's ability to run their own government. As he noted, "Persons acutely aware of the dangers of regimentation when it is imposed by government remain oblivious of the millions of persons whose behavior is regimented by an economic system through whose invention alone they obtain a livelihood" (Dewey, 1998, p. 362). In this kind of system, those in leadership positions take advantage of those governed. Further, this kind of leadership does not follow democratic procedure. Dewey's idea of democracy invites those who are complacent and/or those who are limited as spectators into public realm of action. Perhaps, it is the invitation that can inspire those previously muted voices. This invitation is also what situates democracy as a communication ethic.

A comprehensive consideration of communication ethics as a discipline identifies six approaches to communication. These approaches include: *democratic communication ethics, universal-humanitarian ethics, codes, procedures, and standards in communication ethics, contextual communication ethics, narrative communication ethics*, and *dialogic communication ethics* (Arnett, Fritz, and Bell, 2009). In this chapter, I am concerned with the first approach, *democratic communication ethics*, though there may be areas of overlap from more than one approach that could emerge in this discussion. According to Ronald C. Arnett, Janie Harden Fritz, and Leeanne M. Bell (2009), democratic communication ethics is "a public communication ethic process for discussion of ideas, customs, and rights, protecting and promoting the good of collaborative decision making" (p. 44). Specifically, in the communication discipline, democratic communication ethics trace back to classical Greek democracy. However, significant development of a democratic communication ethic emerged in the early and midpoint of the twentieth century during times of war, "stress points," and growth in the American national fabric (Arnett, Fritz, and Bell, 2009, p. 46).

Earlier in American history, conditions of economic stress and military struggles would come to have impact on the development of a democratic communicative ethic that Dewey's notion of creative democracy embodies. For instance, Karl Wallace's (1955) model of a democratic communication ethic suggested that to ensure the practice of a democratic ethic, the following paradigm ought to be followed: First, be open to new ideas. Second, in the name of justice, gain accurate facts. Third, privilege the common public good over one's own individual preference. Finally, be inviting toward difference in the spirit of learning (Wallace, 1955; Arnett, Fritz, and Bell, 2009). These aspects are essential for a public democratic ethic and Dewey's creative democracy follows this framework, though it is not without criticism.

Critics of Dewey's participatory democracy suggest that he is "hopelessly utopian" in that he maintained an ideal position that perhaps is more of a metaphysical treatise on democracy instead of a practical guide to basic obstacles by developing and elaborating on strategies of engagement in a practical setting (Westbrook, 1991, p. xiv-xv). Other critics suggest that Dewey in general is an anti-essentialist related to his educational theory but not his democratic theory, demonstrating a flexibility in his philosophical suppositions (Bynum, 2005). On the other hand, Dewey is also seen as a "major contributor to the emerging theory of participatory democracy" who recognizes that the condition of conflict is a natural condition situated within human nature (Caspary, 2000). This natural condition of conflict is "inescapable in democratic political life" (Langsdorf, 2003, p. 214).

Recalling Karl Wallace's paradigm for a democratic ethic, there is a distinct similarity to Dewey's creative democracy. First, Dewey's creative democracy is open to new ideas since it is open to all voices having equality. The participation of all voices does not imply that governance has no centrality or stability. Rather, it means that all voices are participatory through listening and contributing to conversations that will ultimately move ideas to action for the common public good. Second, the focus on justice that implies using accurate facts to move toward a justice that privileges truth and the public common good is inherent in Dewey's creative democracy because of the openness to ideas that can lead to truths that may have been formerly hidden. This aspect of creative democracy is significant for the pursuit toward social justice which requires "the active and continual process of inquiring, identifying, and challenging the discourses, structures, systems, and norms that institutionalize poverty, inequality, and the dehumanization of others" (Swartz, Campbell, and Pestana, 2009, p. 28). Next, privileging of the public common good over individual agency is paramount to the ethical nature of both Wallace and Dewey's democratic paradigm. Agency opposes the embedded agent. The difference between one driven by agency and one driven as an embedded agent is that the embedded agent considers her or his connection to others before taking action. The person driven purely by agency is only concerned with what she or he will gain, even at the expense of others. As Ronald C. Arnett (2005) points out, the embedded agent is "located within and responsive to the horizon of a given story and to the historical situation" (p. 44). Finally, Wallace's notion to be inviting toward difference in the spirit of learning is essential for creative democracy because it is the "invitation" that is paramount. The openness of an invitation is not imposing but it does cultivate common ground for people to come together to have a free play of ideas in the spirit of exchange, growth, and perhaps, transformation. The invitation for free play moves this discussion to the question: how can philosophical leisure cultivate Dewey's notion of creative democracy?

Philosophical leisure can cultivate John Dewey's notion of creative democracy because the experience of philosophical leisure begins with a contemplative spirit that ultimately provides the idea-driven content for public participation. Philosophical leisure cultivates one's interiority which resonates with the German concept of *Bildung* in that both concepts focus on the "inner-self cultivation" through the acquisition of comprehensive knowledge" (Bauer, 2003, p. 211). Scholars have identified the connection between *Bildung* and democracy and suggest that this naturally creates a transformation of public lives and community (Bauer, 2003). *Poiesis* permits *Bildung* to thrive, encouraging communicative agents to become active and ethical participants within their citizenry. The outcome of this kind of leisure shapes the active participant that Richard Sennett (1974) advocated being a worthy public citizen. Essential for the cultivation of *Bildung* is an idea developed by Omar Swartz, Katia Campbell, and Christina Pestana (2009) that they refer to as a "critical imagination" that is "concerned with questions of *praxis* and power, issues that we engage with constantly without giving them much thought, thus giving up control of our destinies" (p. 35). Philosophical leisure provides and cultivates theoretical ground from which one can effectively derive content to genuinely and actively participate in decision making and other discussions that have public political implications. Philosophical leisure enables the critical imagination to develop. This happens because, as one attends to ideas contemplatively and attentively, one is also cultivating related ideas that can later emerge in another form or contextual engagement. As Sennett suggests, an active participant becomes "enmeshed in a scene" in public visibility and action (1974, p. 27).

Philosophical leisure is an activity that can help rebuild trust between people and between people and their government. Philosophical leisure cultivates one's ability to work with ideas, to generate new ideas, and to see connections between ideas that are thoughtful contributions to decision making in the public democratic context. A democratic ethic argues for free play of ideas, especially between competing voices, and in order to meet this requirement, one must already have the ability or the capacity to productively and constructively participate this free play. Philosophical leisure hones this ability of free play because the action of free play is not *content* driven; rather, it is *processually* driven. Negotiating free play of ideas regularly fosters the ability to engage the motion of free play in other contexts. For example, in free play, the contemplation of ideas in a particular fashion focuses on the thinking and the idea while not expecting a particular outcome. This negotiation of free play becomes habituated in philosophical leisure and the habituation is what enables the application in other contexts. Finding a leisure activity that is separate from work and from recreation is the ideal condition for experiencing philosophical leisure and free play. This idea of "free play" begins the next section of this chapter that explores a praxis-oriented example.

Participants in Action Through Leisure

Free play can have a multiplicity of meanings (i.e., play limited to physical activity, no cost to engage the activity, or freedom to choose the kind of play one wants). However, for the purpose of this chapter, free play is defined as unrestricted *poiesis*. *Poiesis* is Greek for "making" and implies an active involvement. *Poiesis* in communication has been described as a "communicative dance" that cultivates dialectical texture and complexity necessary for honest communicative exchanges (Arnett, 2005, p. 15). This is when human interlocutors can negotiate differences of opinion constructively and develop common ground while finding common places to continue to hash out responses that can eventually lead toward an appropriate and fitting outcome.

The process of communication is always ongoing and yet, it is often difficult and awkward. The agents involved are embedded within a context that is respectful and tolerant, especially when finding common ground becomes difficult. Having ways of thinking and articulating constructively becomes essential in order to find a healthy and productive response to whatever decision is before the public. This process is not easy because it is easier to ignore the other and her or his ideas. What is more difficult, however, is the endurance it takes to come to an agreement about something through a free play unhampered by agency. If we engage things as in the doing of philosophical leisure, we are engaged in free play as an intellectual activity that is grounded in a contemplative framework. The more philosophical leisure we have in our lives, the easier it is to engage public political communication in a similar manner. The endurance of this action can transform an individual or a nation.

One example of how philosophical leisure can be transformative to an individual and a nation is the story of slavery in the United States. The following section discusses how African slaves, after being unwillingly brought to the United States for the purpose of being bought and sold as property, removed from their own country and home through force and trickery, could find the spirit to continue on in life despite all of the obstacles forced upon them. One might wonder how these individuals survived such an inhumane experience that lasted a lifetime for most. A consideration of how African slaves engaged philosophical leisure through the engagement of music to the point of individual transformation, and subsequently national transformation, exemplifies the argument of this chapter.

Slavery in the Nineteenth Century

Slavery was introduced to the United States in 1619, and by the 1800s the tradition of slavery had become embedded in particular regions with over one million slaves in servitude at that time. Most of the slaves at this time were from West Africa or of Caribbean decent (Koskoff, 2005). Slavery, as a legal institution in the United States, began to change as the abolitionist movement gained support and as class distinctions and ridged hierarchies among whites intensified (Swartz, 2004b). While the victory of the North in the Civil War marked the promise of social and cultural change for the former slaves, the end of legal slavery did not mean the end of discrimination and oppression for African Americans. In order for significant social and cultural change to occur, social and political unrest would remerge one hundred years later in the civil rights movement to reach toward another milestone in history (Koskoff, 2005). Music of the slave culture in the United States was shaped by instruments, such as drums and gourd rattles, that the slaves brought within them to their new surroundings. Slaves also maintained their traditional musical forms that involved their instruments as well as dance and ritual (Koskoff, 2005).

During the transatlantic journey from Africa to the New World, the ship's crew would invite their passengers (slaves) to dance, sing, and play their instruments in order to keep them fit so they get a good wage from their cargo (Burnim and Maultsby, 2006). The intellectual history of the relationship between music and slavery has been garnered from diaries, journals, reports, and memoirs that have been offered from firsthand experience. Initially, African music had very distinct qualities that were outside of the mainstream European musical culture. Of these qualities, most notably, was the use of antiphony in the musical structure.[1] Additionally, the use of drum, dance, verbalization, and different kinds of musical instruments were also identified as the causes of pejorative labels of their music as "barbaric," "wild," and "nonsensical" (Burnim and Maultsby, 2006). To survive in this new hostile, white culture, the black slave culture had to adapt (Hall, 1996). They did so by developing a hymn-singing tradition that incorporated English rhythms (Wootton, 2007). Though, the Negro folk spiritual that originated out of the slavery experience would come to symbolize black cultural identity.

The writing of public history related to the slavery experience may have been seen as insignificant, since spirituals that permeated the slave culture in the nineteenth century have not always been considered by white intellectuals to be a bonafide part of historical discourse (DuBois, 1903/1989; Koskoff, 2005). Today, as histories are being more accurately rewritten, we are more informed about the relationship between music and cultural identity (Koskoff, 2005). For some, the spirituals that were most pervasive during the nineteenth century are simply reminders of earlier, more turbulent times in our country; yet for others, they may resonate with very different feelings. America's slavery years were absolutely "dark times," a term borrowed from Hannah Arendt (1968/1983) that suggests the white dominant culture exploited black people by forcing them into hard labor and a miserable life devoid of most kinds of individual freedoms and basic respect of, and, for others. The dark times of slavery reflect a period of violence against humanity, as slavery removed individual freedom and identity from people placed in captivity. Music and social identity work together for "individuals or groups to help defines themselves in relation to others and as a means for others to define them as well" (Koskoff, 2005, p. 19). Music is a powerful tool that we can use to engage everyday existence and negotiate through dark times.

Blacks in slavery, and the few outside of slavery, lived in a world that confined their ability to grow and transform as human beings. Their self image was shaped through a distortion of their existence in the world as opposed to others. The music that lived in their hearts was connected to their spirit and their community, which often consisted of other slaves. Music that came from the black slave experience told stories of these experiences. Through the telling and sharing of these stories, identification and relationships between slaves strengthened. This strength provided support and motivation for individual slaves that enabled them to cope with their everyday toil. While one could argue that slave spirituals depicted their sense of hopelessness and depression, I maintain that their music was an action of *poiesis* that cultivated their soul or their interiority in order for them to live their lives in hope. These slavery spirituals tell us today about their reactions to their harsh living conditions and what it did to their human condition.

Consider the following example for a spiritual in which the singer exclaims: "I got shoes, You got shoes/All God's children got shoes/And walk all over God's Heaven!" (Jones and Jones, 2001, p. 9). Here, the slave is identifying with other slaves, and perhaps with the slave owners, by revealing that both the I and the Other wear shoes. In the story, all God's children wear shoes and this attribute identifies the slave with Christianity. Since the slave is identified with Christianity, this song also identifies the slave as an equal to the master in the eye of their Christian God, even though not all slaves were Christians. When the first slaves were brought to the United States, they brought along with them their own belief systems and traditions, which were generally not Christian (Jones, 1999, p. 18). So, this slavery spiritual places the slave and master as equals in that they are both God's children and they will both go to heaven. In identifying themselves as Christians through their slave songs, slaves began to fuse their tribal beliefs with Christianity (Berry and Blassingame, 1977; Baldwin, 1984). Additionally, this particular spiritual is liberating to the slave because, in the song, the slave has shoes and walks about freely. In reality, the slave might have shoes but she or he does not have the liberation that the song suggests. So, perhaps metaphorically, the power of the slave songs provides an emotional liberation or a metaphysical catharsis in lieu of an immediate physical liberation.

The spiritual provokes the imagination of the slave in which a new home is discovered, that being Heaven. The author of the spiritual, perhaps the slave who sings the spiritual, is also sending a message to the master, that all people under God are equal in His eyes and that all people have shoes and should be able to walk about freely. By singing this spiritual the slave is also affirming her or his identity by announcing that she or he is somebody. This is an application of philosophical leisure because in the singing of the spiritual the slave is mindful and contemplative, carefully selecting words so as not to anger the master while still gaining relief from the singing of the words themselves. As the slave engages spirituals, a slow cultivation of their interiority begins; it is this nourishment that enables them to maintain their existence within their exploitive environment. Ultimately, these songs have the power to transform slaves into human beings with hope through the practice of performing these contemplative stories.

For instance, in another verse of the same spiritual the slave has the opportunity to be more explicit in her or his reparation toward the master: "Everybody's talkin' 'bout Heaven ain't goin' there/Heaven, Heaven/Gonna shout all over God's Heaven!" (Jones and Jones, 2001, p. 9). Here, the singer is pointing out to the master in a subtle defiance that situates the master as a sinner who will not make it into heaven because of the action of keeping slaves and entangling humanity in that subhuman experience. The slave owner most likely did not pay attention to the words of the slave because slaves were considered subhuman (Jones and Jones, 2001). Therefore, the slave creates a release for him or herself in this act of a public calling out for justice. Slave spirituals enabled slaves to identify with others and be defined by others. Slave spirituals provided a cathartic release when one could use one's voice to make claim of her/his personal freedom, if only momentarily through the spiritual. In this way, spirituals became a tool of empowerment for slaves to begin to redefine their individual and collective existence. For the time of their enslavement, spirituals permitted them solace, gave them identity for themselves and with others, as well as a respite from a living nightmare. A respite would have to be sufficient until they grew in strength and in numbers, until their cause became public, as only then could a public transformation occur. The spirituals enabled the slave narrative to be heard in a public realm that became increasingly sympathetic toward their human condition.

As an act of philosophical leisure, the singing of spirituals began with a contemplative framework through a mindful consideration of the slave's subject position in the world. In this case, mindful consideration was expressed orally through song. The performance of the music came from their hearts and permitted them to express, in a public way, what they could not otherwise communicate. The performance of music as a expressive action enabled a catharsis that released enough of their oppression to give them strength and courage to continue onward. The strength emerged from within the slave her or himself and it was cultivated through the leisure of their singing experience. This action of philosophical leisure was a creative outlet that had the power to transform their daily existence. Singing spirituals enabled many slaves to see through their predicament and build their own intellectual space that would help to transform their interiority and enable them to overcome their despair.

Folk spirituals are stories about their work, home, loves, and losses. As Koskoff observes, "The folk spiritual was an outgrowth of slavery; it was a uniquely African response to an institution which waged a systematic, though unsuccessful, onslaught onto the cultural legacy of black people in America" (2005, p. 198). As a tool, music for slaves offered them hope and encouragement to keep going even in the face of despair. They also developed a sense of selfhood and connection to community by sharing these songs that would ultimately help them transcend their confinement in dark times. Sharing these songs does not mean that music made it all better for them; what it means is that music provided them a common place where they could meet physically and spiritually, to learn to see their way through their darkness. They had to find hope and encouragement within themselves and they did this through their ability to explore in free play of their music. Some might argue that African slave music was reactive, and in some ways, it was. Yet, in an important way the music was an extension of their traditions, their worship, and their spiritual affirmation (Jones and Jones, 2001). Others argue that by the 1830s slavery spirituals "reflected antislavery sentiments of the abolitionist movement, which represented black song in its slave narratives and newspapers as its tragic expression of a noble people caught in a struggle" (Koskoff, 2001, p. 73). Additionally, slavery spirituals reflected the many complexities inherent in the slave culture:

> The Negro spiritual as it was originally conceived was a richly textured mosaic of Christian belief intertwined with African-derived cultural values. To perform the spiritual was to perform one's individual and collective identity as a person of African descent in the New World. To perform these spirituals, whether they exhibited double entendre or not, that is, whether they conveyed subliminal messages understood only by the initiated, or members of the group -- was to wage systematic warfare on the institution that imposed the chains of bondage. To sing the spiritual was to be free. (Burnim and Maultsby, 2006, p. 61)

African slave music portrayed their soulfulness, created communities, and cultivated their identities. In fact, Henry Gates, Jr. (1989) argues that slavery "in the New World, a veritable seething cauldron of cross-cultural contact, however, did serve to create a dynamic exchange and revision" of their culture (p. 4). Their music required imagination, serendipitous interaction, and the ability to play with ideas that would later help them negotiate a different and difficult public space of freedom, all elements of philosophical leisure. Their music gave them the hope to continue in their pursuit for liberation so that they could find their way out of their particular entanglement. Communicative practices are important "means by which society reproduces itself" (Swartz, 2005, p. 12). The communicative practice of slave spirituals emphasized desires of equality, justice, and freedom that shaped how the slaves envisioned a new society might be fashioned. To consider music as a communicative practice, one can envision how music propelled the African community through a transformative experience that emerged from a collective engagement of singing spirituals and, ultimately, provided a cathartic release for the individual slave and larger collective community.

Consider the following works from a spiritual: "Gonna shout/trouble over/When I get home/Gonna shout trouble over/When I get home/No mo' prayin, no mo' dyin/When I get home/No mo' pryin an' no mo' dyin/When I get home/Meet my father/When I get home/Meet my father/When I get home" (Jones, 1999, p. 39-40). Here, the sense of spirituality is revealed through the language that points toward Christianity in the notion of "home," "prayin," and "father." This song portrays a soulfulness, a search for community, and perhaps a Christian faith, either fully Christian or a Christianity blended with African roots. Nevertheless, songs like this revealed much about the individual slave and the slave community in general. For example, this song suggests that the slaves looked forward to "going home," or going to Christian heaven. This spiritual also suggests that the slaves had a strong faith that heaven is peaceful and a better place than the here and now of their daily existence. The song indicates a hopefulness in that the slave will be close to God and no longer will need to pray to him because one day she or he will be able to talk with him. As the slaves remained in captivity with their master, many Africans and other slave cultures began to assimilate into American culture, which is manifest in the large number of slaves sharing a Christian faith, and these songs represented that assimilation. For instance, "Mary, don't you weep an' Marthie don't you moan/Mary don't you weep an' Marthie don't you moan/Pharoh's army got drown-ded/Oh, Mary don't you weep/I thinks every day an' I wish I could/Stan' on de rock whar Mose stood/Pharoh's army got frown-ded/Oh, Mary don't you weep" (Jones, 1999, p. 39).

The above example demonstrates that the slaves could have been aware of Christian and or Jewish traditions because of the use of names and descriptive events that are the same or similar to the Bible or the Torah. Assuming that the slaves were familiar with these traditions, another message in this song could be interpreted as a message for the master, in that just as Pharaoh lost his power someday the master will lose his too. The argument that "Christianity adapts to the communities in which it is practiced" (Swartz, 2004a) accounts for the parallelisms between Jewish, Christian, and slave traditions that enabled the slave owner and the slaves to worship the same God. These parallelisms enabled the slaves to envision a cultural salvation. These shared analogical messages gave them hope and courage to continue the daily struggle.

African spirituals offer evidence that they were able to somewhat insulate slaves from their hostile environment and experiences (White, 1983). African slave music was a participatory action in that it brought slaves together under a common idea, and between/among each other they were able to transform their existence. At first this transformation was symbolic, but later it became a physical transformation in their emancipation from slavery. This transformation, while organic, was not immediate as the engagement of slave spirituals provided ways for individual transformation as well as a collective transformation for black culture and social practices (Eyerman, 2002). A transformation would not come until more than one hundred years later at a time when more cultural changes would occur that would continue the liberation movement toward equality for blacks in the United States.

Conclusion

In our current historical moment, the human community is concerned with an unsettled world economy, political unrest in the Middle East, discussions pertaining to nuclear weaponry, global warming, and genocide in depressed countries (among other horrors). In this contentious environment there ought to be a mechanism that would enable a communication context designed to invite competing narratives into an equitable public space that permits difference and supports endurance as ideas are exchanged. Even if a creative democracy becomes immediately present in our lives today, we must ask ourselves if we are ready to effectively participate. Without the practice of communicating as Dewey envisioned, the reality is that perhaps many of us are not yet capable of this kind of engagement. My main argument in this chapter suggests that a life integrated with philosophical leisure prepares an individual for active and productive engagement in a creative democracy because both philosophical leisure and creative democracy rest their foundations in *poiesis*, a creative making of ideas.

Philosophical leisure cultivates the ground upon which a person stands by teaching him or her how to engage ideas. This engagement of ideas becomes a habituated experience that can be applied in other contexts. So, for example, when a violin player engages philosophical leisure by playing string quartets with three other participants, s/he must learn to listen to the others and respond to others who might interpret the music differently than one's self. In this case, it is helpful to hear from each participant and have a discussion concerning the interpretation of the particular quartet. These discussions might include demonstrating different bow techniques or different interpretations of dynamics at particular places in the composition. There are multiple numbers of interpretive junctures in any given piece of music. Without flexibility in one's perspective, an openness to learning from others, and respect for another person's contribution to the discussion, the successful negotiation of this particular quartet is already limited. These players need to first learn how to play with ideas openly within their own interiority first before they play with ideas of others. Once the embedded agents become successful in the negotiation of the quartet, they will likely be successful with future quartet playing. As this practice becomes habituated, this type of engagement that involves *poiesis* will become a practice in other contexts for the embedded agent. When engaging with others in play, the engagement must be as an embedded agent within the context of the given moment and not as an individual agent driven my individual preferences.

The experience of leisure from a philosophical stance is a starting place for interlocutors who wish to participate in a democracy. In the action of philosophical leisure a person develops an ability to engage others constructively by inviting new ideas; ensuring integrity of information exchange and transactions; privileging the common good over individual expediency; and by engaging in the spirit of openness to learning new things. Experiencing philosophical leisure on a regular basis enables a life-long partnership with learning since the focus shifts to the ideas and the larger message. By embracing philosophical leisure the risk of permitting individual agency to drive our decisions, perspectives, and practices is extinguished. A life imbued with philosophical leisure prepares one to engage practices of a good citizen as it will cultivate one's abilities to participate in public discussions and decision-making. If we want to encourage the development of Dewey's creative democracy as a lived communicative action and not as an unattainable utopian ideal, then we ought to know how to engage ideas with others in a constructive and ethical manner adhering to a public moral good.

Revisiting John Dewey's creative democracy is a worthwhile endeavor at a time of political skepticism that pervades our culture. We can learn to participate in a creative democracy through first learning to play with ideas within our own interiority, which organically provides us with the ability to move our ideas into public engagement. In philosophical leisure we engage ideas for the sake of the ideas themselves. Likewise, in a creative democracy, the engagement is a *poiesis* that is permits serendipitous engagement. In this *poiesis* new ideas emerge, difference is negotiated, and the unexpected happens. There is no better time than the present to begin exploring philosophical leisure so that Dewey's creative democracy can successfully propel ethical and creative communicative engagement in the human community well into the 21st century.

REFERENCES

Arendt, H. (1983). *Men in dark times.* New York: Harvest Books. (original published in 1968)

Aristotle. (2001). Politics. In Richard McKeon (Ed.), *The basic works of Aristotle* (pp. 1127-1324). New York: Modern Library. (original published in 1941)

Arnett, R. C. (2007). Foreword. In Annette M. Holba. *Philosophical leisure: Recuperative praxis for human communication* (pp. 9-18). Milwaukee: Marquette University Press.

Arnett, R. C. (2005). *Dialogic confession: Bonhoeffer's rhetoric of responsibility.* Carbondale: Southern Illinois University Press.

Arnett, R. C., Fritz, J. H., and Bell, L. M. (2009). *Communication ethics literacy: Dialogue and difference.* Thousand Oaks, CA: Sage Publications.

Baldwin, L. V. (1984). "A home in dat rock": Afro-American folk sources and slave visions of heaven and hell. *Journal of Religious Thought, 41 (1)*, 38-57.

Bartels, D. (1999). Metaphor, morality, and Marxism. *Journal of Communication Inquiry, 23(2)*, 118-131.

Bauer, W. (2003). On the relevance of *Bildung* for democracy. *Educational Philosophy and Theory, 35(2)*, 211-225.

Bentham, J. (2005). *An introduction to the principles of morals and legislation.* Whitefish, MT: Kessinger Publishing. (Original published in 1876)

Berry, M. F. and Blassingame, J. W. (1977). Africa, slavery and the roots of contemporary black culture. *Massachusetts Review, 18(3)*, 501-516.

Brown, D. (2007). Songs of slavery. *Index on Censorship, 36(1)*, 138-141.

Burnim, M. V., Maultsby, P. K. (Eds.). (2006). *African American music: An introduction.* New York: Routledge.

Bynum, G. (2005). John Dewey's anti-essentialism and social progress. *Journal of Social Philosophy*, 36(3), 364-381.

Caspary, W. R. (2000). *Dewey on democracy.* Ithaca, NY: Cornell University Press.

Cicero. (1902). *Extracts from Cicero, Part I: Anecdotes from Greek and Roman history: Narrative and description.* Oxford: Clarendon Press.

Dewey, J. (1998). Democracy and America. In L. A. Hickman and T. M. Alexander (Eds.). *The essential Dewey: Ethics, logic, and psychology vol. 2* (pp. 357-365). Bloomington, IN: Indiana University Press.

Dewey, J. (1991). Creative democracy: The task before us. In J. A. Boydston and R. W. Sleeper (Eds.), *John Dewey: The later works, 1925-1953, 1939-1941, essays, reviews, and miscellany, vol. 14* (pp. 227-233). Carbondale, IL: Southern Illinois University Press. (Original published in 1939)

DuBois, W. E. B. (1989). *The souls of black folk.* New York: Bantam Books. (Original published in 1903)

Eyerman, R. (2002). Music in movement: Cultural politics and old and new social movements. *Qualitative Sociology, 25(3)*, 443-458.

Gates, H., Jr. (1989). *The signifying monkey: A theory of African-American literary criticism.* New York: Oxford University Press.

Goodale, T. and Godbey, G. (1988). *The evolution of leisure.* State College, PA: Venture Publishing.

Hall, P. A. (1996). Introducing African American studies: Systematic and thematic principles. *Journal of Black Studies, 26(6)*, 713-734.

Hobbes, T. (1996). *Leviathan.* Oxford: Oxford University Press. (Original published in 1651)

Holba, A. (2007). *Philosophical leisure: Recuperative praxis for human communication.* Milwaukee, WI: Marquette University Press.

Jones, L. (1999). *Blues people: Negro music in white America.* New York: Harper Perennial.

Jones, F., and Jones, A. C. (2001). *Triumph of the soul: Cultural and psychological aspects of African American music.* Westport, CT: Praeger.

Kant, I. (1963). *Lectures on ethics.* L. Infield (Trans.). New York: HarperTorch Books. (Original published in 1930)

Katz, E., and Gurevitch, M. (1976). *The secularization of leisure: Culture and communication in Israel.* Cambridge, MA: Harvard University Press.

Koskoff, E. (2005). *Music cultures in the United States: An introduction.* New York: Routledge.

Langsdorf, L. (2003). Argumentation, conflict, and teaching citizens: Remarks on a theme in recent Dewey scholarship. *Argumentation and Advocacy, 39*(3), 214-221.

Marx, K. (1990). *Capital.* Vol. 1. New York: Penguin Books. (Original published in 1976).

---. (1971). *Critique of Hegel's "Philosophy of right."* New York: Cambridge University Press. (Original published in 1843)

Mill, J. S. (1965). *Principles of political economy.* Vol. III. Canada: University of Toronto Press. (Original published in 1848)

Nippold, M. A., Duthie, J. K., and Larsen, J. (2005). Literacy as a leisure activity: Free-time preferences of older children and young adolescents. *Language, Speech, and Hearing in Schools, 36*(2), 93-102.

Petrarch. (2002). *On religious leisure.* New York: Italica Press. (Original published in 1345-47)

Pieper, J. (1998). *Leisure: The basis of culture.* South Bend, IN: St. Augustine Press. (Original published in 1948)

Postman, N. (1985). *Amusing ourselves to death: Public discourse in the age of show business.* New York: Penguin Books.

Rousseau, J. (1984). *A discourse on inequality.* New York: Penguin Books. (original published in 1755)

Seneca. (2003). *De otio de brevitate.* G. D. Williams (Ed.) (pp. 10-24). NY: Cambridge University Press.

Sennett, R. (1974). *The fall of public man.* New York: Norton and Company.

Smith, A. (1976). *An inquiry into the wealth of nations.* Chicago: University of Chicago Press. (Original published in 1776)

Strate, L. (2006). *Echoes and reflections: On media ecology as a field of study*. Cresskill, NJ: Hampton Press.

Stuckey, S. P. (2006). Afterword: Frederick Douglass and W. E. B. Du Bois on the consciousness of the enslaved. *Journal of African American History*, 91(4), 451-458.

Swartz, O. (2005). *In defense of artisan criticism: Communication studies, law, & social analysis*. New York: Peter Lang.

Swartz, O. (2004a). The African Christ. *The Black Commentator, 112*. Retrieved from http://www.blackcommentator.com/112/112_african_christ.html

Swartz, O. (2004b). Codifying the law of slavery in North Carolina: Positive law and the slave persona. *Thurgood Marshall Law Review, 29(2)*, 285-310.

Swartz, O. (1998). *The rise of rhetoric and its intersections with contemporary critical thought*. Boulder, CO: Westview Press.

Swartz, O., Campbell, K., Pestana, C. (2009). *Neo-pragmatism, communication, and the cultivation of creative democracy*. New York: Peter Lang.

Veblen, T. (1953). *Theory of the leisure class*. New York: Mentor Books. (Original published in 1899)

Wallace, K. (1955). An ethical basis of communication. *Speech Teacher, 4(1)*, 1-9.

Weber, M. (2003). *The protestant ethic and the spirit of capitalism*. Mineola, NY: Dover. (Original published in 1904)

Westbrook, R. B. (1991). *John Dewey and American democracy*. Ithaca, NY: Cornell University Press.

White, J. (1983). Veiled testimony: Negro spirituals and the slave experience. *Journal of American Studies, 17(2)*, 251-263.

Winter, R. (2002). *Still bored in a culture of entertainment: Rediscovering passion and wonder*. Downers Grove, IL: Inter-Varsity Press.

Wootton, J. (2007). Redemption song: Hymns and their relation to social change from slavery to the sex trade. *International Congregational Journal, 7(1)*, 73-91.

Note

[1] Antiphony is a responsive utterance in musical compositions that is generally reflected in the call and response style of singing that is a trademark of Southern

black churches in the United States. This dual nature of slave spirituals emphasized community and the collective interest of slave culture.

CHAPTER 4

En/Countering Frontiers of Moral and Physical Injustice:
Disability Studies as Creative Democracy

Margaret Rose Torrell
SUNY College at Old Westbury

In his brief remarks on the occasion of his 80th birthday, John Dewey (1939/1988) describes what he calls a "frontier" that citizens of the United States must cross if they hope to sustain and advance the democratic principles of freedom, justice, and equality that had been envisaged at the founding of the United States. Such frontier, he notes, is no longer physical; rather, it is "moral" (p. 225). The West had been "won," the great continent "conquered" and settled, and the great resources of our continent made available for development. In the process, the nation had been profoundly transformed from a ragtag collection of loosely affiliated colonies to an emerging superpower with world-historical consequences. The experiment of American democracy, no matter how imperfect it had been to that point, had clearly worked so far. However, as the challenges of the new nation for survival and expansion had been met, the more mature nation now had *new* problems to address, with which Dewey was very much concerned. Specifically, Dewey desired our nation to rethink the social structures that were denying people equal opportunities due to class, ethnic, and gender bias.

Dewey was aware that he was asking a great deal from our country. Crossing the vast frontier of social injustice, Dewey asserts, will make a "heavier demand on human creativeness" (p. 225) than that required to birth the nation, but we should not shrink from our task. Moreover, and most relevant for this chapter, Dewey insists that the central feature of this creativeness is *communication* -- the sharing of experiences so that each cultural group can be understood and validated as part of the enriched multiplicity of the larger community. This free flowing vocalization of individual citizens is necessary for bringing greater diversity into the cultural consciousness, altering prejudicial thinking, and propelling the nation on its trek across the moral frontier.

Dewey's ideas on communication and citizenship have proven insightful: the transmission of experience, whether in a political, artistic, personal, or other medium, has resulted in making progress toward easing insufferable class, ethnic, and gender bias in the United States. In the decades following Dewey's speech, significant civil rights activities have indeed begun to propel the nation across the moral frontier. As we progress, we expose more terrain that must be covered, more prejudicial thinking that must be countered by the communication of experience. One field that is actively performing such communicative work is disability studies; insights offered by disability studies scholars can help to chart out the territory that must be covered and provide examples of how to accomplish our journey toward greater social justice and equity.

Disability studies scholars understand "disability" as a culturally created identity category, much like class, ethnicity, and gender. Much of the work of disability studies is dedicated to examining and deconstructing the abled-disabled binary that underlies mainstream thinking about the body. The binary facilitates the association of the able-body with such culturally desirable traits as strength, control, attractiveness, independence, and happiness. The disabled body, by implication, is subject to weakness, limitation, ugliness, dependence, misery, and a variety of other socially unfavorable characteristics. The abled-disabled binary enforces the inferiority and alterity of the disabled body and excludes disabled people from participation in the range of opportunities available to able-bodied people. In disability studies, this binary is understood as a harmful social fiction that must be challenged and re-written. In placing the stress on the constructedness of disability, scholars explore the shifting cultural conceptions of embodiment and the emancipation that become possible when disabled people define themselves on their own terms.

Those working in disability studies frequently identify two barriers to social justice for disabled people: *attitudinal barriers* and *environmental barriers*. Both barriers have begun to be challenged and dismantled through the active communication of disabled experience; but, paradoxically, both barriers also function as blocks to such communication. *Attitudinal barriers* are the prejudicial ways disability is transmitted in cultural media and conceived in mainstream mindsets. These discriminatory attitudes become internalized by disabled people and can impede or prevent the free exchange of experiences. The idea is that the act of communicating life experiences is predicated on the belief that one's outlook is significant enough to share. Cultural attitudes often suggest otherwise and present formidable obstacles to the communication of disabled experience. *Environmental barriers* are the ways the physical setting segregates disabled people, keeping them from having access to the same space and opportunities as nondisabled people. These physical barriers make the communication of disabled experience challenging: they prevent disabled people from being present in all sorts of public spaces to share their experiences or simply to be a visible presence in the surrounding community. Thus, both attitudinal and environmental barriers impede the communication of disabled experience. An important task of disability studies, therefore, is how to use communication to challenge and dismantle these barriers and move toward greater equal rights for disabled people.[1] As we will see, the communication of disabled experience also has rewards for nondisabled people as well.

In this chapter, I make the most of Dewey's metaphors of the "moral" and "physical frontier," arguing that where disability is considered, the nation has *both* a moral and a physical frontier to cross. In disability studies, these frontiers translate to the attitudinal and environmental barriers encountered by disabled people and the "human creativeness," communication, and community needed to counter them are centerpieces of both Dewey's creative democracy and the tenets of disability studies. I examine how disability studies builds from the communicative action and community spirit of Dewey's creative democracy to work toward a general vision of social justice. Cornerstones of disability studies theory and art which reflect Dewey's principles include the communication of the lived experiences of disabled people in order to bring about equality in accessibility and provide a diversity of models of disabled experience, as well as the linguistic work of re-seating the disabled-abled binary and re-composing disabled identity on disabled people's own, often empowered, terms. As I consider the aims of disability studies alongside Dewey's theories of communication, some complications will emerge. I discuss these to further define disability studies and to consider ways Dewey's theories are precursors to the multicultural movement.[2] I conclude by considering the far-reaching, universal benefits of the communicative action project of disability studies -- not just for disabled people, but for all.

Frontier Crossing and the Communicative Turn

As a first step toward drawing connections between the communication projects of disability studies and Dewey's creative democracy, I begin by foregrounding central concepts in Dewey's "Creative Democracy -- The Task Before Us" (1939/1988). There, Dewey outlines his theory of creative democracy and demonstrates its use in overcoming social prejudices. The mechanisms of his theory are applicable to disability studies, as we will see in the subsequent sections of this chapter.

In his provocative essay, Dewey (1939/1988) begins by identifying two types of frontiers: one which had a central place in the founding of the United States and a second which is necessary for the continuance and revitalization of American democracy. The first, the physical or geographical frontier of the United States, inspired the conception of the nation as "a country of physical opportunity and invitation" because of the prospect of expansion into "free lands that seemed boundless" (p. 225). This sense of physical possibility prompted a small group of politically gifted men to design a democratic system for their fledgling nation.

In 1939, when Dewey penned his remarks, a change had occurred that affects the terms of democracy initially set out by its founders: the project of western expansion has been completed, and so the physical frontier no longer existed as a space of possibility for the nation. Cognizant of this significance, Dewey identifies another frontier in its place, which he terms "the moral frontier," a conceptual space of vast potential in terms of human resources, but one which social prejudices prevent us from tapping into. As Dewey explains, "Unused resources are now human rather than material. They are found in the waste of grown men and women who are without the chance to work, and in the young men and women who find doors closed where there was once opportunity" (p. 225). In calling attention to the shift from the physical to the moral frontier, Dewey recognizes a reallocation of the country's resources, from the geographical to the social: territorial expansion accompanied by the perception of unlimited natural resources no longer creates a sense of possibility for the country. In its place is untapped human potential with few opportunities for work, something that seems more like a social problem than a possibility, especially when it is coupled with definite geographical borders. Conditions such as these under which natural resources are perceived to be limited can germinate prejudice and stigma (Coleman, 1997, p. 229).

Dewey's use of the frontier metaphor relies on a careful selection of language and re-conceptualization. For instance, in framing this problem in terms of another frontier to cross as opposed to focusing on the closing down of the physical frontier, Dewey calls needed attention to a social problem -- the claustrophobic, prejudice-generating sense that there are more people than there are prospects for life sustaining employment. Moreover, he rewrites the problem as an opportunity for the advancement of the country and an enhancement of the democratic principles upon which it had been founded. Dewey thus provides the nation with a *new goal* and a *new direction* for expansion when he points the way toward the still-to-be-crossed moral frontier.

Dewey includes in his theory of creative democracy a set of guidelines for how to cross the moral frontier. First, democracy is no longer to be crafted by a small group of politically gifted men as it had been at the founding of the nation. Instead, democracy is now "the task before *us*" -- democracy is the personal responsibility of each of its members. Second, Dewey's concept of democracy is reliant on social diversity and equality. To have a creative democracy, there must be "faith in the potentialities of human nature as that nature is exhibited in every human being irrespective of race, color, sex, birth and family, or material cultural wealth" (p. 289). Third, interpersonal and intergroup communication is the primary means of advancing this model of democracy. As he notes, to "cooperate by giving differences a chance to show themselves because of the belief that the expression of difference is not only a right of the other persons but is a means of enriching one's own life-experience, is inherently in the democratic personal way of life" (p. 228). When personal experiences are shared, an individual's desires and opinions are made known, enriching the recipients' knowledge base. This promotes understanding of diverse standpoints and is an impetus for affecting change on a personal, community, and national level. Dewey outlines the mechanisms of this theory in *Democracy and Education* (1916/1955):

> A democracy is more than a form of government; it is primarily a mode of associated living, of conjoint communicated experience. The extension in space of the number of individuals who participate in an interest so that each has to refer his own action to that of others, and consider the action of others to give point and direction to his own, is equivalent to the breaking down of those barriers of class, race, and national territory which kept men from perceiving the full import of their activity. (p. 101)

Thus, the more people who communicate their experiences and the more people who are available to be recipients of these ideas, the more equal a society we become because these communications will help to direct the interests and concerns of the country. This is the foundation of Dewey's concept of creative democracy, which Omar Swartz, Katia Campbell, and Christina Pestana (2009) define as "a society that through the active participation of all its citizens, continues dynamically to evolve in its ability to be inclusive, fair, and just" (p. 12). As diverse experiences are shared and enter into collective national thought, democracy evolves and is reinvigorated.

Gert Biesta (2006) understands Dewey's emphasis on the sharing of experience as a kind of "communicative turn" in his philosophy that marks his realization "that mind, consciousness, thinking, subjectivity, meaning, intelligence, language, rationality, logic, inference, and truth . . . only come into existence through and as a result of communication" (p. 24). Otherwise stated, the "communicative turn" in Dewey's writing places a stress on the role of individual expression and the potential of language itself to alter the ways social groups are perceived. The assumptions about the way language works in creative democracy are articulated by Swartz, Campbell, and Pestana (2009) thusly, that "language in literature, art, and politics generally is an important resource of power for individuals and communities." On the one hand, language can "be used to institutionalize cruelty, poverty, hatred, and alienation"; on the other hand, language can be far more emancipatory in that it can "shape our understandings of reality; as humans change the way they talk about things, their attitudes, beliefs, and actions also change" (p. 107). As such, language can be used as a tool to "emphasize human connectedness and facilitate redescription, transformation, and liberation" (pp. 107-8).

Indeed, the emphasis on the transformative power of communication and its building block, language, has been central to the ongoing project of gaining equal rights and social justice across race, ethnicity, gender, sexuality, and class divisions. A belief in the liberating potential of language has also been a mainstay of re-defining disabled identity. An exploration of the communicative turn in disability studies leads to greater awareness of how the language of disability can, with mainstream usages, enforce inferiority, often across many marginalized identities, and also how language can be carefully reworked through the critical lens of disability studies to have emancipatory potential -- for disabled people and for the entire population.

Encountering Disability Studies, Countering Attitudinal and Environmental Barriers

Many groups of citizens celebrated on the night of President Barack Obama's election, among them, disabled people. Early in President Obama's victory speech, he recognized disabled people as a cultural group alongside a variety of other cultural groups, and did so by configuring his sentence so that "disabled" became a positive term: "young and old, rich and poor, Democrat and Republican, black, white, Hispanic, Asian, Native American, gay, straight, disabled and not disabled" (¶4). In these lines, President Obama eschewed the expected hierarchical pair "abled" and "disabled," where "disabled" is the negative term. Instead, he opted for the more neutral pairing "disabled and not disabled," where the use of "not" calls into question the ability-disability hierarchy.

The cause for the exuberance on election night was not that this public naming would magically enact equal rights for disabled people across the board and make environmental barriers disappear. The President-elect's mention, however brief and embedded in a larger social commentary, suggests progress has been made -- that the disability studies movement to talk and write about disability, make disability issues known, and chip away at mainstream conceptions of disability -- has begun to perform its cultural work.[3] The use of "disabled and not disabled" is a small piece of creative democracy caught in action, a moment that took arduous behind-the-scenes work by many people with experience in various disciplines, a moment that, albeit cause for celebration, should not eclipse the work that still remains to be done. Much of this work reflects the communicative action plan outlined in Dewey's theories of democracy. In what follows, I provide a primer in disability studies that includes some consideration of how the communicative work of disability studies reflects and augments Dewey's theories of creative democracy.

Disability Studies: A Primer

At fundamental levels, the field of disability studies raises crucial questions about "normalcy," the body, identity, and language, questions which have become essential to communication and identity scholars (see, Davis, 2006b; Garland-Thomson, 1998 and 2004b; Linton, 1998). The central work of disability studies is based on the recognition that "disability" is a social construct that has carried with it predominantly negative associations. For example, in mainstream communication, "disabled" often takes on pejorative meanings such as "freakish," "broken," "pitiful," "useless," "dependent," and/or "asexual," among others. Disability studies explores the genesis and implications of these negative associations and challenges them, advancing alternative ways to understand physical, cognitive, and psychological difference. In her study of the literary and cultural representation of disability, for example, Rosemarie Garland-Thomson (2004a) writes of the importance of challenging "entrenched assumptions that 'able-bodiness' and its conceptual opposite, 'disability,' are self-evident physical conditions" and instead understands them as productions of "legal, medical, political, cultural, and literary narratives that comprise an exclusionary discourse" (p. 6). Garland-Thomson's tracings of how mainstream perceptions of disability have been produced by culture supports her objective to "recast [disability] from a form of pathology to a form of ethnicity" (p. 6).

A major project of disability studies, in fact, has been to understand disability according to the terms set by the *Social Model* of disability in which disabled people form an oppressed minority group that advocates for equal rights.[4] A key factor in doing so is the recognition that cultural attitudes and physical environments are organized according to the needs and beliefs of the able-bodied. Therefore, the set-up and the practices of the culture around one are disabling and disempowering, not the actual impairment itself. Garland-Thomson (2004a) explains this concept:

> Disability studies points out that ability and disability are not so much a matter of the capacities and limitations of bodies but more about what we expect from a body at a particular moment and place. Stairs disable people who need to use wheelchairs to get around, but ramps let them go places freely. Reading the print in a phone book or deciphering the patterns on a computer screen is an ability that our moment demands. So if our minds can't make sense of the pattern or our eyes can't register the print, we become disabled. In other words, we are expected to look, act, and move in certain ways so we'll fit into the built and attitudinal environment. If we don't, we become disabled. (p. 524)

As Garland-Thomson does, much of the work of disability studies reveals how cultural practices -- as opposed to the physical conditions of the body -- deny disabled people equal respect and access. Kenny Fries (1997) reinforces this concept by noting that "it is the barriers, both physical and attitudinal, that need to be changed, not the impairments or the bodies with which we live. I have asked many disabled persons what causes them more difficulty, the disability itself or the discriminatory barriers put in their way. The answer is overwhelmingly the latter" (p. 8). Thus, while the mainstream focus may be on eliminating the disability from the person or on making the person more "able-bodied," a main objective in disability studies is on eliminating barriers of prejudice and environmental inaccessibility from society. These barriers have a disabling influence on bodies. Removing the barriers -- not "fixing" the bodies -- will lead to a change in social status for disabled people and create a more socially just world.

The work of disability studies is enacted on many fronts: there are projects which call for greater accessibility and political representation, inquiries into the ways physical, cognitive, and psychological difference are historically understood, and studies which focus on mainstream environments and communication to re-evaluate the meanings of "disability" and "ability" (for example, see Charlton, 1998; Davis 2006a; and Stiker 1999). There are also projects of recovery which explore the contributions that people with disabilities have made to all fields in order to recognize and historicize disabled identity. Still another branch examines the intersection of disability with other cultural groups -- there are sub-fields such as disability and gender studies, disability and race studies, and disability and queer theory, for example.[5] Through these efforts and others, a central goal of disability studies is equality through communicative action. Simi Linton (2004) eloquently describes this goal:

> Disability studies' project is to weave disabled people back into the fabric of society, thread by thread, theory by theory. It aims to expose the ways that disability has been made exceptional and to work to naturalize disabled people -- remake us as full citizens whose rights and privileges are intact, whose history and contributions are recorded, and whose often distorted representations in art, literature, film, theater, and other forms of artistic expression are fully analyzed. (p. 518)

Linton identifies a two-fold approach used in disability studies: one analyzes, interrogates, and re-works mainstream assumptions in order to dismantle attitudinal and environmental barriers for disabled people. The other approach focuses on "the vibrant self-explorations . . . that are found in memoir and cultural expressions of various kinds" (p. 518), in itself another type of re-working of disabled identity. Both approaches are ways of making disabled experience known, of using communication to affect a change in both the social perception of disabled culture and the accessibility of built environments. Such communicative action for disabled people requires traversing both moral and physical frontiers. In the following section, I provide examples of attitudinal barriers and discuss the communicative work that is underway to dismantle them; the section after that will address environmental barriers.

Attitudinal Barriers as Moral Frontiers

For disability studies, the moral frontier might be a group of insidious attitudinal barriers about disability that have far-reaching effects for disabled people and nondisabled people alike. Attitudinal barriers are similar to the moral frontier Dewey describes in which prejudice must be overcome in thought and language in order to make progress toward social equality. While viewed in varying ways, physical, cognitive, and psychological difference has always carried telling cultural significances. Shifts in attitudes about disability can be historically observed. For example, Henri-Jacques Stiker, in his foundational study *A History of Disability* (1997), provides an anthropologically based history of disability, starting from earlier moral models, in which disabilities are linked to "sin" and "transgression," charity models which understand disability as a personal misfortune which might be aided by the pity, service, and financial donations of the nondisabled, and medical models which view the disabled body as broken and in need of repair (see also Mitchell and Snyder, 2001; Barnes, Mercer, and Shakespeare, 2000).

The moral, charity, and medical models all put a stress on the disabled body as being abnormal and preference the able-bodied. For example, underlying the moral model is the idea that disability is a punishment and indicator of sin, a construction that presumes the morality of the able-bodied and traces the cause of a person's disability to the moral indiscretion of that person. The charity model creates a hierarchical relationship between the "helpless" disabled and their "more fortunate" able-bodied benefactors. The medical model is driven by the goal of modifying the disabled body so that it reaches -- as much as is possible -- the "gold standard" of abled-embodiment. An underlying implication of these models is that mainstream society does not have to change; instead, disabled people must be made to fit in or be subject to social rebuff and isolation. Some current attitudes about disability reflect a similar belief. As Garland-Thomson (2004) explains, "Even though those of us with disabilities are a visible and vocal constituency, we are also a profoundly economically disenfranchised and excluded group . . . . Our society emphatically denies vulnerability, contingency, and mortality" and there is currently a movement to "standardize" bodies through technology, medicine, and eugenics which perpetuates the devaluing of disabled bodies (2004a, p. 524).

Much of the disability literature launches an attack on these attitudinal barriers, both on the level of language -- reworking the pejorative meanings of words -- and on the level of narrative -- telling new, more emancipatory stories about disabled experience. To demonstrate how such communication takes place, I have selected as an example Nancy Mairs's disability autobiography,

Waist High in the World: A Life among the Nondisabled (1996), a disability studies classic for its comprehensiveness and trenchant re-defining of disabled experience. In using Mairs's text, I approach art, particularly disability art, as a type of cultural and political work that responds to, and subverts, mainstream attitudes. In this sense, I am following Scott Stroud (2007), whose Dewey-inspired theory of art maintains that "art can be used as communicative in the sense that it can be employed by an agent (the artist) to *evoke* a certain experience in an auditor (the receiving audience member)" (p. 7). As such, the communicative medium of art performs democratically in ways similar to those Dewey identifies. In fact, in *Experience and Nature* (1938/1966), Dewey understands that arts such as literature can "do more than all else to determine the current direction of ideas and endeavors in the community. They supply the meanings in terms of which life is judged, esteemed, and criticized" (p. 204). The outpouring of disability art in the past two decades, then, is a good indication of the progress being made to infiltrate mainstream attitudes about disability and the body in general. To be sure, there is more work to be done, but these changes in themselves are indications that when individual voices express themselves in the public medium of art, they can affect the thinking of a diverse nation.

Mairs's *Waist High in the World* is an excellent example of the communicative power of disability studies work. Consider, for example, the linguistic revision Mairs performs when she challenges the hierarchical structure embedded in words themselves. As she determines the names by which she will refer to herself, a person with Multiple Sclerosis (MS), she refines the meaning of "disabled": "Like all negative terms, 'disability' is part of a binary, existing in relation to a privileged opposite: that is, one is 'disabled' only from the point of view of another defined by common social values as 'able'" (p. 13). While binaries may provide a sense of organization because they allow everything to fit neatly into one of two categories, they are "merely a habit of the mind" and too narrow to express the "frightful jumble" of abilities people have. She continues, stressing the arbitrary and shifting nature of words. "'I' am disabled, then, only from 'your' point of view (and 'you' from 'mine'). Whoever gets to define ability puts everyone else in place, which (human nature tending to define one's own as the proper place) then becomes other, outside: a cheerless and chilly spot" (p. 13-4).

Emphasized in Mairs's linguistic reconstruction is the sense that disabled identity is a social fiction created through language. Disability is, therefore, a pliable, malleable identity that can be crafted and re-crafted with words. To illustrate this point, she develops the term "the nondisabled" for people who lack disabilities, "since in relation to me, they are the deficient ones" (p. 13). In this way, Mairs tells us, she "begin[s] to reconstruct the world" (pp. 14). As we see with President Obama's speech, Mairs pushes the term "disabled" into a more positive linguistic seat. The "reconstruction" she performs occurs at a basic linguistic level and suggests that those who have the power to use words (in spoken or written medium) can affect a change in perception. In particular, Mairs's re-definition of the group label "disabled" allows her to begin to revise how her group is seen on her own terms (for more discussion of the power of re-naming, see Swartz, 2009, p. 291). Just as an identity can be constructed pejoratively to enforce a social hierarchy, an identity can also be reconstructed as valid and central through harnessing the creative potential of language.

In addition to confronting attitudinal barriers on the level of language, Mairs also challenges them on the level of narrative. She shares narratives of her life in order to alter the expected cultural stories -- the bleak and fearful "myths and legends" -- that are told about disability. As she recounts her experiences as mother, wife, sexual woman, charitable Christian, and writer, she offers an account of her thinking process that combats mainstream attitudes ingrained in her own (and her readers') consciousness, reflects on the physical and emotional contingencies of her life, and describes her own pleasurable experiences and accomplishments. Her goal is not to write a sugar-coated "feel-good" book, but instead to write a "feel real" book in which she can tell readers "that a life commonly held to be insufferable can be full and funny." As she declares, "I'm living the life. I can tell them" (pp. 18, 10-11). These narratives allow readers to trace her thoughts as she moves through her own process of dismantling negative assumptions and exploring the ways her life is "full and funny." By providing realistic and positive accounts of her various experiences, she adds to, and alters, the stories about disabled lives that are culturally available.

Mairs's use of communication to dismantle attitudinal barriers is the type of arduous work that is central to Dewey's concept of democracy. Attitudinal barriers can severely restrict the communication necessary for creative democracy; the absorption of these attitudes by disabled people can effectively shut down the impetus to share experiences. Thus, with these barriers in place, the free sharing of information Dewey counts on for creative democracy can be difficult to achieve.

Here, I would like to identify some complications in the communication process that diffuse the straightforwardness of Dewey's theory and make some adjustments based on what is at stake in the communication of marginalized experience. Dewey theorizes how central and educational communication is in *Democracy and Education* (1916/1955) where he writes that communication is a learning experience for both the communicator and the receiver of information. On the part of the receiver, "One shares in what another has thought and felt and . . . has his own attitude modified" (p. 6). On the part of the communicator, the process of converting thoughts into words and then sharing them is itself a way of understanding the person to whom she is communicating: "To formulate requires getting outside of [one's mindset], seeing it as another would see it, considering what points of contact it has with the life of another so that it may be got into such form that he can appreciate its meaning" (p. 6). Thus, in sharing one's experience with another person, the communicator forecasts how the recipient will view her information and calibrates her presentation to maximize her meaning. In this way, Dewey celebrates the communicator's knowledge of her audience. To share one's experience with others helps the communicator to understand others because she must internalize the perspective of the person with whom she is communicating. As Dewey notes, "one has to assimilate, imaginatively, something of another's experience in order to tell him intelligently of one's own experience" (p. 6).

However, when disabled people communicate their experience to nondisabled people, the situation may be more oppressive than educational due to attitudinal barriers. Living among able-bodied culture, disabled people often internalize an acute awareness of mainstream perspectives. These mainstream attitudes often include assumptions about the inferiority of marginalized people that are almost unconsciously embedded in the cultural representation of disabled people. Therefore, a communicative experience is not necessary to give disabled people an education in the perspectives of mainstream culture. In fact, knowledge of such attitudes may prevent marginalized people from feeling free to share their experiences. G. Thomas Couser (2002) makes this clear in his study of the obstacles to writing a disability memoir which are applicable to sharing life experiences in other modes of communication. Couser argues that social and cultural barriers contribute to making disabled people "less likely to live the sorts of lives considered narratable" and "less likely to be encouraged to display" those lives. This is in part due to "the internalization of prejudices. Those who accept society's devaluation of them are less likely to consider their lives worthy" to be shared (2002, pp. 78-9).

Even for Mairs, who staunchly answers back mainstream perceptions of disability, concerns such as those raised by Couser about the importance and narratability of the disability life experience initially prevent her from beginning *Waist High in the World*. Her writer's block was generated by assumptions about the uselessness of her life: "In embarking upon this book about disability, I have committed myself to spend months contemplating issues and experiences that mark mine as an undesirable, perhaps even an unlivable, life" (p. 4). After speaking to a young woman who may have multiple sclerosis, Mairs realizes the importance of her project; this realization, and her profound need to communicate, drives her forward: "What I'm supposed to do about [the young woman], of course, is to write a book: one in which she can recognize and accept and even celebrate her circumstances, but also one that reveals to those who care about her what needs and feelings those circumstances may engender in her" (p. 6).

Likewise, later in her memoir, Mairs poignantly discusses the detrimental effect her awareness of mainstream attitudes has on her desire to share her experience, but she vigorously pushes past them for the sake of social change. As she notes, "To know that one arouses dismay and fear and pity simply sickens the spirit of anyone, whether sound of limb and mind or not. One is tempted to withdraw altogether, at least from the company of 'normals,' so as to avoid the indignity; but disappearance from the scene, however welcome to both parties, won't lead to change" (p. 104). It is crucial to recognize and debunk mainstream perceptions of disability, although an awareness of social prejudices can shut down communication as opposed to enhance it. Thus, Dewey's notion that the communicator's knowledge of her audience is educational for her and advances democracy may need to be adjusted based on the complications of communicating from a marginalized position.

For some disabled people, there is an associated barrier to communication: the rules of communication themselves presume ablebodiness. In other words, face-to-face communication is governed by a set of expectations that involve physical ability in areas such as speech, hearing, facial expression, and body posture and movement. Linton (2004) reflects on these rules of communication, noting that we "learn that we will be accepted and will succeed to the extent that we move, speak, and look like the majority culture . . . Disabled people are expected to mask the behaviors that would disturb the public and certainly not to exaggerate or call attention to our odd forms or the way our forms function" (p. 519). As a result of the pressure to conform to able-ist conventions of communication, a disabled person may opt not to communicate at all or to communicate as an able-bodied person would, effectively keeping her disability from the observer's view.

This concern also complicates Dewey's theory of communication because it reveals additional barriers to the self-expression of marginalized people. In her feminist evaluation of Dewey's philosophy, Frances Maher expresses similar reservations about Dewey's hope for free-flowing communication: "To simply encourage the expression of everyone's experiences, or voices, is in fact to encourage the more privileged voices, and often, to contain the marginalized voices within the terms set by the most privileged" (2001, p. 20). For Maher, communication of experience cannot be free flowing because the conditions of discourse are governed by privileged groups. Therefore, marginalized people may find themselves either shut out of opportunities to communicate or without the means to communicate effectively. To apply Maher's theory to disability studies, the suggestion is that in communication, disabled people are encouraged to pass as mainstream -- to use language, vocalization, and comportment in a way that the nondisabled person can identify with, at the expense of communicating and being comfortable with their identities as disabled people.

The removal of attitudinal barriers though communication, then, includes changes to the rules governing communication itself. These changes can only occur by efforts to communicate in a diversity of ways; as Mairs writes in her memoir, "disappearance from the scene… won't lead to change" (p. 140).

As we have seen in this section, the existence of attitudinal barriers, which I link to Dewey's notion of the moral frontier, has dire social consequences for the development of creative democracy: without the honest exchange of experience, creative democracy cannot exist. Disability studies' incisive dismantling of attitudes in language and narrative underscores the central role of communication in achieving social justice and reveals some of the contingencies of communicating from a marginalized position that complicate Dewey's theories.

Environmental Barriers as Physical Frontiers

For disabled people, the lifting of attitudinal barriers is only one-half of the work necessary to progress toward equality. In addition to the moral frontier formed by negative conceptions of disability, there is also a physical frontier that must be crossed. This is not the expanse of land and resources which Dewey has identified as being closed in his speech. Instead, the physical frontier is public space of many types that is, at best, unwelcoming to disabled people. This space is richly adorned with, among other things, opportunities for employment, education, public visibility, transportation to work, family, and friends, shopping, travel for business and enjoyment, entertainment, intellectual thought, art appreciation, and interpersonal communication. However, even with changes in public accessibility made necessary by the Americans with Disabilities Act (ADA) of 1990, there still remain physical frontiers with a cache of benefits which have yet to be made fully available to some disabled people, as we will see with examples supplied by Mairs. In disability studies, these are termed "environmental barriers," and they have just as significant an impact on communication as do attitudinal barriers.

The ADA was created to enforce equality in "employment, public accommodations (access), transportation, state and local government, and telecommunications" for disabled people (Barnes, Mercer, Shakespeare, 1999, p. 161). The Act required changes to the accessibility of pre-existing public spaces and mandated that the architecture of newly built public spaces take accessibility issues into account. For example, the installation of ramps at building entrances, the creation of curb cuts at intersections, the posting of building directories and room numbers in Braille, prompted by the ADA, all make built environments more easy to navigate, depending on an individual's disability. However, there are limits to the ADA in a variety of areas. The ADA does not apply to the private spaces of houses and apartments and it does not apply to some public spaces, such as airplanes (see Mairs, pp. 190-195) or some cases in which the structural alterations required to allow disabled people access would create an economic hardship. There are also complications and delays in fully implementing the requirements outlined in the ADA, many of them cost-driven.[6] Thus, while the ADA is instrumental in making public space more accessible, environmental barriers continue to prevent disabled people from having the same access and opportunities as do non-disabled people. Among these denied opportunities is the chance to communicate about disabled experience.

The problems environmental barriers pose become clear as Mairs (1996) shares her observations. For instance, she writes that the "world as it is currently constructed does not especially want -- and plainly does not need -- me in it" (p. 88). Following up, she explains, "I mean simply that much of the time, as a disabled woman, I find that my physical and social environments send the message that my presence is not unequivocally either welcome or vital. I am not looking for reassurances just now. I want to change the world" (p. 88). To reveal how uninviting the environment can be, she performs a "thought experiment" where she asks, very simply, "Suppose I came to call [in my wheelchair] . . . could I get onto the front porch to ring the door bell?" (p. 88). What follows is an enlightening tour of public space from the perspective of a person in a wheelchair and an illumination of the challenges to leading a day-to-day life that includes work, transportation, shopping, dining, entertainment, using bathrooms, and being a guest in someone's home. More is at stake here than simple access to public space, although having to struggle to gain that access is itself a social equality issue and energy-draining reality. Public presence is a form of communication, as Mairs suggests: "If I want people to grow accustomed to my presence, and to view mine as an ordinary life, less agreeable in some of its particulars than theirs but satisfying over all, then I must routinely roll out among them" (p. 104). The idea is that the public presence of disabled people sharing space and activity in and amongst nondisabled people can be a form of communication about disabled identity that subverts mainstream attitudes about disability.

The hard-to-cross physical frontier for disabled people even includes the very locations that Dewey singles out as ideal for the enactment of creative democracy. He asserts, "I am inclined to believe that the heart and final guarantee of democracy is in free gatherings of neighbors on the street corner to discuss back and forth what is read in uncensored news of the day, and in gatherings of friends in the living rooms of houses and apartments to converse freely with one another" (1939/1988, p. 227). The presence of environmental barriers on the street and in the home makes communication of this nature difficult -- in some cases impossible. I do not mean to ignore the spirit of Dewey's lines which imagine a free-flowing exchange between people. I *do* mean to promote an awareness of the detrimental effects environmental barriers can have on such free-flowing exchange. When environmental barriers are in place, communication, the central component of Dewey's democracy, fails. As Dewey explains, for "every way of life that fails in its democracy limits the contacts, the exchanges, the communications, the interactions by which experience is steadied while it is also enlarged and enriched" (1939/1988, p. 229).

In my discussion of attitudinal and environmental barriers in this and the previous section, I have been arguing that participation in the communication necessary for Dewey's creative democracy is complicated for disabled people. Attitudinal and environmental barriers prohibit disabled people from sharing their experiences honestly and keep disabled people more isolated, more unavailable to participate in the free exchanges Dewey finds so central to democracy. As I have suggested, some elements of Dewey's theory of communication might reflect an incomplete knowledge of the dynamics of communication for socially marginalized groups. To be sure, Dewey's theory predates the formation of disability studies and the multicultural movement in general, but his work can be seen as a precursor to this movement. Maher (2001) offers two ways to understand Dewey in this context:

Notions that Dewey didn't deal with multiculturalism, that his ideas of democracy have been succeeded by Freirian concepts of oppression and liberation, could be read in two ways: that these newer struggles are basically natural outgrowths and extensions of Dewey's search for democracy and community or, on the other hand, that they represent a reformulation, even a rejection, of some key aspects of this thought. (p. 13)

In this chapter, I favor the first possibility and consider Dewey's theories as important impetuses to the multicultural movement. Notably, Dewey does demonstrate an awareness of the categories of cultural identity for his time, as he does when he asserts the need for equality regardless of "race, color, sex, birth and family, or material cultural wealth" (1939/1988, p. 226). Even so, for the sake of communication, I think it is important to identify and discuss complications to Dewey's theories. After all, an author's silences, omissions, and gaps -- however unintentional -- are also a form of communicating about a culture. I have called attention to such omissions as part of disability studies' project to revise language, perception, and environment with the goal of moving toward equality for disabled people.

Conclusion

In her memoir, Mairs suggests that the movement toward equality for disabled people will have a positive impact on the population at large: "There are rewards for making the world physically and emotionally accessible to all people, including benefits that accrue to society as a whole. The more perspectives that can be brought to bear on human experience... the richer that experience becomes" (p. 106). As Mairs argues, the presence of disabled people will not only enrich the diversity of the culture, but it will also facilitate an alteration in thinking about the body that will also benefit all people. Crossing both moral (attitudinal) and physical (environmental) frontiers as a culture has far-reaching rewards, particularly because disability is a universal and eventual cultural identity, one that includes almost everyone at some point in life. I conclude by considering the universality of disability in two ways.

First, the language of disability oppression has been used to justify the social oppression of many groups, a mechanism that is observable dating at least from Ancient Greek times (see Garland-Thomson, 1997). There is an ability-disability binary at the core of cultural constructions of marginalized identity, whether these identities are sex, sexual, ethnic, or class-based, as Garland-Thomson (2004b) argues. A group's claim to social dominance relies on two simultaneous ability-based constructions: the privileged group's construction of themselves as able-bodied and predominantly disassociated from their bodies, and their construction of the inferior group as disabled and embodied. Douglas C. Baynton (2001) and Lennard J. Davis (2006b) make similar points: historically, disability characteristics were often used to define the racial, ethnic, or gendered line between the minority and the majority. For example, Baynton reads the arguments for and against citizenship for women's suffrage, African American freedom and civil rights, and immigration, among other things, as reliant on discourses of mental and physical disability. In an attempt to bar people from equal participation in United States democracy, minority groups were associated with characteristics of cognitive, psychological, and physical disability. In turn, equal rights activists reacted against these constructions, insisting that marginalized groups were not disabled and "were not proper subjects for discrimination" (pp. 33-44). The underlying assumption for both sides of the debate is that disabled people do not have the same rights as others. Disability studies' work on the social barriers for disability, then, can have an effect on the ways marginalized groups in general are depicted, undermining the linguistic hierarchy used to suggest their inferiority. As Davis explains:

> Disability studies can provide a critique of and a politics to discuss how all groups, based on physical traits or markings, are selected for disablement by a larger system of regulation and signification. So it is paradoxically the most marginalized group -- people with disabilities -- who can provide the broadest way of understanding contemporary systems of oppression. (p. 240)

Second, disability is not only the largest minority group, but it is also a most fluid cultural identity. If a person is not born disabled, s/he will most likely become disabled if not by accident or illness then by age.[7] Because most everyone can become disabled and most likely will, disability, not ability, is the more normative state. Garland-Thomson (2004b) explains, "Our collective cultural consciousness emphatically denies the knowledge of vulnerability, contingency, and mortality" but disability "insists otherwise, contradicting such phallic ideology." The reality is that we "evolve into disability. Our bodies need care; we all need assistance to live" and so "we are better off learning to individually and collectively accommodate bodily limits and evolutions than trying to eliminate or deny them" (p. 92). As disability studies performs its cultural work to revise mainstream attitudes and make public space accessible, a far-reaching hope is that disability will eventually be understood as more normal and in more positive ways.

This project of re-defining disabled experience is an ultimate goal of Mairs's memoir. She explains that she means it to be a type of travel guide to the country of disability, "a country to which no one travels willingly" (p. 6). However, once a diversity of disabled experiences is shared, this country will "seem less alien, less perilous, and far more amusing than the myths and legends about it would suggest" (p. 6). Notably, she recognizes that she is "not alone" in this country, and is expecting much more company: "as the population ages, more and more people -- a significant majority of them women -- may join me in it, learning to negotiate a chill and rubble-strewn landscape with impaired eyesight and hearing and mobility, searching out some kind of home there" (p. 63). Because of the inevitability of disability as an identity category for a majority of the population, her task is not so much "to conceptualize . . . a habitable body" but instead "a habitable world: a world that wants me in it" (p. 63). In sharing her own experiences and in imagining a habitable world, Mairs performs important communicative work -- not just in terms of re-envisioning her own identity, but in terms of revising the negative concepts that others, disabled and nondisabled, may have about disability. In doing so, she advances social justice by "reconstruct[ing] the world" (p. 14).

These revisions to hegemonic, able-ist thinking challenge constrictive thought patterns about the body and provide examples of the types of "human creativeness" and communicative action needed to traverse the moral and physical frontiers of social injustice for the disabled community. Because the field of disability studies interrogates general assumptions about bodies that uphold other social hierarchies such as class, ethnicity, and gender, we can, therefore, turn to disability studies for additional information on how to use communication to counter other frontiers of social injustice and -- in Mairs's words -- "reconstruct the world" or -- in Dewey's words -- to form a creative democracy that provides "a freer and more humane experience in which all share and to which all contribute" (p. 230).

REFERENCES

Albrecht, G. L., Seelkan, K. D., and Bury, M. (Eds.) (2001). *Handbook of disability studies.* Thousand Oaks, CA: Sage.

Barnes, C., Mercer, G., Shakespeare, T. (2000). *Exploring disability: A sociological introduction.* Malden, MA: Blackwell.

Baynton, D. C. (2001). Disability and the justification of inequality in American history. In P. K. Longmore and L. Umansky (Eds.), *The new disability history: American perspectives* (pp. 33-57). New York: New York University Press.

Biesta, G. (2006). "Of all affairs, communication is the most wonderful": The communicative turn in Dewey's *Democracy and Education.* In D. T. Hansen (Ed.), *John Dewey and our educational prospect: A critical engagement with Dewey's* Democracy and Education (pp. 23-38). Albany: State University of New York Press.

Bickenbach, J. E. (2001). Disability human rights, law, and policy. In G. L. Albrecht, K. D. Seelkan, and M. Bury (Eds.), *Handbook of disability studies* (pp. 565-584). Thousand Oaks, CA: Sage.

Charlton, J. I. (1998). *Nothing about us without us: Disability oppression and empowerment.* Berkley: University of California Press.

Coleman, L. M. (1997). Stigma: an enigma demystified. In L. J. Davis (Ed.), *The disability studies reader* (pp. 216-231). New York: Routledge.

Couser, G. T. (2002). Conflicting paradigms: The rhetorics of disability memoir. In J. C. Wilson and C. Lewiecki-Wilson (Eds.), *Embodied rhetorics: Disability in language and culture* (pp. 78-91). Carbondale: Southern Illinois UP.

---. (1997). *Recovering bodies: Illness, disability, and life writing.* Madison: University of Wisconsin Press.

Davis, L. J. (2006a). Constructing normalcy: The bell curve, the novel, and the invention of the disabled body in the nineteenth century. In L. J. Davis (Ed.), *The disability studies reader* (pp. 3-16). New York: Routledge.

---. (2006b). The end of identity politics and the beginning of dismodernism: On disability as an unstable category. In L. J. Davis (Ed.), *The disability studies reader* (pp. 231-242). New York: Routledge.

Dewey, J. (1939/1988). Creative democracy -- The task before us. In J. A. Boydston (Ed.), *John Dewey: The later works, 1925-1953, Volume 14* (pp. 224-230). Carbondale: Southern Illinois University Press.

---. (1916/1955). *Democracy and education: An introduction to the philosophy of education.* New York: Macmillan.

---. (1938/1966). *Experience and nature.* New York: Dover.

Fries, K. (1997). Introduction. In *Staring back: The disability experience from the inside out.* (pp. 1-12). New York: Plume.

Garland-Thomson, R. (2004a). Disability and representation. *Conference on Disability Studies and the University PMLA, 120(2)*, 522-527.

---. (1997). *Extraordinary bodies: Figuring physical disability in American culture and literature.* New York: Columbia University Press.

---. (2004b). Integrating disability, transforming feminist theory. In B. G. Smith and B. Hutchison (Eds.), *Gendering disability* (pp. 73-106). New Jersey: Rutgers University Press.

Hershey, L. (2008). *What the Obama victory means to me.* Retrieved from www.laurahershey. com

Linton, S. (1998). *Claiming disability: Knowledge and identity.* New York: New York University Press.

---. (2004). What is disability studies? *Conference on Disability Studies and the University PMLA, 120(2)*, 518-522.

Longmore, P. K., and Umansky, L. (2001). Introduction, Disability history: From the margins to the mainstream. In P. K. Longmore and L. Umansky (Eds.), *The new disability history: American perspectives* (pp. 1-31). New York: New York University Press.

Maher, F. (2001). John Dewey, progressive education, and feminist pedagogies: Issues in gender and authority. In K. Weiler (Ed.), *Feminist engagements:*

Reading, resisting, and revisioning male theorists in education and cultural studies (pp.13-32). New York: Routledge.

Mairs, N. (1996). *Waist-high in the world: A life among the nondisabled.* Boston: Beacon Press.

Miles, A. (2008, Nov. 6). Obama mentions disability in his speech [Msg 10116]. Message posted to the Disability Studies in the Humanities electronic mailing list, archived at https://listserv.umd.edu/archives/index.html

Mitchell, D. T. and Snyder, S. L. (2001). Representation and its discontents: The uneasy home of disability in literature and film. In G. L. Albrecht, K. D. Seelkan, and M. Bury (Eds.), *Handbook of disability studies* (pp. 195-218). Thousand Oaks, CA: Sage.

Obama, B. (5, Nov. 2008). Victory Speech. *New York Times.* Retrieved from http://www.nytimes .com/2008/11/04/us/politics/04text-obama.html

Shakespeare, T. (2006). The social model of disability. In L. J. Davis (Ed.), *The disability studies reader* (pp. 197-204). New York: Routledge.

Snyder, S. L., Brueggemann, B. J., and Garland-Thomson, R. (2002). Introduction, Integrating disability into teaching and scholarship. In *Disability Studies: Enabling the Humanities* (pp. 1-14). New York: Modern Language Association.

Stiker, H. (1999). *A history of disability.* Ann Arbor: University of Michigan Press.

Stroud, S. R. (2007). Dewey on art as evocative communication. *Education and Culture 23(2)*, 6-26.

Swartz, O., Campbell, K. and Pestana, C. (2009). *New-pragmatism, communication, and the culture of creative democracy.* New York: Peter Lang.

Swartz, O. (2009). *Persuasion as a critical activity: Application and engagement.* 2nd ed. Dubuque, IA: Kendall Hunt.

Wilson, J. S. (2008). The language of disability in the media, politics, and policy in 2008. Retrieved from www.cipa.cornell.edu/doc/wilson.pdf

Notes

[1] Throughout this chapter, what I mean by "disabled person" is a person who has a cognitive, psychological, or physical impairment. As I discuss environmental barriers later in the paper, I focus on the barriers experienced by people with physical impairments.

[2] Fueled by the Civil Rights Activities of the 1960s, the multicultural movement recognized and celebrated the diverse cultural makeup of the United States.

[3] For example, see the following responses to the president-elect's victory speech: Hershey (2008), Miles (2008), and Wilson (2008).

[4] The Social Model of disability sees people with disabilities as an oppressed group and stresses the difference between impairment, which is a condition of the body, and disability, which is the social perception of impairment. The latter leads to oppression and exclusion (Shakespeare, p. 198, 2006).

[5] For an overview of the field, see Albrecht, Seelman, and Bury (2001), Simi Linton (2004), and Longmore and Umansky (2001).

[6] For discussions of the ADA and other antidiscrimination legislation, see Barnes, Mercer, and Shakespeare (1999) and Bickenback (2001).

[7] For more discussion of this, see Snyder, Brueggemann, and Garland-Thomson, 2002, p. 2; and Couser, 1997, p. 16.

Part II: Applying Creative Democracy

CHAPTER 5

Appreciating Conduct and Consequences Through Communication:
Revisiting Community Through a Deweyan Lens

Musetta Durkee
University of California, Berkeley

"Community" is a deceptively simple concept with a rich and complex history. How and why certain conceptions of community are accepted and others rejected not only reflect historical values, geographic location, and socio-political norms but also solidify the framework -- democratic or otherwise -- within which interpersonal relations and civic engagement can take place. In ancient Greece, for example, citizens were bonded in a political community by ideals of justice and rationality. Through active participation and deliberation of all rational citizens, which did not include women or slaves, the people shaped public decisions and policies (Swartz, Campbell, and Pestana, 2009, p. 12). Throughout later antiquity, religious ideals and sacred symbols displaced rational deliberation as the primary bonding force for homogenous communities (Anderson, 1991, p. 13). In the dynastic era, by contrast, trade and warfare created heterogeneous communities with the far-reaching sovereignty of vast empires, providing boundaries between communities. Finally, in the modern era -- and especially with increased mobility and globalization -- communities have been overshadowed by nation-states with an emphasis on nationalistic bonding of its citizens (Anderson, 1991, p. 19).

However, with the threats of extreme nationalism such as those experienced during the Balkan Wars of the 1990s, ideologically-driven political regimes such as North Korea and Cambodia during the Khmer Rouge, and religious extremism in the late 20th century in places like Iran, Afghanistan, and Saudi Arabia, the virtues (and vices) of community have regained a prominent place in public discourse. Discussions of community today subsume community's varied history into two competing camps. On the one hand are those who idealize the virtues of, and advocate a return to, a pre-modern and communitarian conception of a *gemeinschaft* community.[1] On the other are those representing liberalism who criticize such utopian visions as exclusionary and intolerant. Both camps, in my opinion, are problematic in their attempts to achieve democratically inclusive and diverse communities, especially in today's global, hyper-mobile, and heavily technology-driven age. The former because it places constraints on individual freedoms, encourages prejudice against nonmembers by drawing strict cultural boundaries, and employs rigorous social control to enforce conformity (Brint, 2001, p. 16). The latter because it depends on the idea of an individual that exists prior to, and independent of, the community to which s/he belongs and the social relations that form it (Mouffe, 1989, p. 42). In this chapter I reject both the ahistorical utopia of *gemeinschaft* communities and the universalism of human reason as the foundational values for a revival of the concept of community. Instead, I theorize the importance of community starting with the Deweyan belief, as summarized by Sandel (1996), that the loss of community is "not simply the loss of communal sentiments." Rather, it is "also the loss of the common identity and shared public life necessary to self-government" (p. 208).

In rethinking community as neither an exclusionary *gemeinschaft* community nor merely a collective of pre-formed individuals, I must be cautious not to divorce community from democratic political values. As John Dewey stresses, regarded "as an idea, democracy is not an alternative to other principles of associated life. It is the idea of community life itself" (1998, p. 331). This idea of the community life, more than mere association or a transactional society based in anonymous economic interactions, depends on communication for several reasons. The first reason is linked to the benefits of community pursuant to pragmatic goals of self-governance and increased moral obligations. Using Richard Rorty's image, the "more featherless bipeds you include in your list of who counts, who matters, the people to whom you have obligations, the more morally advanced you are" (Rorty, 2000, p. 110).

While "elective communities" or communal relations of interests may provide some of the bonding and trust lacking in modern society, reconciling the two competing concepts of community requires more than merely inserting social capital into problem spots. Such "elective communities" include "readers of romance literature, gamblers, and devotees of demimonde subcultures" (Brint, p. 5). As Steven Brint makes clear, communal relations occur in

> bowling and soccer leagues; in singing and book clubs; in children's play groups; in groups of men and women who make a point of seeing each other on a regular basis; among the regulars at local taverns; in the interchanges of sore members or usenet groups; among the active members of churches, synagogues, and mosques; among those who are fans of a particular television show, sports team, or philosophical movement and are in sympathetic contact with their fellow partisans. (p. 8)

Though "social capital" is a long-standing concept (if not phrase) tracing back at least to Alexis de Tocqueville (1835/1994), Robert D. Putnam (2000) has become the modern champion of social capital as a measure against the deterioration of modern relationships. According to Putnam, who draws on data showing that Americans are signing fewer petitions, participating in fewer community organizations, and even bowling alone instead of in bowling leagues, Americans in the past quarter century have become more isolated and disconnected from family, friends, neighbors, and civic community structures. That is, Americans are lacking crucial forms of social capital. James Farr describes Putnam's version of social capital as "complexly conceptualized as the network of associations, activities, or relations" -- like the aforementioned elective communities -- "that bind people together as a community via certain norms and psychological capacities, notably trust" (p. 9). However, Farr criticizes this version of social capital as a cure-all for communities' ills, citing evidence that, first, poor and marginalized communities have often been left out of such trust-bonded communities, and, second, such trust-based social capital lacks what Dewey calls an "active sympathy" which is required for communities defined by appreciating one's consequences on others (p. 27).

Instead, in pursuit of democratic inclusion and participation (which requires an informed populace, as Dewey reminds us), community founded on communication is essential. As Dewey writes, everything "which bars freedom and fullness of communication sets up barriers that divide human beings into sets and cliques, into antagonistic sects and factions, and thereby undermines the democratic way of life" (1976, pp. 227-28). The pursuit of an informed populace was "the problem of the public" according to Dewey. As he explains,

> the improvement of the methods and conditions of debate, discussion and persuasion. That is the problem of the public . . . . It is not necessary that the many should have the knowledge and skill to carry on the needed investigations; what is required is that they have the ability to judge on the bearing of the knowledge supplied by others upon common concerns. (p. 365)

My ultimate goal in this chapter, therefore, is to revive the virtues of community in this modern age and to identify practical means, especially through communication as distinct from mere deliberation, and through uses of new information and communication technologies (ICTs), to incorporate those virtues into everyday life. In so doing, I will describe a positive concept of community distinct from *gemeinschaft* communities and their critics as well as offer practical examples of communication tools working towards inclusive, informed, democratic communities. At stake for policy- and decision-makers, activists, artists, community organizations, NGOs, educational and other public institutions, as well as individuals leading their everyday lives, is a concept of community which protects against violence and oppression of out-groups or "others" in the name of an in-group or "self." My goal is, thus, to theorize a way of understanding community that acknowledges how communities are produced through the practices and participation of individuals, as well as through individuals' responses to external economic, political, and social forces. Such an understanding of community would not only balance the interests of individuals and the community, it would allow for individuals to have memberships in multiple communities, to cultivate varied interests, and to foster hybrid identities and activities that are becoming increasingly common and important in this global, mobile, and modern age.[2] This ideal community structure, situated at the intersection of *gemeinschaft* communities and liberal individualism, I would like to classify as "relational communities of differentiated inclusivity."

By relational communities of differentiated inclusivity, I mean that, on a horizontal level (that is, addressing how communities relate to each other), such communities must exist in open relation with one another instead of in closed boundaries. I call this the *relational* aspect of community. On a vertical level (that is, how individuals relate to the community of which she/he is a part), individuals must be allowed to cultivate the multiple memberships, hybrid identities, and varied interests that are characteristic of this modern age. I call this the *differentiated* aspect of community. Finally, in terms of mobility (that is, individuals' co- and cross-existence in multiple communities), individuals must be able to move freely within and among communities and must be included both within community boundaries and included in hybrid spaces in-between and among communities. Such co-/cross-existence must exist in both communities with which individuals share defining characteristics of membership and communities with which individuals have no shared characteristics. I call this the *inclusive* aspect of community. In order to serve Dewey's call for an informed and interconnected public, my classification combines the work of Chantal Mouffe's (1992) notion of a "radical democracy" with Iris Marion Young's (2000) "communicative democracy."

In contrast to liberal democracy (which is based in equality) and deliberative democracy (which is based in consensus) Mouffe (1993, 2000; Mouffe and Laclau, 1985), proposes a radical, third way which embraces difference and dissent as essential to democracy and to changing oppressive power dynamics. For her part, Young uses the term "communicative democracy" in contrast to "deliberative democracy" which, she remarks, "carries connotations of the primacy of argument, dispassionateness, and order in communication." She uses the term "communicative democracy" to "denote a more open context of political communication" including minority speech cultures, emotional and gestural expression, and artistic communication (pp. 39-40).

We are currently faced with a number of pressing situations that seem to require a revamping of community structures and forms of communication. James Bohman, for one, describes the current "fact of globalization" as precisely the "sort of problematic situation [that] requires 'creative democracy,' in Dewey's terms, where deliberation is about transforming both the means and ends of democratic institutions" (pp. 29-30). Young identifies exclusion and forced inclusion in a global world as problematic, cautioning that "[n]ationalist interpretations of the distinctness of peoples . . . tend to be inappropriately essentialist and exclusionary" and suggesting that "[i]nstead, peoples should be understood as relationally constituted, and the political recognition of the distinctness of peoples should be able to accommodate the millions of people who think of their identities as hybrids of national membership, or who construct cosmopolitan identity" (p. 237). Finally, Mouffe emphasizes the need for democratic rights to be exercised collectively and not individually writing that "the necessity of democratic rights, rights, which, while belonging to the individual, can only be exercised collectively and presuppose the existence of equal rights for others" (1989, p. 42). In order to better understand this proposed rethinking of community, I situate relational communities of differentiated inclusivity between *gemeinschaft* communities and communitarianism, on the one hand, and liberalism and deliberative democracy, on the other. I will then rehearse criticisms of these two camps. Finally, I will show how Mouffe, Young, and Dewey reconcile these positions and how my conception of community fits into their schema. To conclude, I explore how communication and ICTs aid the pursuit of informed communities and pragmatic problem-solving.

"Communities of Exclusion": Criticisms of Communitarian Fraternity

Gemeinschaft communities are defined as a kind of spontaneous and organic relationship between peoples with strong bonds of kinship, reciprocal sentiment, and a common tradition (Mouffe, 2000, p. 29). Often, such communities are evocative of nostalgia for a premodern, harmonious, fraternal community that is today threatened by modern communities and "internal homogeneity" and is, therefore, favored over "cross-cutting communal allegiances and collective identities" (Bader, 1995, p. 217).

These *gemeinschaft* communities, while seemingly providing valuable personal interactions and communication, have been attacked by a number of poststructuralist and postcolonialist critics (Joseph, 2000, pp. xviii-xxvi). For example, such critics are hesitant to sing the praises of communities defined by a homogenous communal characteristic, instead of individual experience, because of tendencies towards fascism (Nancy, 1991) or cultural absolutism (Fanon, 1961). Common to all these criticisms is the claim that, even though *gemeinschaft* communities promise to foster values of inclusivity, solidarity, and trust, these communities are actually laden with power imbalances that serve to exclude those who are not "like" included members and to give meaning to the group in and through that exclusion. Such communities of exclusion, Joseph plainly states, "immediately . . . raise questions of belonging and power" (2000, p. xxii). These exclusionary tendencies have led to three main criticisms of *gemeinschaft* communities. First, that celebrating and participating in such communities can create "internal and external enemies" who "are then elided, excluded, or actively repressed" (Joseph, p. xix) and can even result in "constituting and legitimating violences" (Joseph, p. xx) against those of the out-group. Second, that rigid boundaries of exclusion do not allow for persons to "have multiple memberships" and/or for persons to "not fit any characterization" (Young, 2000, p. 225) without facing prejudice, oppression, and/or invisibility. Third, because individuals do, in fact, live in a geographically-defined world, individuals need to find ways of protecting individual rights and concerns without a wholesale denial of a communities' benefits.

Such communities of exclusion prevent individuals from exercising their potentialities in multiple groups, a hallmark of democracy, at least in its ideal form. As Omar Swartz, Katia Campbell, and Christina Pestana remark, even though "the common assumption is that we as a society actually value and support both democracy and diversity," this "is not always the case" (2009, p. 9). Because there is opportunity to monitor the actions of their members, constrain individual freedoms, and "employ strong forms of social control to enforce conformity" (Brint, 2001, p. 17), communities of exclusion are especially dangerous as elective belief-based communities in which there are "high levels of interaction among physically co-present members" (p. 17). Such exclusionary communities not only severely restrain individual rights and freedoms that are legally guaranteed in democratic society, they also create factions of individuals within society, thereby undermining general safety and readily respected standards for behavior. While on the one hand, "the fact of globalization" is a problem because it is difficult to ensure that everyone's voices and viewpoints are being addressed, on the other hand, negative versions of conjoined communities deny such multifaceted memberships and identities and inter-/intra-group movement. From teenage gang violence to religious extremism to virtually-co-present hate-group websites, such exclusionary communities that deny multiple group memberships are difficult to reconcile with the need for an informed, participatory, communicative public.

However, while critics of *gemeinschaft* communities succeed in revealing the insidious tendencies of communities that are not acknowledged by those who understand community in its utopian, pre-modern ideal, they fail to provide a positive form of community to replace these communities of exclusion. I am not, here, concerned with elective communities of interest, identity, activities, and association, as described above, as a replacement for such communities of exclusion. Even though Dewey would undoubtedly include such interactions in his understanding of group memberships as related to individual capacity and participation, these kinds of communal relationships -- especially when they stand in for informed public debate and interaction -- lack, in my view, the "interacting flexibility" that is a condition of democratic groups (Flamm, 2006, p. 47). Thus, in this chapter, I look to multifaceted communities which are both created and sustained through individual members' appreciation of consequences toward a commonly recognized good.

I should emphasize, in this vein, that in no way do I mean to reject and condemn all forms of community as responsible for creating enemies and subsequent in-group/out-group violence. Clearly, communities are important for shared problem-solving, for working together, and for fostering shared experiences (Sunstein, 2007). They are, as was mentioned above, indivisible from democracy and an informed and participatory public. For Dewey, especially, community is essential, not for mere political empowerment, but for bringing naturally-occurring group loyalties into harmony with each other and with the surrounding environment (Flamm, 2006, p. 48). I mean only to charge communities which prize and pursue homogeneity and essential sameness at the exclusion and denial of difference and particularity. For instance, I reject communities whose social practices "presume or attempt to enact and produce identity, unity, communion, and purity"(Joseph, 2000, p. xviii-xix) or communities that constrain individuals to "a single idea of the common good" (Mouffe, 1989, p. 44). That is to say, it would be wildly unfair and tendentious to condemn any and all gatherings of like-minded people who share similar interests and participate in similar activities, or people of shared ethnic or racial backgrounds, or to accuse them with inciting violence or hatred against those not within their groups. Nevertheless, if a key element uniting these people and reinforcing their likeness is the exclusion of others -- that is, if without an identifiable "other" such a group would lose its cohesion -- then such a community risks falling into intolerance of, marginalization of, and violence against those not "like them," be it in interests, background, or activities.

Beyond Deliberative Democracy and Liberal Individualism

In communities of exclusion, individuals are defined according to one dominant characteristic comprising the community in question. For example, the fervent nationalism of the early 20th century, which led to the rise of totalitarian and communist regimes, made individual citizens subordinate to the state's interests as a whole. Similarly, the identity-politics communities which gained political currency in the 1970s and 80s or the communitarians who view community as "constituted by shared moral values and organized around the idea of 'the common good'" (Mouffe, p. 29), both subsume the individual under the overarching characteristic of the community as well as deny the individual's own diversity in pursuit of a cause. This overarching cause both creates the need for the particular community and gives the community a purpose to continue. That is to say, in communities of exclusion the individual is sacrificed to the community and the ideal of the communal cause and defining characteristics are both descriptive of the community and gives the community its meaning. Such a community will persist, fundamentally unchanged, even as its individual members die or otherwise exit the community.

I realize that some may dispute the above description, contending that it is not necessarily bad for the individual to take second place to the vision of community, for one could imagine an overarching vision that would bond peoples of diverse backgrounds together in pursuit of a virtuous common goal: human rights, global peace, ending needless suffering, loving thy neighbor all seem like timeless ideals worth pursuing, sometimes at the sacrifice of individual wants and needs. However, not only is such a re-creation of *"gemeinschaft* community cemented by a substantive idea of the common good . . . clearly premodern and incompatible with the pluralism that is constitutive of modern democracy" (Mouffe, 1992, p. 29), pursuing such universal goals risks forced inclusion of the other into the supposedly enlightened sphere. In other words, *gemeinschaft* communities force belonging and sameness at the expense of individual diversity and hybrid interests, identities, and associations.

One corrective to the relationship between individual and community as found in communities of exclusion is staunch liberalism in which the private and public spheres are necessarily and importantly distinct and which "affirms that there is no common good and that each individual should be able to define her own good and realize it in her own way" (Mouffe, 1992, p. 29). In this view, individual and private interests are paramount, the purpose of public institutions is to protect individual interests, rights and freedoms, and regard for others' needs and wants is limited to political and economic management and negotiation. Also, instead of individuals being sacrificed to communities, communities are merely aggregations of pre-formed, independent individuals who are free to pursue their own interests under the protection of societal conventions and contractual guarantees. However, as de Tocqueville warned, such extreme liberalism risks falling into an unchecked individualism in which individuals are placed "side by side, unconnected by any common tie" and "general indifference [is] a sort of public virtue" (1835/1994, p. 102). For de Tocqueville, therefore, and Dewey would likely agree, some degree of sacrifice of personal liberties are necessary for establishing a democratic and participatory public.

Another corrective is rational discourse in the public sphere aimed at reaching consensus through correct procedural parameters. Inevitably, a discussion of deliberation will come up in a chapter on communities defined as relational, inclusive, diverse, and arrived at through communication of the community members. Deliberation has a storied place in theories of communication and democracy, with the standard model succinctly described by Young as implicitly championing "norms of orderly and dispassionate reason-giving" (p. 168). In such deliberation, truths, or at least consensus, can be arrived at only if informed individuals deliberate, dispassionately, the issue at hand. Deliberation thereby promises inclusivity through the equal participation of those who will be governed by the collective decisions made through deliberation. However, similar to the above critiques of liberalism as providing unencumbered individual freedom, Bohman remarks that deliberation is also problematic in two main ways. He writes that "either deliberation is conformed to the institutions of liberal democracy and thus inherits all their problems of legitimacy," for example, pervasive asymmetries of gender, class, and race, practical problems in actually conducting such deliberation, and even reducing democracy to mere seminar discussions. Or, he continues, deliberation "proposes its own institutions and decision-making procedures, at the cost of making its own democratic legitimacy infeasible" (pp. 23-24). Therefore, deliberation, as it has been commonly championed (Gutmann and Thompson, 1996; Page, 1996), suffers from the same problems of legitimacy and individualism as liberalism.

So what are the alternatives? What form can community take in which individual freedoms and rights are protected by common ties and equality, marked by consideration for fellow individuals, is also cultivated? How can such a community avoid falling into exclusionary practices which would fracture public virtues and encourage inequality between in-groups and out-groups? To answer these questions, let us turn to the work of Young (2000) and to Mouffe (1992).

Young (2000) suggests there is way of understanding the relationship between individuals and communities which does not depend on "the distinctness of peoples" (p. 237). Rejecting such "inappropriately essentialist and exclusionary" distinctions between peoples as belonging to one group or another, Young suggests that "peoples should be understood as relationally constituted, and the political recognition of the distinctness of peoples should be able to accommodate the millions of people who think of their identities as hybrids of national membership, or who construct cosmopolitan identity" (p. 237). In other words, in order to ensure differentiated inclusivity on a community level, individuals can neither be subsumed under the overarching goals of a distinct community nor can individuals be seen as independent entities, completely divided from one another except through the cohesion provided by social contract. By contrast, individuals should be recognized as constituted in relation to one another and in relation to the myriad of communities of which they are a part. In this way, Young provides a means for understanding inclusivity that neither sacrifices the individual to the common characteristic or goal of the community nor forcefully integrates varied individuals in a celebration of democratic pluralism. Instead, Young provides a way of both allowing individuals to group with other "like" individuals and protecting individuals' diversity and possible hybrid identities, interests, activities, and memberships in multiple communities or groups.

Mouffe (1992) offers a similar conception of differentiated yet inclusive communities. Even though her inquiry is exploring the relationship between individual identity and political communities instead of communities more generally, her acknowledgement that individuals have varied memberships in different communities but must also submit to certain overarching governing rules of conduct, is a helpful synthesis of the communitarian and liberal views of individuals' relationship to communities and society. Mouffe argues that persons are "engaged in many different communities and have differing conceptions of the common good" but nevertheless "accept submission to certain authoritative rules of conduct" (p. 31). This form of community is held together "not by a substantive idea of the common good but by a common bond, a public concern. It is therefore a community without a definite shape and in continuous reenactment" (p. 31). In other words, it is a form of community defined through the constantly shifting practices of the members of the community itself yet governed by the overarching rules and boundaries of the geographically-determined, political districting. In such a community, individuals are both free to pursue their own interests and have their freedoms protected as they act together in pursuit of goals that are defined in and by the community itself, instead of independent from the community.

Unlike communitarian and liberal understandings of communities in relation to pre-formed individuals, Young and Mouffe describe a community that cannot exist prior to, or independent of, individuals; that is, its common values, goals, and characteristics cannot be developed or persist without the membership, participation, and engagement of specific individuals. Furthermore, the community identity and individual identities of its members are created in and through the participation of its members and their relationships to each other and to other communities. Swartz et al similarly argue that democracy "is creative when literature (in its most general sense) not law, ideas not power, and hope not faith sustain a community that is continuously redescribing itself -- always unsure of its future but aware of its past and, for that reason, committed to and optimistic for the present . . . . A democratic society," and, I would add, a creative community, "thus, is incomplete" (p. 14).

Finally, individuals are recognized as holding multiple memberships in differing kinds of communities -- of language, of background, of interests, etc. However, both Young and Mouffe's accounts of relationally-constituted communities bound by a conception of public problem and a common solution, require further steps to achieve such communities. Borrowing from Dewey, I would like to argue that, common to Young and Mouffe's descriptions of community relations, is the implication that the members of these communities appreciate the consequences of their actions on fellow members of the community and are, in turn, affected by the actions of others in their communities. Boldly stated, I am arguing that the boundaries of communities are neither the mere geographic boundaries that incidentally connect independent individuals to each other nor the bounds of previously-formed, common ideologies, identities, interests at the exclusion of uncommon ideologies, identities, and interests. Instead, the boundaries of communities are formed in and through the scope of which persons can appreciate the consequences of each other's actions, along the three axes I originally described: vertically (how individuals appreciate consequences within their own community), horizontally (how communities are related to each other through the collective appreciation of community members towards other communities), and in terms of mobility (how individuals appreciate the consequences of multiple communities).

There are, of course, a number of factors affecting how far and in what manner such appreciation can reach, including geographic boundaries, language, interests, associations, identities, activities, technologies for communication, and mobility. However, such factors, instead of being dispositive -- a claim which many theorists and social scientists have argued, as seen above -- place a limit on the available scope of shared consequences. By contrast, actually appreciating these consequences and creating "a community of action saturated and regulated by mutual interest in shared meanings" (Dewey, 1988, p. 331) requires individuals to both participate in communal activities, problems, and goals and to share in their results.

Armed now with both a concept of community and a test for determining its boundaries and members, the questions become: How is such a community cultivated? How are such consequences appreciated? How does this side-step the pitfalls of the above-described versions of community while moving toward democratic communities?[3]

Appreciating Consequences: Communication is Key

For Dewey, communities are formed when the consequences of individuals' actions "are intellectually and emotionally appreciated [by the members of the community], a shared interest is generated and the nature of interconnected behavior is thereby transformed" (p. 252). But without communication among individuals, the consequences of an individuals' actions on others cannot be perceived and varied; therefore, relational, inclusive communities would not be generated. Expanding on Young's view of deliberation and considering it in light of Mouffe's account of radical democratic communities and Dewey's creative democracy, I would like to suggest that, in order to avoid such utopian and "formal" instantiations, communication and deliberation would need to be put in the service of relational communities of differentiated inclusivity in the ways described below.

First, regarding the relational aspect of community, deliberation and forms of communication must enable communities to exist in open relation with each other. Multiple avenues of communication and opportunities for problem-solving and collaboration should be cultivated by private companies, government incentives and subsidies, community organizations, NGOs, and innovative uses by individuals. A number of organizations and individuals have begun to create such avenues of communication. Noteworthy examples include: *National Issues Forum*, which brings people together to discuss and learn about important issues in forums from small study circles to large town-hall meetings; *Everyday Democracy*, which helps local communities talk and work together to solve problems); the *Harwood Institute*, which provides affordable access to communication and organizing tools in the hopes of cultivating public innovators); and the *Youth Innovation Fund*, which uses multiple action pathways to foster youth engagement and youth-led civil action projects in local communities. Journalism schools have also begun programs that empower local communities and gather community stories and ideas. For example, MyMissourian.com, in conjunction with the Missouri Journalism School's faculty-run, student-staffed daily newspaper, is a citizen journalism project where the readers serve as writers and the journalism students serve as editors and guides. Another example is Northwestern's Medill School's "News Mixer" which was developed from the 2008 New Media Publishing Project. "News Mixers" allow citizens in Eastern Iowa to comment on news articles, ask questions that other readers as well as the reporter can answer, and send letters to the editor which can themselves be commented on, or asked about, by fellow readers.

Underlying this goal is the precarious balance between communication as a means for cultivating shared experiences, and dispassionate, starkly rational deliberation that depends on participants leaving personal differences and diversities "at the door." As Bohman notes, the ideal of a "multi-perspectival polity" is based in non-domination and seeks "to take into account the positive and negative dimensions of current social conditions as well as to incorporate the various perspectives of relevant social actors in attempting to solve a problem" (2004, p. 24). Sunstein (2007) agrees, arguing that "a heterogeneous society benefits from shared experiences" which "provide a kind of social glue, facilitating efforts to solve shared problems, encouraging people to view one another as fellow citizens, and sometimes helping to ensure responsiveness to genuine problems and needs, even helping to identify them as such" (p. 117).

Successfully walking this line between shared experiences and incorporating various perspectives of diverse actors in the deliberative and communicative processes that cultivate community is described, in part, in Dewey's insistence on recognizing individuals' actions' far-reaching consequences on fellow individuals and communities. Such communicative processes are also described, in part, by Young's reformulation of deliberation as encompassing varied, informal, participatory, expressive, and even "messy" (2000, p. 168) modes of communication. In Dewey and Young's frameworks, deliberation is not merely coming to rational consensus via communicative means; rather, it is participatory problem-solving and decision-making that is concerned with the consequences on fellow individuals and communities. Practiced as such, deliberation can aid in preserving open avenues of communication between and among various communities and individuals belonging to varied communities.

Examples of such open channels of communication are digital public square projects that have been emerging in recent years. PublicSquare.net ("common ground, uncommon debate"), provides forums for discussion, reports and analyses from around the globe to foster debate, a series of video-blogs and blog posts with ability to comment. American Towns is a company building an online "public square" for every town in America. Union Square Online is an online version of youth culture and community in New York's Union Square. Such online public forums for discussion, especially when the option for commenting on fellow community members' posts and for posting video and audio components (which addresses some of Young's concerns of deliberation as privileging certain modes of communication over others), have the potential to foster community discussion in less formal, more interconnected ways. The hope is that such communicative deliberation (borrowing from Young's phrase "communicative democracy") can aid in identifying common problems, cultivating shared experiences, and encouraging intra- and cross-community decision-making. Instead of being forced to adhere to the constraints of formal deliberation which limit participation to certain kinds of discourse on restricted topics, these open avenues of communication, especially when combined with social networking tools, enable individuals to introduce both the concerns of and provide solutions to varied and overlapping communities' issues.[4] Individuals are thereby neither reduced to one form of communication at the expense of another nor to one community membership at the expense of another.

Second, speaking to the differentiated aspect of community, free forms of individual and communal expression and communication are essential to cultivating individual diversity, varied interests, hybrid identities, and multifaceted collaborations. From artistic expression to more self-conscious definitions of identity via social networking sites to DYI videos illustrating unique talents or background experiences, creative expression and communication with others via such expression is important for both cultivating diversity and for making such diversity known to others in the community and to community representatives. The crux of creative expression in terms of cultivating community through appreciated consequences is not so much the creation of the products but the sharing and dissemination of these products. Sending links to friends, blogging and reading blogs, embedding streaming video on social networking profile pages, posting links as "statuses" on online instant messaging services, and peer review services like Delicious (www.delicious.com) or Digg (www.digg.com) are all ways of sharing products of creative expression. This sharing is, in fact, communication in its own right. Unlike the formal deliberation of city council meetings or testimonies to government bodies (which are important for making community concerns known to those in power), sharing creative products of expression are vital forms of community life. The scope of such sharing -- that is, how large the network is that will ultimately come in contact with the product -- is one way of determining the bounds of community: those who appreciate the effects of the creative product will continue sharing the product; those who do not appreciate the creative product will end such sharing. In this way, the community's shared values are determined through the specific act of communication (sharing) and the community boundaries are formed through the appreciation of the effects of the creative products.

I should emphasize that it is not the *kind* of technology that determines if the communication that technology enables is "communicative" or "deliberative" (to use Young's distinction). Streaming video can be used as easily in propaganda campaigns to exclude others from a community as it can be opening diverse and varied channels of communication so that individuals can actively participate in developing multiple and overlapping community relations. Henry Jenkins' (2007) work on "civic media" as any medium engaged with fostering and enhancing popular civic engagement echoes my assertion: the key to fostering communities that are relational, differentiated, and inclusive is appreciating consequences of one's actions and recognizing each other's actions as affecting oneself; such appreciation can occur in a multitude of forums. However, ICTs, because of their current tendency towards openness, interconnectedness, and user-friendliness, have a unique propensity toward fostering such mutually-recognized and appreciated communication and interaction.

Finally, concerning the inclusive aspect of community, communication is essential in providing individuals with the ability to move in, and among, different communities, both those with which they share defining characteristics and those in which they do not. Flamm remarks that because, according to Dewey "we are born organic beings associated with others" but not "members of a community" (Dewey, 1998, p. 330), "the establishment of community entails a successful working out of the appropriate democratic relation between individuals and groups" (Flamm, 2006, p. 47). Cultivating relationships between communities, between the varied and multiple groups of an individual's relations, and between individuals as they move in and among these different communities are all, I propose, important facets for working out the appropriate interconnectedness between groups and individuals in democratic society. Instead of pursuing a homogenous grouping of like-identity individuals (communities of exclusion, communitarianism) or rational consensus as to a common good (deliberative democracy, liberalism), relational communities of differentiated exclusivity are both appreciative of and cultivated through "conjoint activity whose consequences are appreciated as good by all singular persons" (Dewey, 1988, p. 295).

Communities, in other words, do not exist as islands unto themselves; the mobility of individuals among communities -- both geographic and of interest, identity, association, etc. -- is necessary for allowing individuals to have multiple memberships. Alternative and independent news outlets have long served as means of communication and interconnection between and across various communities. Alternative weeklies have served sub-groups of communities of interest (for example, underground music and art scenes) as well as minority communities (for example, foreign-language newspapers). Independent media outlets have also served communities that transgress the boundaries of mainstream modes of communication. Recently, not only have these media outlets for intra- and cross-community communication and information sharing moved to online forums and incorporated various new ICTs, a number of organizations have developed which give citizens themselves the tools needed to engage in such interconnected communication. From the Independent Media Institute and the Women's Media Center to New American Media (focusing on ethnic communities), previously excluded communities are being provided with ways to communicate with each other while still being part of the dominant community group. This kind of intra- and cross-communication, as defined by Dewey and distinct from deliberation's traditional notions of consensus-building, is necessary to ensure not only that individuals within discrete communities are appreciating the consequences of their actions, but also that individuals moving in and among different communities appreciate such consequences instead of merely engaging with others in a transactional or indifferent way. As Swartz, et al remark, criticizing marketplace -- or what Dewey would call transactional -- diversity in democratic communities: "When the richness of diversity is limited to the appeal of commodities, and when we tend to define ourselves in terms of the commodities we consume, diversity is reduced to little more than powerful identification devices to sell products and to create the façade of inclusion and acceptance" (2009, p. 16).

Communication in Action: Real-World Examples

Moving away from the theoretical, I would like address ways to cultivate group memberships which avoid both exclusionary practices and forced inclusion and instead make possible individuals' "conduct as a member of [the] . . . group [to be] enriching and enriched by [their] participation in family life, industry, scientific and artistic associations" (Dewey, quoted in Flamm, 2006, p. 47). How can we establish such communities? How can we ensure that differentiation is voluntary and that individuals' memberships in multiple communities is respected? How can we come to develop and recognize a common bond, a public good, without sacrificing the individual to this goal? How can we fight indifference to public concern while still allowing for individual liberty and equality? To answer these questions, I turn to three real-world examples in which communication aided in creating and maintaining relational communities of differentiated inclusivity. These examples are culled from testimonies of current conditions and hopeful suggestions for improvement from meetings and community forums for the Knight Commission on the Information Needs of Local Communities in a Democracy (KnightComm). My hope is to provide a hopeful formula for looking at and rethinking these communities while also creating a template at which empirical research can be aimed.

New ICTs have the potential to both expand the scope of appreciated consequences but also, and perhaps most importantly for achieving Dewey's creative democracy, to enhance the quality and force of local interactions. Evidence of a trend toward locality is present on both sides of the political spectrum, with both Democrats and Republicans showing support for things like shopping at local farmers' markets to supporting small businesses to energy conservation on a community level. Common to both sides is the emphasis on appreciating the actions of others on one's own life; for example, knowing purchases at farmers' markets and small business are directly supporting the person with whom one is making the transaction and that person is directly supplying goods affecting one's everyday life. This trend is also evident in the innovative uses of new technologies, not merely to improve movie recommendations and keep tabs on long-lost friends, but in identifying local problems and working towards common solutions.

The first example of communication used in ways that cultivated a community of differentiated inclusivity is a story recounted by Raj Jayadev, Founder of Silicon Valley De-Bug, who spoke at the KnightComm's Mountain View Community Forum (2008). Jayadev discussed the need for an inclusive media landscape in which marginalized communities were able to create their own reflections of themselves in larger society. He argued that, in order for there to be a civically engaged generation, individuals need to be able to "define themselves in [and through] their own terms" -- that is, through new ICTs and not through the formal deliberation of City Hall. (Jayadev, 2008). He described such a hope for a community of youth, bounded by both geography and shared -- albeit diverse -- identities and interests, to be cultivated in and through new tools for communication and information sharing. Individuals who had previously not recognized others within their geographic spaces as "like them" discovered shared interests and joined together to affect changes that mattered to them, as youth, and to their shared communities.

As suggested above, Jayadev made it clear that certain youth communities developed out of shared goals which were developed from shared geographic location and shared concerns of potential permitting processes. A diverse yet unified community of "rockers and rappers" in Silicon Valley did not exist prior to their organization against the proposed permit; instead, the community was developed in and through their united goals, concerns, and proximity. Therefore, not only were these individuals neither sacrificed to the community nor completely independent and indifference to "pubic virtue," but also, like Young's and Mouffe's formulations of individuals' role in communities, which require continuous participation and engagement of the individuals in establishing and reestablishing a common bond, these Silicon Valley rockers and rappers established a common bond in response to a public concern. Furthermore, the continued common interest in free public association which the proposed permit would have prohibited ensures the continued existence of this community.

In addition to communication and ICTs enabling new communities to develop based around common problems and collective solutions, many community leaders at the KnightComm meetings remarked on the need to arm existing politically-defined and geographically-bound communities with tools to enable collective communication and problem-solving. Repeatedly, individuals and community spokespersons testified that community members lack only the tools of communication, research, information-sharing, and collaboration, and the top-down technical support and subsidy to keep those tools working. They do not lack initiative or commitment to fellow community members in moving toward democratic, inclusive, differentiated, and mobile communities. "Give us the tools, the templates, the means" they seemed to say, "and we, as a community, will do the rest."

Flowing from the above leads me to the second example of communication being used to cultivate and support inclusive and diverse communities. When Local Initiatives Support Corporation (LISC), a community organization whose goals include providing hyper-local information to Chicago neighborhoods via websites, first posted projects online, there was a dramatic, positive response by community members. Soon after this initial launch, however, community members were saying they wanted their own websites, instead of a single site for 16 neighborhoods, and they wanted to be the ones in control of the content on their neighborhood's site. So, LISC created a website for each neighborhood community and now teaches citizens how to use the websites and report their own news. Almost immediately, community members were making clear to LISC exactly the communications and information tools they wanted -- e-newsletters, video, online radio -- and LISC teaches them how to do these things (Barry, 2008).

A third example of ICTs put in the hands of community members and successfully fostering inclusivity and collaboration is a neighborhood communications tool called Front-Porch Forum (FPF). FPF provides neighborhood email services so that community members can post inquiries, make community announcements, ask questions, organize around municipal issues, etc. The template is more restrictive than the LISC-supported, neighborhood-run websites just described. Members are not permitted to post anonymously to the e-newsletters, thereby requiring individual responsibility and accountability within the community. I would like to emphasize that DYI communication and information-sharing tools do not necessarily cultivate relational, diverse, and inclusive communities, nor do more formalized ICTs necessarily lead to communities of exclusion. Instead, ICTs can be put in the service of either form of community. FPF is an example of a strict template that, through requiring user information, thereby creates accountability and fosters inclusivity because it allows community members to recognize the effects of individual actions and requests on the community as a whole (Wood-Lewis, 2008).

These examples of community potential and community needs provide evidence that relational communities of differentiated inclusivity are both a practical possibility and an anticipated, though hopeful, reality. The two competing concepts of community offered in this chapter are meant to provide a way of both evaluating existing communities and to provide an ideal form of community which celebrates and cultivates individual flourishing and community development in ways motivated by democratic principles of liberty, equality, and association. Such an ideal form balances on the delicate line between communities as inclusionary spaces and relationships that foster trust, solidarity, and democratic engagement and the negative effects of communities as exclusionary mechanisms that create boundaries of an "us versus them" nature that breed distrust and blind loyalties. While democratic principles need not be the dominant principles of governance for any potential community, these principles should motivate the creation and continued performance of various kinds of relational communities of differentiated inclusivity. I would like to hope that, adopted from the ground-level up instead of imposing values from the top-down, these principles could be broadly adopted and aid in fostering shared recognition of common goals as well as appreciation of consequences of collective and individual action. Such communities would, thereby, be both consistent with, and formative of, the communities' own histories, politics, place, and changing values.

Evidenced in the testimonies at the KnightComm meetings and community forums, communication -- through new and old media channels, through social networking sites, through blogs and DYI videos and reporting, through mobile communications technologies -- is paramount in two ways. First, communication and new communications technologies enable communities to present a vision of themselves to themselves. Secondly, prominent decision-makers and local communities are able to interact and engage with each other in powerful and innovative ways. As we have seen, the dominant theme of the KnightComm testimonies is that they do not need to be told that they need information or channels of communication, nor do they need to be told how to communicate; instead, communities need the power of information and communication technologies and tools. With means of communication guaranteed, individuals within discrete and multiple communities will be confident in their abilities to cultivate the shared experiences and identities they need while also remaining connected to their politico-geographic spaces and issues attendant to those spaces. Individuals are able to recognize the effects of their actions, of their expression, of their own needs and values, and they are able to be affected by the actions, expressions, and needs of others. Through these shared effects and consequences via communication tools, individuals identify common goals, interests, geographic-spaces, identities and are able to work collectively towards common goals. In this way, a community is formed.

Why Community?

I would like to conclude by answering a fundamental question to this chapter: Why do we need community at all? Why not reject all communities as *gemeinschaft* communities of exclusion -- both supposedly organic, utopian communities and supposedly corrective ones driven by singular aims of identity-political groups -- and merely act as independent individuals in society? While I do not imagine myself to have the definitive answers to these questions, there are a couple of realities to take into account which make me unable, in good conscience, to turn my back on communities altogether.

First, we need communities because we necessarily exist in geographically-bound spaces which, in the United States, determine our political stakes and distribution of material resources. From bonding together with shared interests and experiences comes political capital. If we do not recognize this fact and we languish in our responsibilities to fellow citizens within our shared political communities, then individuals and groups alike risk losing their voices in the republic.

Second, and relatedly, politico-geographic communities cannot be and are not individuals' sole ways of relating to others. In these contemporary times -- in part because of ICTs that enable virtual and hyper-mobile modes of communication, inter-relation, and expression -- there are communities of interest, identity, association, and activities that are cultivated and exist independent from the geographically-bound world. If, however, on the other end of the spectrum from rejecting community altogether, the only concept of community is one divorced from the necessary politico-geographic boundaries, then we likewise risk political incapacitation. Geographically boundless communities do not, as the current voting and electoral system in the United States is organized, provide representatives necessarily accountable to an individual's geographically-independent (i.e., her/his vote-independent) interests.

Finally, we need community because of the simple and powerful reason that we cannot escape: "community generates not an attitude of 'whatever' but rather the strongest of passions" (Joseph, p. xxx). Individuals will seek common interactions and shared meanings; the question is if there are better and worse forms -- for our democracy, for civil and human rights, for future generations -- for such communities to take.

As I saw and heard at the KnightComm community forums and meetings, people have fierce passion for, and dedication to, their communities, both geographically-defined and communities defined by interest, identity, association, or activities. In order to reconcile the geographically-determined communities with elective communities of interest, identity, activity, and association, policy-makers, politicians, CEOs and others working from the top-down must pair with NGOs, community and educational organizations, everyday people empowered by ICTs working from the bottom-up. They must reconcile these seemingly opposing versions of communities while still realizing that communities are necessary to guarantee that all individuals are included in having their own shared interests, concerns, and needs recognized. They must realize that relational communities of differentiated inclusivity are necessary in overcoming the potentially violent and exclusionary results of *gemeinschaft* communities and the indifference of liberal individualism. Finally, they must realize that communication, appreciation of one's own and others' actions, and recognition of individuals' multiple memberships will create communities that reflect the passion, not the indifference, of individuals. Such communities will breathe new life into local and elective communities alike.

REFERENCES

Anderson, B. (1991). *Imagined communities: Reflections on the origin and spread of nationalism.* New York: Verso.

Bader, V. (1995). Citizenship and exclusion: Radical democracy, community, and justice, or what is wrong with communitarianism? *Political Theory, 23(2)*, 221-246.

Barry, P. (2008). Content manager for LISC/Chicago's new communities program, Testified at KnightComm Meeting, Chicago, November 17. Retrieved from www.knightcomm.org.

Bohman, J. (2004). Realizing deliberative democracy as a mode of inquiry: Pragmatism, social facts, and normative theory. *Journal of Speculative Philosophy,* 18(1), 23-43.

Brint, S. (2001). *Gemeinschaft* revisited: A critique and reconstruction of the community concept. *Sociological Theory, 19*(1), 1-23.

Dewey, J. (1988). The public and its problem. In J. Boydston (Ed.), *John Dewey: The later works, 1925-1953, volume 2* (pp. 235-372). Carbondale, Il: Southern Illinois University Press. (Original published 1927).

-- (1976). Creative democracy: The task before us. In J. Boydston (Ed.), *John Dewey: The later works*, 1925-1953, volume 14 (pp. 224-230). Carbondale, Il: Southern Illinois University Press. (Original published 1939).

Fanon, F. (1961). *The wretched of the earth*. New York: Grove Weidenfeld.

Farr, J. (2004). Social capital: A conceptual history. *Political Theory(1)*, 32, 6-33.

Flamm, M. (2006). The demanding community: Politicization of the individual after Dewey. *Education and Culture*, 22(1), 35-54.

Gutmann, A. and Thompson, D. (1996). *Democracy and disagreement*. Cambridge: Harvard University Press.

Hicks, D. (2002). The promise(s) of deliberative democracy. *Rhetoric & Public Affairs*, 5(2), 223-260.

Jayadev, R. (2008). Founder, Silicon Valley De-Bug, Testified at KnightComm Meeting, Silicon Valley, September 8. Retrieved from www.knightcomm.org.

Jenkins, H. (2007). What is Civic Media? Confessions of an Aca-Fan, Oct. 3. Retrieved from http://henryjenkins.org/2007/10/what_is_civic_media_1.html.

Joseph, M. (2002). *Against the romance of community*. Minneapolis: University of Minnesota Press.

Knight Commission on the Information Needs of Local Communities in a Democracy, A Project of the Aspen Institute Communications and Society Program and the John S. and James L. Knight Foundation. June 2008-October 2009. Retrieved from www.knightcomm.org.

Laclau, E. and Mouffe, C. (1985). *Hegemony and socialist strategy: Towards a radical democratic politics*. New York: Verso.

Mead, G. H. (1934). *Mind, self, and society*. Chicago: University of Chicago Press.

Mouffe, C. (1992). Citizenship and political identity. *October, 61,* 28-32.

---. (1989). Radical democracy: Modern or postmodern? *Social Text, 21,* 31-45.

Nancy, J. (1991). *The inoperative community*. Minnesota: University of Minnesota Press.

Page, B. (1996). *Who deliberates?* Chicago: University of Chicago Press.

Putnam, R. (2000). *Bowling alone: The collapse and revival of American Community.* New York: Simon & Schuster.

Rorty, R. (2000). The moral purposes of the university: An exchange. The *Hedgehog Review, 2*, 106-120.

Sandel, M. J. (1996). *Democracy's discontent.* Cambridge: Harvard University Press.

Sunstein, C. (2007). *Republic* 2.0. Princeton: Princeton University Press.

Swartz, O., Campbell, K., and Pestana, C. (2009). *Neo-pragmatism, communication, and the culture of creative democracy.* New York: Peter Lang Publishing.

Tocqueville, A. (1994). *Democracy in America.* New York: Alfred A. Knopf. (Original published in 1835).

Wood-Lewis, M. President and Co-founder of Vermont-based Front Porch Forum, Testified at KnightComm Meeting, Washington, D.C., June 24, 2008. Retrieved from www. knightcomm.org.

Young, I. M. (2000). *Inclusion and democracy.* New York: Oxford University Press.

Notes

[1] As noted by Brint, German sociologist Ferdinand Toennies developed the concept of *gemeinschaft* communities in his theoretical essay entitled *"Gemeinschaft* end *Gesellschaft"* ("Community and Society") (1887). Brint describes how Toennies' definition of community "represented the childhood of humanity" by being defined by "common ways of life . . . concentrated ties and frequent interaction . . . small numbers . . . [and] emotional bonds." This is in contrast to *gesellschaft* society which represented the ills of modern, legalistic, and transactional society (p. 2).

[2] Bader, citing Carens and others, distinguishes between "group culture" (i.e., things that reflect society's history, traditions, forms of life distinct from political culture) and "public political culture" (i.e., the principles necessary to a liberal democratic society, such as an informed and active populace) (p. 223). The concept of community I am proposing must encompass both types of cultural forces, not merely the political ones.

[3] George Herbert Mead describes this test as such: "The question of whether we belong to a larger community is answered in terms of whether our own actions call out a response in this wider community, and whether its responses is reflected back into our own conduct" (1934, p. 217).

[4] While originally thought to threaten strong social ties and community bonds, social networking sites have actually been found to strengthen the bonds between family and friends by supplementing (rather than replacing) face-to-face interaction and by helping connect individuals to trusted resources and information to help them make informed decisions.

CHAPTER 6

Reimagining Community Through Julie Laible's "Loving Epistemology"

Valerie Palmer-Mehta
Oakland University

Diminishing global resources, predatory globalization, toxic industrial waste and pollution, and ethnic-religious conflict have generated a maelstrom of problems resulting in mass human suffering and the corrosion of the physical environment that we rely upon to sustain us. Critics have long discussed the consequences of unproblematized consumption and the exploitation of resources and people (Carolan, 2004; Fernandez, 2004; Singer, 2002, 2009), but it is perhaps the global financial crisis of 2009 that has most recently prompted citizens of the world to reflect on their interdependence and the need for a comprehensive and effective moral framework to combat the politics and practices of distrust, selfishness, and greed (Kochler, 2009, pp. 3-6; Wargo, Baglini, & Nelson, 2009, pp. 2, 12). As David Rothkopf asserts, "we need to remember that capitalism is an amoral system and that a society without a moral basis is unsustainable" (2008, ¶4). While capitalism is not inherently a malevolent or corrosive structure, without a moral framework, it can be manipulated by those who view people's lives and the environment as nothing more than products to be manipulated, exploited, and spoiled for personal profit.[1]

In an interdependent global society, the imperative for an ethical framework that can be used as a corrective for oppressive and exploitative relationships is more relevant than ever. As Peter Singer (2002) maintains, "when different nations led more separate lives, it was more understandable -- though still quite wrong -- for those in one country to think of themselves as owing no obligations, beyond that of non-interference, to people in another state. But those times have gone" (p. 197). Singer argues that the new global dynamic not only *requires* rethinking our relationships to one another, but it also provides the *conditions* upon which to reinvigorate our commitment to the ethical. Specifically, our "newly interdependent global society, with its remarkable possibilities for linking people around the planet, gives us the material basis for a new ethic" (p. 12). If we are to actualize an international democratic community where human suffering is confronted and struggled against rather than taken as commonplace, and where we leverage our interrelatedness to benefit and enhance our humanity, we need a framework to serve as a foundation for sustainable ways of living in the world. As Grace Lee Boggs (2003) notes, "We need a vision that recognizes that we are at one of the great turning points in human history when the survival of our planet and the restoration of our humanity require a great sea change in our ecological, political, and spiritual values" (p. 28).

Communication scholars and students are strategically situated to help bring into being such a vision, and have the privilege and opportunity to do so in democratic cultures. As Omar Swartz (1997) notes of Western cultures like the U.S., "Institutional practices of social inequity are supported in large part by rhetorical, rather than military, means" (p. 8). Consequently, he argues, those who study communication "have a special responsibility for illustrating to others how rhetorical tensions mediate the way people think, feel, and interact within society" (p. 9). Swartz notes that because people in the United States live in a society where brutal repression against democratic reform is not totalizing, "the potential for peaceful redescription and change is greater in American society than in many non-Western societies" (pp. 8-9). Such potential for interruption and redefinition of the status quo is hardly conceivable in cultures where repression is institutionalized, as Harry Redner (2001) illuminates: "In a society where the state is overpowering, the law all-embracing, and people less given to the promptings of conscience or other ethical feeling, a condition of demoralization ensues with unforeseeable social consequences" (p. 12). Consequently, "those who live in democratic societies have the unique opportunity and, I would argue, *obligation*, to enhance the ethical quality of our lives and to reform society in the service of creating a "cultural condition reducing marginality and human suffering" (Swartz, 1997, p. 4). Being self-reflexive about the values we negotiate in society and in our scholarship, and generating new values by which to strengthen our democracy and sense of responsibility to our communities, can edify our discipline's theorizing and enhance our impact on and relevance to the broader society. Such edification, therefore, is an interest of the highest order.

A scholar committed to social justice and the promotion of policies that dismantle oppressive practices, Julie Laible (2000) coined the term "loving epistemology" to describe a theory of knowing Others that does not subsume Others into dominant apparatuses and structures and serves as a corrective for academic practices that mute or distort the voices of the non-dominant. Laible hoped that the loving epistemology would provide "an ethical way of producing knowledge about other human beings" (p. 688) while speaking to her overall vision of "accounting for and transforming existing forms of dogmatism, oppression, and despair" (p. 686). The components of a loving epistemology, which I extend and advance as a fundamental element of progressive social change in the service of what contributors to this edited volume, following John Dewey, call a "creative democracy," requires a relentless self-reflexivity and responsibility to Others that are essential to counteracting a culture of pernicious individualism, religious bigotry, racial prejudice, and an ethic of "survival-of-the-fittest." This transformational approach lays the groundwork for rethinking and reshaping our democracy into a sustainable and fully participatory society that long has been part of the American cultural mythos but which has been difficult to bring about in political practice. As Swartz (2006) has argued, "Human beings have the potential to create a society that is kind, just, healthy, and fair, but often are discouraged from doing so by the rhetorical and legal environments in which our society is situated, compromising many of the admirable values the United States claims in its normative narratives to represent" (p. 3). Indeed, if we are to reconceptualize democratic community in both theory and practice, we must begin with assessing the practices of inquiry that lie at the heart of, and shape, civic life.

To demonstrate how the loving epistemology serves as a launching point for re-imagining democratic community and communicative practice in the 21st century, I begin with an elucidation and reconsideration of Laible's loving epistemology. Specifically, I present Laible's original contours of the loving epistemology and build upon them. In Laible's original conception of a loving epistemology, love remained undefined. Thus, in the second section of the chapter I define and present love as a transformational modality, drawing on Martin Luther King, Jr.'s conception of agape love. Finally, I conclude this chapter with a discussion of how the loving epistemology and love as a transformational modality are pivotal facets of Swartz, Katia Campbell, and Christina Pestana's (2009) discussion of creative democracy.

Reconsidering Laible's Loving Epistemology

Laible's work expresses a deep concern with improving the ability of those who inhabit dominant identities to understand the everyday lived reality of marginalized peoples whose experiences have been rendered mute or made invisible by long standing power disparities in U.S. society (Laible, 1997, pp. 201-215; Laible, 2000, pp. 683-692; Scheurich & Laible, 2002, pp. 101-108; Young & Laible, 2000, pp. 374-415).[2] In her work on the loving epistemology, Laible was focused on encouraging those who inhabit dominant identities to take greater responsibility for understanding the experiences of the marginalized, and she argued that social theorizing should work toward disrupting institutions and practices of oppression. However, as she admitted, her work on the loving epistemology was in a fledgling state, and due to her untimely death she was unable to develop her ideas further.[3] My examination is an attempt to both illuminate Laible's original conceptions and proceed with their development in an effort to situate the loving epistemology within the broader project of re-imagining democratic community.

Other-Centered Ethic: As originally conceived, the loving epistemology had three main thrusts (Laible, 2000, p. 690). First, Laible sought to create an ethical relation between the self and Others by making the Other constitutive of the self. Laible had misgivings that those who inhabit dominant identities would ever be able to understand the experiences of the marginalized; consequently, she sought to create an unflinching responsibility to the marginalized by making Others an integral part of the self. Inspired by the work of Emmanuel Levinas (1981), who advanced the radical idea that ethics come before philosophy, Laible argued for placing ethics before ontology and epistemology, because she desired to turn concern for others into a precursor to our ways of knowing, infusing the research process. She saw this as the best way to guard against epistemological bias. Laible was drawn to Levinas's thought because his theorizing "does not dominate or subsume the Other" but, instead, "articulates a clear and extensive responsibility to and for the Other" (p. 689). Following Levinas, Laible attests to the importance of going "back one step before consciousness or existence to state what is pre-phenomenological, pre-ontological. In this state, we the subjects are exposed to Others" which forms the "bedrock of our selfhood; it is the condition of subjectivity, not an aspect of it" (p. 689). By placing ethics before ontology and epistemology, she sought to create ways of knowing and being that already accounted for and included Others because, in this arrangement, Others become a central conditioning component of the self.

It is not surprising that Laible desired to place ethics before epistemology and ontology because she indicated that her race and class based epistemological bias led to inadequate outcomes despite her best efforts to engage in ethical research practices.[4] Laible's intention is admirable, but how to bring such a vision into practice is elusive and, consequently, some scholars have criticized this approach and questioned what such a configuration would look like in practice. For example, while acknowledging the primacy of ethics in research, Michelle D. Young and Linda Skrla (2003) question whether there must be a linear and hierarchical progression from ethics to ontology and epistemology: "Does this mean that before one engages with issues of ontology or epistemology, one must have his or her ethical principles clarified? . . . If so, the implication would be that ethics supersedes our understanding of reality and our view of knowledge" (p. 202). Our ethical commitments rest upon our ontological and epistemological assumptions and, as such, Young and Skrla find Laible's approach of placing ethics before ontology and epistemology untenable, impractical, and naïve (pp. 202-203).[5] They offer an alternative conceptualization that still valorizes the place of ethics, but does not situate it prior to one's understanding of reality and view of knowledge. As they note, one's "ethics would envelope and guide one's thoughts and actions -- permeating the entire research process like a fine mist. Researchers would work consciously and conscientiously to keep their ethical principles, their responsibilities to the Other, at the forefront of their work" (p. 203). In order to ensure ethical practices throughout one's research, Young and Skria argue that researchers must constantly "trouble" and question one's ideas to ensure accuracy, avoid assumptions, and always consider the impact of research on Others: "We as researchers must constantly consider our own complicity in power arrangements and in other oppressions that structure the lives of the people in our settings for research and . . . we must always ask ourselves how our presence and our research affect our participants" (p. 208). Young and Skrla also argue that researchers must be accountable for their knowledge claims, responsible to those on whom they are conducting research, and consistently scrutinize the process and outcome of research, rather than view themselves as disinterested researchers who are disconnected from the research process (pp. 203-204).

It may be tempting to become mired in a discussion of whether ethics should precede and ground philosophy or vice versa; however, it is more productive to focus on *what kind* of ethics should guide our efforts. An Other-centered ethic, such as an ethic of care, would edify the loving epistemology. Joan Tronto and Berenice Fisher (1990) define an *ethic of care* as an activity "that includes everything we do to maintain, continue, and repair our 'world' so that we can live in it as well as possible. That world includes our bodies, our selves, and our environment, all of which we seek to interweave in a complex, life-sustaining web" (p. 40). Based on the work of second generation care theorists such as Tronto (1993), Fiona Robinson (1999), and Olena Hankivsky (2004), progressive care theorizing rejects essentialist notions of care centered on female biology and the private sphere in favor of a public, political care observed by all citizens.[6] This approach is marked by a relational ontology, recognizing that we "are not fully autonomous, but must always be understood in a condition of interdependence" (Tronto, 1993, p. 162). The approach focuses on people in their "dense contexts," recognizing that individuals are situated in particularized historical, political, economic and social milieus, which have a resounding effect on their lives (Hankivsky, 2004, p. 34). An ethic of care requires that citizens learn "how to listen and be attentive and responsive to the needs and suffering of others." Further, such an ethic "forces us to think concretely about people's real needs and to evaluate how those needs will be met" (Robinson, 1999, pp. 30-31). Indeed, an ethic of care has the potential to produce a greater understanding of the conditions that shape our lives across our differences because it reveals contextual factors that debunk the time-worn myth that humans have equal access to experiences, opportunities and advantages even in a democracy (see Palmer-Mehta, 2009). This Other-centered care ethic works symbiotically with Laible's desire to improve the ability of those who inhabit dominant identities to grasp the experiences of the marginalized.

An ethic of care is formed through reciprocal engagement with Others, enabling the researcher to recognize the historical and contextual contingency of her or his understanding of social life. Traditional philosophy focuses on the abstract, homogenous, universal subject disconnected from social and political life and all its complexities and effects. In contrast, the loving epistemology, edified by an ethic of care, requires recognition of one's location in distinct social arrangements based on privilege and difference and the effect such situatedness has on how we produce and consume knowledge. Because connectivity, interdependence, and relationship are central parts of knowledge production, and of our collective understanding of the situatedness of our knowledges, we are called to be actively engaged with Others in order to consider how power and privilege might mark our relationships and our understanding of the social world. This means reaching out to our research subjects in *their* world and on *their* terms, and being accountable to *their* perspective of the social world. Marsha Houston (1992) advocates this kind of approach in her discussion of feminist research, which is clearly applicable to other intellectual projects. As she notes, "Research on women's communication differences must be grounded in direct, not vicarious, relationships with women who are different from us; we must *earn* the right to speak about them, by learning who they are as they communicate in their own ethnic cultural contexts, their world, not simply in ours" (p. 55). Part of earning the right to speak about Others is actively listening to marginalized groups, particularly their criticisms of the status quo and the practices of dominant groups, with the knowledge that "attentive listening is especially difficult for members of dominant groups" (Johnson, 2006, p. 141). To ensure we have an appropriate grasp on the social world, Johnson recommends making a decision to engage in ongoing reading about the matrix of privilege and domination as well as sharing one's writing with those who possess similar commitments to destabilizing the vortex of power "because seeing things clearly is tricky" (p. 139). This is particularly relevant in a corporate democracy where the roots of ideological conditioning are so deep and pervasive that it is difficult to penetrate the depth of its disorientation in order to generate meaningful, substantive critique (see Herman and Chomsky, 2002; Hedges, 2009).

Laible (2000) sought to generate "a theory of knowing others" that would address "general human imperatives of living in the world as compassionate, loving human beings" (p. 685). An ethic of care is an Other-centered ethic that is well suited to actualizing the kind of "theory of knowing others" that Laible sought because it recognizes our interdependence as a central feature of life and it requires recognition of the distinct contexts in which humans function. Part of understanding our distinct socio-political context is engaging our research subjects on *their* terms and in *their* space, but there is no substitute for physical displacement, which is discussed in the next section, to gain a better sense of the form and force of our social location.

Traveling vs. Physical Displacement. The second and third components of Laible's loving epistemology deal with epistemological criteria for ethical theorizing and the idea of traveling to different spaces to develop a critical consciousness, elements that work symbiotically. Drawing on Patricia Hill Collins' (1998) criteria for critical social theory, Laible (2000) argues for a loving epistemology that would produce social theory (and I extend this to research generally) that reflects the reality of research subjects' lives, equips people to resist oppression, and moves people to take action (p. 690). Rather than elaborating on these three items, Laible moves to a discussion of the last element of the loving epistemology, which is traveling to different worlds in order to identify with the experiences of Others and to see the self through Others' eyes (p. 691). As Laible states, "Many times people like us have traveled to different worlds and have conquered them, taken their resources, and claimed them for our own. At the very least, we have traveled and not understood. The traveling that I am encouraging us to do is very different" (p. 691). Laible advocates a kind of traveling that serves as a method of connecting with, and understanding, the lives of Others while gaining a deeper, more critical understanding the self. As she notes, traveling "to someone else's world is a way of identifying with them because by traveling to their 'worlds' we can understand what it is to be them and what it is to be ourselves in their eyes. Only when we have traveled in each other's worlds are we fully subjects to each other" (p. 691). Traveling, as Laible conceives the process, provides a vehicle through which to gain humble identification with and recognition of Others that is "constitutive of a new understanding of love" (p. 691). Finally, Laible advises her reader to "travel knowing that you are responsible for others -- they are a part of you -- you do not exist without them" (p. 691).

Here I would like to capture, complicate, and deepen Laible's conception of the importance of moving into other spaces in order to generate humane theorizing. The concept of "travel" as it functioned in literary travel writing and anthropological research has been the focus of scrutiny and criticism for its Euro-American centrality, patriarchal ideology, and class privilege (see for example Clifford, 1997; Pratt, 1992; Wolff, 1993). Janet Wolff (1993) argues that travel writing and travel theory "exclude or pathologize women" (p. 225) and Mary Louise Pratt (1992) maintains that travel writing promoted a "Eurocentered form of global or . . . 'planetary' consciousness" (p. 5). James Clifford (1997) discusses travel's "historical taintedness" (p. 39), acknowledging that it has never been successfully freed "from a history of European, literary, male, bourgeois scientific, heroic, recreational meanings and practices" (p. 33). Further, Clifford argues that racism is implicit and explicit in travel writing: "[I]n the dominant discourses of travel, a nonwhite person cannot figure as a heroic explorer, aesthetic interpreter, or scientific explorer" (p. 33).[7] In her indictment of travel writing and travel theory, Wolff argues, "some discourses are too heavily compromised by the history of their usage" (p. 225). There is an obvious tension that exists between Laible's desire to de-center the dominant and create an extensive responsibility for Others and a concept that historically has been associated with imperialism, dominance, and irresponsibility. Consequently, I wish to disentangle the loving epistemology from the limitations of the term and instead draw upon the theoretical concept of displacement.

The idea of being displaced into "other spaces" as a mode of critical consciousness -- indeed as a central unit of thought itself -- has been illuminated by James W. Perkinson (2004, 2005), a scholar committed to identifying and decoding white and patriarchal dominance in its various manifestations in modernity. Complicating traditional notions of "traveling," Perkinson (2004) advises that "white experience of material space -- in the suburb, the gated community, the university, the mall -- we could gloss as an experience of 'gossamer,' a kind of living and moving and having one's being inside a delicate halo that protects and buffers" (p. 177). This buffer distorts the experience and understanding of those who enjoy it, subsuming and encoding that which is different into a Euro-centered vortex of meaning. This shields white experience (we might extend this to dominant subjectivities in general) from having to grapple with or understand the difficulties, dangers, and complexities of moving into spaces experienced by those who are non-white (or non-dominant), while empowering white existence to remain centered, privileged, and uninterrogated. Thus, space in this sense is "not an obstacle to be overcome" as it can be for those who are non-dominant, "but an invitation to sample" (p. 178). Sampling is unhindered by the burdens of marginality. The specter of sampling conjures up images of those who would "travel" to an "exotic" location and enjoy exposure to appealing and agreeable parts of a culture without having to negotiate the noxious elements of a culture's everyday lived existence or grapple with the problems associated with being oppressed, marginalized, threatened, or disempowered (p. 178). Perkinson asserts that this buffer is institutionalized and a part of everyday life:

> [The buffer] is in part a function of police and immigration law, of access to inheritance and city hall, of free movement across the pavement and through the air without encountering interrogation. Certainly not all white people may experience such, but the pattern and history are there: white skin, by itself, will never in America as currently constituted, draw down on its head the baton of rejection *because it is white*. Space cooperates with whiteness; white people have "place." (p. 177)

Space is structured in ways that reflects, reinforces, and perpetuates the dominance and subjugation that exists in the broader culture, and these conditions shape our interactions with Others and our sense of self. Merely "traveling" to different spaces does not necessarily enable illumination for those who embody privilege because one's whiteness (or one's dominance) can confer a different experience of space than that which is experienced by those who are non-white (or non-dominant). One's positionality may unwittingly constrain the dominant from fully absorbing and understanding the everyday lived experiences, the complexities and privations, of those who do not similarly benefit from normativity, power, and privilege.

As opposed to traveling, which suggests the possibility of agency, privilege, and exploitation associated with the "sampling" enabled by dominance, Perkinson (2005) emphasizes the importance of *physical displacement*, especially for those who inhabit dominant identities: "For those whose subjectivity already encodes dominance and normativity at the level of the body, physical displacement becomes a prerequisite for critical thinking and ethical struggle" (p. 200). Physical displacement involves meeting "the oppressed not at the center, but in the margins, on their own turf" (p. 200), where "others have majority power and whiteness can thus begin to be *experienced* as the minority identity it really is globally and *owned* as the mythology of supremacy that the majority have rightly grown to hate" (Perkinson, 2004, p. 215). Perkinson (2004) argues that the hallmark of displacement is the "experience of terror and loss -- of position, of privilege, of power, of identity -- as the precursor to a new identity, new position, new vulnerability" (p. 215). Becoming vulnerable to the ferocity of privilege and power, and recognizing how dominance can be and has been violently etched on the bodies of Others, enables the "radical vision" that leads to "ethical precision," which can propel us toward "motivated struggle" (Perkinson, 2005, p. 200). Thus, "closing the gap" between dominance and marginality requires inhabiting the margins in order to gain a deeper sense of how one's dominance has the "power to rearrange" the lives of Others and considering how one's practices and ways of being will change to accommodate this new insight (pp. 200-201). Recognizing the form and force of one's own discursive and material dominance is central to ethical engagement because it demonstrates how persons inhabiting dominant identities are affecting the lives of Others, even unwittingly, since power is never not complicit in the marginalization of others. Having explained and extended Laisle's loving epistemology, I now turn to the problem of defining "love."

Agape Love as a Transformational Modality

In Laible's conception of a loving epistemology, love itself remained unelaborated. It is essential to clarify what is meant by love in this context and develop an understanding of the utility of love in social transformation. This is important not only because "love" can be a nebulous construct, but also because academics may perceive it as mawkish and activists may see it as a form of capitulation. As King (1972) has indicated, "One of the great problems of history is that the concepts of love and power have usually been contrasted as opposites -- polar opposites -- so that love is identified with a resignation of power, and power with a denial of love" (p. 1071). Consequently, I provide an elaboration of love as a powerful transformational modality to discern what it may offer our renewed understanding of the loving epistemology and to demonstrate its utility to a creative democracy.

Perhaps the most convincing proponent of love as a tool for understanding and changing the social world was the late Martin Luther King, Jr. Along with Swartz, Campbell, and Pestana (2009), I believe that King's vision is even more relevant today as cultural communities move toward continued fragmentation and isolation, despite our ever-increasing mediatized connectedness (this phenomenon is discussed in Kolko, Nakamura, & Rodman, 2000; Nakamura, 2002). Reflecting on the years that have passed since King's death, Detroit-based Boggs (2003), a noted activist in her own right, argues that we have seen an increasing tendency towards dehumanization and a decline in the quality of life for people across cultures:

> Our communities have been turned into wastelands by economic disinvestment . . . and the youth in our de-industrialized cities have become increasingly desperate. Transnational corporations have spread their tentacles around the world, widening the gulf between the rich and poor, robbing local communities of their sources of food, fuel, and local cultures. (p. 27)

These conditions have prompted Boggs to suggest that we "seem to have drifted further from anything resembling a beloved community in this nation" (p. 24). Boggs's social change activities centered around the Black Power "Movement" in the 1960s, but the hands of time have led her current thinking toward King because of the depth of his critique of democracy. As she notes, King "envisioned a nonviolent revolution that would challenge all the values and institutions of our society, and combine the struggle against racism with a struggle against poverty, militarism, and materialism" (p. 26). Boggs proposes looking to King's perspective on organizing, global citizenship, and especially love in order to reinvigorate community activism in the service of developing more sustainable relationships across our differences.

King spoke about the vitality, utility, and power of love in a variety of his works, deploying love as the foundation for his enduring commitment to transfigure U.S. society (see, for example, King, 1963, 1972, 1986a, 1986b, 1986c, 1986d, 1986e). In his powerful treatise on love, "Loving Your Enemies," King argued that, "love is the most durable power in the world . . . [It] is the most potent instrument available in mankind's quest for peace and security" (1963, p. 56). King argues that the difficulty and complexity of our times call for a new approach: "Far from being the pious injunction of a Utopian dreamer, the command to love one's enemy is an absolute necessity for our survival. Love even for one's enemy is the key to the solution of the problems of our world" (pp. 49-50). King argues that one should love one's enemies because the spiral of destruction must be broken before we are all annihilated. Half a century later, King's words are even more relevant: "Hate multiples hate, violence multiples violence, and toughness multiples toughness in a descending spiral of destruction" (p. 53). In his essay, King discusses both *how* to love one's enemies as well as *why* one should attempt to do so. In the process, he reveals that the kind of love he is espousing is not "some sentimental outpouring" or "emotional bosh" (p. 52). Instead, drawing on the Greek New Testament's conception of agape, he defines love as "understanding and creative, redemptive goodwill for all men. An overflowing love which seeks nothing in return" (p. 52). In "An Experiment in Love," King (1986a) argues that the kind of love he espouses does not make distinctions between people and functions altruistically: "*Agape* does not begin by discriminating between worthy and unworthy people, or any qualities that people possess . . . [it] makes no distinction between friends and enemy; it is directed towards both" (p. 19). Like the ethic of care, agape love recognizes that "all life is interrelated" (p. 20) and it "springs from the *need* of the other person -- his need for belonging to the best in the human family" (p. 19). King (1963) advises that we should show our love through our capacity to forgive, through recognizing that those elements of our enemy that we dislike "never quite expresses all that he is" and by "not seek[ing] to defeat or humiliate the enemy but to win his friendship and understanding" (p. 51). This kind of love thwarts the hatred and disregard that nourishes the mentality of oppressors and empowers the marginalized to overcome the powerlessness and alienation that dehumanization and repressive social structures can engender.

Although in his speeches and sermons King (1963c) often advised his audiences to approach situations of hatred with love, he did not suggest the marginalized should accept their oppression or "love their oppressor in an affectionate sense" (p. 8). Rather, King suggested that love should be deployed to defeat unjust and evil systems (1986b, p. 47), to redeem enemies (1963, p. 51), and to fight against the deterioration of the self in the face of hate and injustice (1963, p. 53). For example, in "Loving Your Enemies," King (1963) stated that it is "almost impossible to like some people . . . How can we be affectionate towards a person whose avowed aim is to crush our very being and place innumerable stumbling blocks in our path? How can we like a person who is threatening our children and bombing our homes?" (p. 52). King makes a distinction between *liking* people, which he defines as a "sentimental and affectionate word" and *loving* people, with an agape form of love, which is a powerful, far reaching modality that can prompt transformation in the face of great constraints. Similarly, in "Love, Law, and Civil Disobedience," after defining love as agape, and making the distinction between liking and loving people, King (1986b) states that "one seeks to defeat the unjust system, rather than the individuals who are caught in that system ... [one seeks] to get rid of the evil system and not the individual who happens to be misguided" (p. 47). King (1963) sees love as a way to redeem oppressors. He advises his followers to recognize that the oppressor's hate "grows out of fear, pride, ignorance, prejudice, and misunderstanding" and that there are competing tensions within all of us toward both the good and the bad (p. 51). By focusing on the possibility that there exists goodness in our enemy, just as there exists some badness within the self, we might begin to love our enemies and open them up to the redemptive power of love (p. 51). Finally, King (1963) deploys love to fight against the desecration of the self, since hate distorts our powers of perception, our principles, and our open-mindedness: "Hate destroys a man's sense of values and his objectivity. It causes him to describe the beautiful as ugly and the ugly as beautiful, and to confuse the true with the false and the false with the true" (p. 53). Focusing on the havoc hate can wreak on the self, King (1986a) argues, "If I meet hate with hate, I become depersonalized" (p. 20).

King advanced agape love as the key to combating the deleterious effects of hate, but he also saw love as a method for compelling social change and enhancing community, especially through nonviolent mass mobilization. Rather than being an ineffectual emotion confined to the private sphere, the kind of love King advocates is an active, public force focused on reducing marginality and achieving human equality. In "An Experiment in Love," King (1986a) states that the love he espouses is "not a weak, passive love. It is love in action. Agape is love seeking to preserve and create community" (p. 20). In "Where Do We Go From Here," King (1972) stated, "What is needed is a realization that power without love is reckless and abusive, and love without power is sentimental and anemic. Power at its best is love implementing the demands of justice, and justice at its best is power correcting everything that stands against love" (p. 1071). In "The Power of Nonviolence," King (1986d) similarly underscores the importance of love in moving forward the movement for racial equality:

> Some people are saying we must slow up . . . They are saying we must adopt a policy of moderation. Now if moderation means moving on with wise restraint and calm reasonableness, then moderation is a great virtue that all men of good will must seek to achieve in this tense period of transition. But if moderation means slowing up in the move for justice and capitulating to the whims and caprices of the guardians of the deadening status quo, then moderation is a tragic vice which all men of good will must condemn. We must continue to move on . . . We must keep moving with wise restraint and love and proper discipline and dignity. (p. 14)

King saw love as the organizing principle around which he would advance the objective of mass social transformation in the midst of major upheaval, violence, and hate. He did not deploy love to slow down the movement, to capitulate to oppressors, or to advance a sappy sentimentalism that would deny the raw reality of racism and oppression. Instead, King saw love as an agent for change and as a nonviolent mode of subversion that would enable him to achieve his goal of upending the "deadening status quo." Far from using love as a conciliatory gesture, as an impotent signifier of capitulation, King sees love as an active force in the ongoing drive for social transformation.

King clearly viewed love as a powerful modality for instigating radical change, but love also is central to sustaining social change efforts over time. An activist for sixty years, Boggs (2008) has wrestled with how to create a lasting commitment to improving our communities and our world, while combating violence and apathy.[8] Central to understanding the necessity of love in nourishing and maintaining such efforts, Boggs asserts, is grasping the difference between *rebellions* and *revolutions*, which lends insight into the necessary adjustment in tactics and perspective. While rebellions represent "massive uprising and protest of the oppressed," and throw "into question the legitimacy and supposed permanence of existing institutions," they only last a few days and merely set the stage for revolution; they are not the revolution (p. viii). After the rebellion dies down, Boggs suggests (arguably) that rebels often feel victimized and "expect those in power to assume responsibility for changing the system" (p. viii).[9]

Alternatively, revolutions "go beyond struggling against oppressive institutions and go beyond victim thinking" and make "an evolutionary/revolutionary leap toward becoming more socially responsible and more self-critical human beings" (Boggs, 2008, p. viii). Boggs envisions a two-sided transformation, of the self and institutions, with self-transformation extending out to the community in a longer, more involved struggle that is part and parcel of producing lasting social change:

> Thus, unlike rebellions which are here today and gone tomorrow, revolutions require a patient and protracted process that transforms and empowers us as individuals as we struggle to change the world around us. Going beyond rejections to projections, revolutions advance our continuing evolution as human beings because we are practicing new, more socially responsible and loving relationships to one another and to the earth. (p. viii)

While rebellions are represented by a momentary surge of energy, a revolution is a commitment to a long-term struggle that *requires* a loving relationship to the self and Others in order to sustain it over time and to edify the humanity of those involved in the struggle. To that end, Boggs (2003) argues we need "movement builders who, confident of their own humanity, are able to recognize the humanity in others, including their opponents, and therefore the potential within them for redemption" (p. 28).

Any system of injustice can provoke among the marginalized a desire to wrest power away from the oppressor and to dominate as they have been dominated, replicating endlessly the system of oppression and force that they fought. That is because, following David R. Hawkins (2002), "Force always creates counterforce; its effect is to polarize rather than unify" (p. 133). Consequently, the centrality of agape love in achieving lasting, peaceful social change cannot be overstated. As Sean Chabot (2008) argues, "If participants in emerging and future revolutions do not learn to translate anger and despair into love, or domination into peaceful dialogue, we will eventually fall into the same trap as all past revolutions . . . and merely replace one tyranny with another" (p. 824). Reconfiguring our traditional, mundane notions of power from the "win/lose dichotomy" into more complicated, time-consuming modes is, therefore, essential in the struggle for change (Hawkins, 2002, p. 133). Love as agape shifts our focus from simply *transferring* power to *transforming* power, from domination to cooperation, from exclusion to inclusion, from exploitive to valuing. Herein lies all the difference in the world.

Transforming our communities and our notions of power require dismantling and disabling cultural mythos surrounding technology and the marketplace that have for so long bound us together, but in dysfunctional and hierarchical ways. Drawing on King, Boggs (2008) argues that we must grapple "with the contradiction between our technological and economic overdevelopment and our human and political underdevelopment" (p. ix). Paradoxically, Americans historically have looked at technology and the marketplace as magical elixirs to solve our problems, without recognizing the myriad ways in which they are the sources of alienation, isolation, and devastation. As Chabot (2008) argues, "Because we rely on money and commodities for our sense of well-being, we grow disconnected from the material world (e.g., from the land we live on), lose the capacity to lead thoughtful lives, fail to learn how to solve our own problems, and become more passive in our personal relationships" (p. 806). Resolving this paradox requires that we mine our community's resources to address the problems that plague us, recognizing that "we are the leaders we are looking for" (Boggs, 2008, p. xxxv), rather than outsourcing our solutions to captains of industry whose profit motive is paramount, or allowing the "free" market to determine our fate with its invisible hand. This is not to suggest that dismantling macro-level systems and structures of oppression is unimportant. Rather, it is meant to direct our attention to the idea that meaningful and creative social change begins from the bottom and works its way up: "huge steps will be the accumulation and culmination of small steps" (p. xxxiv). Agape love shifts our focus from the marketplace to the human race, focusing our thinking and values on what enables long-term survival and a quality of life for humans and the environment that sustains us. This shift in focus from consumption and wealth generation to creating sustainable living arrangements requires that individuals begin to rethink the structures that diminish our humanity. To that end, Boggs argues that we must "reject the old American Dream of a higher standard of living based upon empire, and embrace a new American Dream of a higher standard of humanity that preserves the best in our revolutionary legacy" (2008, pp. xxxiv-xxxv).

This examination of love as agape has shown that love is a powerful political modality that disrupts dysfunctional arrangements and serves as the framework for promoting sustainable relationships and ways of living in the world. A method, a moral principle, a vision, a language, rules for engagement -- love is an active political force that can generate crisis, command attention, and demand dialogue, with the ultimate purpose of achieving reconciliation, equality, and the end of human suffering. Arguably, no other modality has the power, endurance, or ability to sustain a revolution over an extended period of time. Rather than being an impotent signifier of capitulation, agape love can be a powerful instrument that is particularly adept at enabling citizens to identify, address, and reform multiple points and structures of burden, distress, and marginalization.

A Loving Epistemology as a Tool for Sustainability and Transformation

Having reviewed Laible's loving epistemology and the transformational potential of agape love, I aim to revise the loving epistemology in the service of a creative democracy. Swartz, Campbell, and Pestana (2009) describe a creative democracy as "a society that continues dynamically to evolve in its ability to be inclusive, fair, and just through the active participation of all its citizens, a society without . . . a dejected underclass or 'surplus' population of unusable and dispensable people" (p. 12). A creative democracy seeks a condition in which citizens may "dissent meaningfully, challenging selfishness, greed, exclusivity, and policies that reflect a general disregard for social inequities" (p. 14). This vision of democracy does not take human suffering as a given, but rather sees it as something citizens can eliminate if the political will demands it (p. 14). Citizens are compelled to take "personal responsibility" for such social transformation (p. 43). Ultimately, a creative democracy is "an experiment in the human potential, enlarging our ability to imagine and nurture new expressions of our common humanity" (p. 14). A loving epistemology has the potential to be a fundamental component of a vibrant creative democracy. Below I provide some additional inflections and modifications to move the loving epistemology out of its sole location in the academy as a practice of inquiry and into our communities in order to further the goal of a creative democracy.

The loving epistemology as reconceived here includes a variety of constituent elements. First, the loving epistemology insists that an Other-centered ethic such as an ethic of care be placed at the forefront of our research and civic participation. Such an ethic calls for reciprocal relationships and active listening, focusing our attention on the nexus of privilege and difference, and it urges us to actively work in communities committed to de-centering the self from privilege and disassembling the structures of power that strangle our humanity. Through reciprocal relationships with Others we encounter the difficult questions that assist in our intellectual and moral development and prompt more thorough-going moments of self-reflexivity regarding the form and force of our privilege. Similarly, an Other-centered ethic recognizes our situatedness in distinct historical and socio-political arrangements and the effect such positioning has on how we produce, consume, and evaluate knowledge. Finally, following an Other-centered ethic in our work and in our civic life means that we should make an active commitment to reading about the matrix of domination and privilege and live in communities where our perspectives are continuously challenged in an effort to combat the ideological conditioning of our corporate democracy.

The second contour of the reconsidered loving epistemology is physical displacement in the service of humane theorizing. The aim of critical theorizing and research, public policy, community organizing -- indeed, daily life itself -- should be identifying and disassembling the vectors of power that create structures of suffering and oppression, informed by inhabiting the spaces of Others and recognizing the form and force of our privilege and/or marginalization. The *Beloved Communities Initiative* developed by the *Boggs Center* in Detroit offers participants the opportunity for growth and development by connecting with "beloved communities" (based on Martin Luther King's notion of community) across the U.S. that are profoundly justice oriented and committed to social and individual transformation.[10] Some of these communities, like the *Poverty Initiative* at the *Union Theological Seminary* in New York, offer immersion seminars to deepen one's connection to the struggles of Others. Such immersion provides the context for self-assessment by demonstrating how dominant subjectivities, in general, serve as an institutionalized buffer and by offering opportunities to step outside that buffer into spaces where one is not the majority and is vulnerable to the experience of Others. Such experiences provide the opportunity to become sensitive to one's power to rearrange the lives of Others, if only by recognizing how one's inaction can have a dramatic impact. Inhabiting the margins gives researchers and citizens the fecund experience and requisite humility necessary to understand the motivations and challenges faced by Others.

Reflecting on agape love informs the loving epistemology and democratic community in multiple ways. First, agape love urges us to rethink traditional, outmoded conceptions of power, moving from the traditional win/lose dichotomy to more complicated forms of power sharing based on cooperation, inclusion, and valuing. Rethinking modes of power fits neatly with and enhances the loving epistemology, which has at its core the questioning of power structures and the relationship between difference and privilege. Agape love enriches the loving epistemology by urging us to move beyond simply interrogating privilege to transforming the very way we think about power. Second, agape love motivates us to question ideologies that place economic and technological considerations over human development and well being, while also urging active participation in civil society, because "we are the leaders we are looking for" (Boggs, 2008, p. xxxv). Consider, for example, how Americans continue to look to the marketplace to solve our problems, rather than examining how our over-dependence on the economic domain and preoccupation with consumption are the source of so many of our problems, such as overwhelming debt, health care and war profiteering, the poisoning of the environment, and the exploitation of workers in the U.S. and abroad (Swartz, 2005). Agape love illuminates how Americans fetishize the marketplace, enabling our ways of being and thinking to be dictated by market motivations. By extending this understanding of agape love to the loving epistemology, we are urged to think in ways that place people and the environment before the market and profit margins and question ways of knowing that do not sustain humanity. Because agape love is active, it exhorts individuals to take part in solving the problems we may not have generated but exacerbate by sustaining the status quo, and modulate our behavior accordingly, while pushing for structural change. This kind of collective effort is necessary to counterbalance a culture in which greed is the prevailing value of the transnational marketplace and corporations have no allegiance to people, nation-states, or the environment, only to bottom lines (Hedges, 2009).

Agape love and a loving epistemology, as powerful modalities of a creative democracy, have infinite potential to inform and enhance the ways in which we conduct research and organize democratic community. We recognize that love has been the only modality that has sustained us in moments of personal crisis and collapse. However, only now are we beginning to recognize that love can enrich us in the most overwhelming of circumstances, not only personally, but also politically and intellectually, as King and Boggs suggest. Barbara A. Holmes and Susan Holmes Winfield (2002) argue:

> When we are confronted by the infrastructures of malignant social systems, love seems frail at best and irrelevant at worst. Yet the lessons of history teach us just the opposite. In defiance of our logic, love has sustained whole communities. With nothing more than love, besieged people confront radical evil, endure losses, bury their dead, and console each other during and after devastation. (p. 189)

A loving epistemology is a powerful mechanism for fighting against the subversion of morality resulting from the Othering of humans that has permitted varying forms of injustice and has enabled moral people to commit, and witness in silence, immoral things. A loving epistemology, in shaping the way we know Others and ourselves in relationship to Others and the environment, is a revolutionary tool for cultivating compassion in our communities and responsibility in the academy and the marketplace. Further, it can set the stage for recasting our national values in an effort to achieve human solidarity and struggle against oppression and unnecessary suffering, which are essential goals of a creative democracy. For too long we have allowed traditional ways of knowing to extinguish from our conceptual universe the very idea of a loving epistemology, despite its ability to enrich our lives. We have allowed traditional conceptualizations to generate abject subjectivities through which we are divorced from ourselves and Others. This elaboration of a loving epistemology is an effort to contribute to the broader project of reconceptualizing democratic life, and decolonizing our minds, so that rather than continuing to witness what happens in the absence of love, we might discover what we can construct in its presence.

REFERENCES

Boggs, G. L. (2003, January/February). From Marx to Malcolm and Martin. *The Other Side, 39(1)*, 24-28.

---. (2008). Introduction to the new edition. In J. Boggs and G. L. Boggs (Eds.), *Revolution and evolution in the twentieth century* (pp. vii-xlvi.). New York: Monthly Review Press.

---. (1998). *Living for change: An autobiography.* Minneapolis: University of Minneapolis Press.

Carolan, M. S. (2004). Unmasking the commodity chain. *Peace Review, 16(1)*, 193-198.

Chabot, S. (2008). Love and revolution. *Critical sociology, 34(6)*, 803-828.

Clifford, J. (1997). *Routes: Travel and translation in the late twentieth century.* Cambridge: Harvard University Press.

Collins, P. H. (1998). *Fighting words: Black women and the search for justice.* Minneapolis: University of Minnesota Press.

Fellner, J. (2000, May). Punishment and prejudice: Racial disparities in the war on drugs (Volume 12, number 2). *Human Rights Watch*. Retrieved from http://www.hrw.org/ legacy/reports/2000/usa/

Fernandez, C. C. (2004). Justice, globalization, and human rights. *Peace Review, 16(1)*, 199-205.

Gilligan, C. (1982). *In a different voice.* Cambridge: Harvard University Press.

Hankivsky, O. (2004). *Social policy and the ethic of care.* Vancouver: UBC Press.

Hawkins, D. R. (2002). *Power vs. force: The hidden determinants of human behavior.* Carlsbad, CA: Hay House.

Hedges, C. (2009). *Empire of illusion: The end of literacy and the triumph of the spectacle.* New York: Nation Books.

Herman, E. S., and Chomsky, N. (2002). *Manufacturing consent: The political economy of the mass media.* New York: Pantheon.

Holmes, B. A., and Winfield, S. H. (2002). King, the constitution, and the courts: Remaining awake through a great revolution. In L. V. Baldwin (Ed.), *The legacy of Martin Luther King, Jr.: The boundaries of the law, politics, and religion* (pp. 173-212). South Bend, Indiana: University of Notre Dame Press.

Houston, M. (1992). The politics of difference: Race, class, and women's communication. In L. F. Rakow (Ed.), *Women making meaning: New feminist directions in communication* (pp. 45-59). New York: Routledge.

James, C. V., Salganicoff, A., Thomas, M., Ranji, U. Lillie-Blanton, M., and Wyn, R. (2009). Putting women's health care disparities on the map: Examining racial and ethnic disparities at the state level. *Race/Ethnicity and Health Care Program at the Henry J. Kaiser Family Foundation.* Retrieved from http://www.kff.org/minorityhealth/ upload/7886.pdf

Johnson, A. G. (2006). *Privilege, power, and difference* 2nd ed. Boston: McGraw Hill.

King, M. L. (1963). Loving your enemies. *Strength to love* (pp. 49-57). Philadelphia: Fortress Press.

---. (1972). Where do we go from here? In P. S. Foner (Ed.), *The voice of black America: Major speeches by Negroes in the United States, 1797-1971* (pp. 1068-1077). New York: Simon & Schuster.

---. (1986a). An experiment in love. In J. M. Washington (Ed.), *A testament of hope: The essential writings and speeches of Martin Luther King Jr.* (pp. 16-20). New York: Harper One.

---. (1986b). Love, law, and civil disobedience. In J. M. Washington (Ed.), *A testament of hope: The essential writings and speeches of Martin Luther King Jr.* (pp. 43-53). New York: Harper One.

---. (1986c). Nonviolence and racial justice. In J. M. Washington (Ed.), *A testament of hope: The essential writings and speeches of Martin Luther King Jr.* (pp. 5-9). New York: Harper One.

---. (1986d). The power of nonviolence. In J. M. Washington (Ed.), *A testament of hope: The essential writings and speeches of Martin Luther King Jr.* (pp. 12-15). New York: Harper One.

---. (1986e). Remaining awake through a great revolution. In J. M. Washington (Ed.), *A testament of hope: The essential writings and speeches of Martin Luther King Jr.* (pp. 268-278). New York: Harper One.

Kochler, H. (2009, October). *Solidarity and economic interdependence: Religious analysis of the financial crisis.* Paper presented at the Seventh Doha Interfaith Dialogue Conference on Human Solidarity. Doha, Qatar.

Kolko, B., Nakamura, L., and Rodman, G. (2002). Race in cyberspace: An introduction. In B. Kolko, L. Nakamura, and Rodman, G., (Eds.), *Race in cyberspace* (pp. 1-14). New York: Routledge.

Laible, J. (1997). Feminist analysis of sexual harassment policy: A critique of the ideal community. In C. Marshall (Ed.), *Feminist critical policy analysis* (pp. 201-215). Bristol, PA: Falmer Press.

Laible, J. (2000). A loving epistemology: What I hold critical in my life, faith, and profession. *International Journal of Qualitative Studies in Education, 13(6),* 683-692.

Levinas, E. (1981). *Otherwise than being: Beyond essence.* Boston: Martinus Nijhoff.

Mauer, M. (2009, October). Racial disparities in the criminal justice system. *The Sentencing Project. 1-8.* Retrieved from http://www.sentencingproject.org/doc/publications/rd_ mmhousetestimonyonRD.pdf

Nakamura, L. (2002). *Cybertypes: Race, ethnicity, and identity on the Internet.* New York: Routledge.

Palmer-Mehta, V. (2009). Aung San Suu Kyi and the rhetoric of social protest. *Women's Studies in Communication, 32(2)*, 151-179.

Perkinson, J. W. (2004). *White theology: Outing supremacy in modernity.* New York: Palgrave Macmillan.

Perkinson, J. W. (2005). *Shamanism, racism, and hip-hop culture: Essays on white supremacy and black subversion.* New York: Palgrave Macmillan.

Pratt, M. L. (1992). *Imperial eyes: Travel writing and transculturation.* London: Routledge.

Redner, H. (2001). *Ethical life: The past and present of ethical cultures.* Lanham, MD: Rowman & Littlefield.

Robinson, F. (1999). *Globalizing care: Ethics, feminist theory, and international relations.* Boulder, CO: Westview Press.

Rothkopf, D. (2008). What's next for capitalism? *Carnegie Endowment for International Peace.* Retrieved from http://www.carnegieendowment.org/publications/index fm?fa=view&id=22434

Scheurich, J. J. and Laible, J. (2002). The buck stops here in our preparation programs: Educative leadership for all children (no exceptions allowed). In J. J. Scheurich (Ed.), *Anti-racist scholarship: an advocacy* (pp. 101-108). Albany: State University of New York Press.

Shuler, S. (2007). Autoenthnographic emotion: Studying and living emotional labor in the scholarly life. *Women's Studies in Communication, 30(3)*, 255-283.

Singer, P. (2002). *One world: The ethics of globalization* 2nd ed. New Haven: Yale University Press.

Singer, P. (2009). *The life you can save: Acting now to end world poverty.* New York: Random House.

Swartz, O. (1997). *Conducting socially responsible research: Critical theory, neo-pragmatism, and rhetorical inquiry.* Thousand Oaks, CA: Sage.

Swartz, O. (2005). *In defense of partisan criticism: Communication studies, law, & social analysis.* New York: Peter Lang.

Swartz, O. (2006). Reflections of a social justice scholar. In O. Swartz (Ed.), *Social justice and communication scholarship* (pp. 1-20). Mahwah, NJ: Lawrence Erlbaum Associates.

Swartz, O., Campbell, K., & Pestana, C. (2009). *Neo-pragmatism, communication, and the culture of creative democracy.* New York: Peter Lang.

Staveteig, S., and Wigton, A. (2000). Racial and ethnic disparities: Key findings from the national survey of America's families (Number B-5 in Series, New Federalism: National Survey of America's Families). *Urban Institute.* Retrieved from http://www.urban.org/ Publications/309308.html

Tronto, J. (1993). *Moral boundaries: A political argument for an ethic of care.* New York: Routledge.

---, and Fisher, B. (1990). Toward a feminist theory of caring. In E. K. Abel & M. K. Nelson (Eds.), *Circles of care: Work and identity in women's lives* (pp. 35-62). Albany: State University of New York Press.

Wargo, D. T., Baglini, N. and Nelson, K. (2009, Spring). The global financial crisis -- caused by greed, moral meltdown and public policy disasters. *Forum on Public Policy Online*, Retrieved from http://forumonpublicpolicy.com/ spring09papers/archivespr09/wargo.pdf

Wolff, J. (1993). On the road again: Metaphors of travel in cultural criticism. *Cultural Studies 7(2)*, 224-239.

Wood, D. (2005). *The step back: Ethics and politics after deconstruction.* New York: State University of New York Press.

Young, M. D. and Laible, J. (2000). White racism, antiracism, and school leadership preparation. *Journal of School Leadership, 10*(4), 374-415.

---, and Skrla, L. (2003). Research on women and administration: A response to Julie Laible's loving epistemology. In M. D. Young and L. Skrla (Eds.), *Reconsidering feminist research in educational leadership* (pp. 201-210). Albany, NY: State University of New York Press.

Notes

[1] I am not opposed to the capitalist's profit per se, but I am opposed to profit that is gained through the harm, spoilage, suffering, and exploitation of people and the environment. Free-market capitalism, as manipulated by greedy and self-serving capitalists, can become homicidal as people's lives and the environment become irrelevant "playthings" for unethical business people to manipulate, exploit, and spoil for their personal profit. Such immoral capitalists may choose to exploit a

people's need for jobs to feed their families by having them work in unsafe environments or poison the community's environment with toxic waste and pollution; or such capitalists might "weigh" whether or not to provide life-saving health services to an ill individual based on a profit-loss margin, rather than on the value of maintaining a human life. Such practices are homicidal because money takes precedence over the value of human life. Of course it would be disingenuous to suggest that the workers are complicit or "willing" participants in this arrangement when they do not have the power to control the choice of where to work, live, or receive health care due to economic constraints. In a society with a moral foundation that believes that *human life is valued more than profit*, capitalists would work to militate against harm and create jobs and services that work in productive harmony with human life and the environment. In such a configuration, profits, in my view, are not contemptible and could be used to edify and sustain humanity and the environment.

[2] For a discussion of these disparities, see Fellner (2000); James et al (2009); Johnson (2006); Mauer (2009); and Staveteig & Wigton (2000).

[3] Laible, who dedicated her life to the causes of social justice and anti-racism, was an Assistant Professor of Educational Leadership and Policy Studies at the University of Alabama when she was tragically killed on March 27, 1999. She was traveling on Interstate 75 when a young man dropped a 22 pound piece of concrete off a highway overpass, striking her windshield and killing her instantly. Her work on the loving epistemology that I draw upon was delivered as a keynote speech to the Campus Ministers' Association Faith Seeking Understanding Lecture and was later published in *Qualitative Studies in Education*. It was delivered in March of 1999 and represents one of her last scholarly contributions. Ironically, the conference organizer had asked her to pretend that this was the last lecture that she would ever give and to focus on what she holds most important in her life. I did not know Laible personally, but learned about her from my friend and former University of Alabama colleague, Sheri Shuler, who was the first person to introduce me to Laible's idea of the loving epistemology. Shuler (2007) briefly references the loving epistemology in her award winning article "Autoethnographic Emotion: Studying and Living Emotional Labor in the Scholarly Life."

[4] While Laible (1999) was committed both intellectually and personally to improving the lives of Others, she also wrestled with how her "middle-class, Euro-American standards" influenced the development and execution of her research (p. 686). Laible particularly was disquieted with the infinite potential to distort or silence the experiences of Others and she drew on the words of bell hooks to underscore how researchers can affect the voices of their subjects: "No need to hear your voice when I can talk about you better than you can speak about yourself. No need to hear your voice" (as cited in Laible, p. 687). For Laible, comprehending and learning from the voices of those who are different from us are central to one's humanity in

general and one's ability to be an effective scholar or knowledge maker in particular. However, despite her conscious effort to give proper consideration to how her privileged status as a white, middle class scholar influenced her research, Laible (2000) was troubled by the fact that, in her dissertation, she still tended to evaluate the experiences of her young Mexican-American female research subjects based on her class and race based intellectual framework. Laible ultimately viewed this research project as inadequate because "my epistemology, how I come to know different realities, is racially biased -- I can only see things through my Euro-American middle-class lens" which resulted in her "reshaping the girls' experiences (the Other) to either positively or negatively fit with my notions (the Same) of what it means to be an adolescent, a female, and a Mexican-American" (pp. 686-687). So disturbed was Laible by her perception that she had not done justice to the young women's experiences, she ultimately decided that: "My desire to gaze upon the Other and reinscribe him/her in my words, in my opinion, is no longer valid or ethical. My research victimizes others, although this is not my conscious intent . . . .And unfortunately, a great deal of this type of research takes place in this university by incredibly caring and well-meaning individuals and in universities just like this one . . . . *I hope it is clear by now that I believe research on Others is unethical*, especially Euro-American research on people of color" (p. 687). Laible pushes her self-reflexivity outward, compelling scholars to consider whether their epistemologies enable them to fully grasp the lived reality of those who are different from them. This moral dilemma served as the impetus for Laible's queries: "Is there an ethical way to continue producing knowledge about other human beings? Is there such a thing as a 'loving epistemology?'" (p. 689).

[5] For a critique of Levinas's conception of placing ethics before ontology (which Laible follows to suggest placing ethics before both ontology and epistemology), see Wood (2005).

[6] I follow Hankivsky (2004) in my delineation between "first generation" and "second generation" care theorists (pp. 9-40). *First generation* care theorists, spurred by Carol Gilligan (1982) with her influential writing *In a Different Voice*, tended to focus on women's caring capacity and linked care to the female gender as a function of mothering and nurturing instead of focusing on how care should be a fundamental aspect of all human life (p. 11). These writings are important to the development of our understanding and theorizing of care, but they limited care to a female activity and thus essentialized and limited both women and caring.

[7] Clifford offers the expedition to the North Pole by Robert Peary as an example. The American explorer Peary was given credit for having reached the North Pole (although Frederick Cook claimed to have reached it one year earlier and some have questioned whether Peary actually reached the pole). However, virtually nothing was spoken about Matthew Henson, the African American explorer who accompanied him, or the Inuit travelers, without whom the trip may not have been possible.

Clifford argues that because of their race and class, those who accompanied Peary were not deemed "proper travelers" (p. 33).

[8] See the *Boggs Center* in Detroit at www.boggscenter.org/.

[9] Of course this is a generalization, and must be read in the context of Boggs's sixty-year commitment to revolution and community organizing, much of it in active collaboration with her activist husband of forty years, James Boggs. While Grace may be best known for her involvement in the Black Power Movement and her community organizing in the city of Detroit, she also has been involved in the Labor, Feminist, Asian American, and Environmental Movements. Given her long-term commitment to creating social change (see her autobiography, *Living For Change*), I think it would be fair to assert that Boggs might feel frustrated with those who do not maintain such a commitment. By selecting this quote from Boggs, I do not mean to suggest that I believe all those involved in rebellions possess a victim mentality and expect the system to change itself, but I do agree that a lasting commitment to struggle is necessary if social change is to occur.

[10] See the website at http://www.race-democracy.org/New_initiative.htm.

CHAPTER 7

Click on Deweyan Democracy:
John Dewey Joins the Online Literacy Debate

Shane J. Ralston
Pennsylvania State University-Hazleton

According to John Dewey, "democracy is more than a form of government" (1916/1996d, p. 93). By this he means that democracy is an *attitude*, an ethos, a way of being vis-à-vis others in the world. Thus, the burden of improving democracy falls heavily on the shoulders of average citizens or the mass of persons who accept the duties and obligations of citizenship. Such people are important to ensure, whether through their direct participation or indirect oversight, that technological and institutional innovations exemplify the democratic ideal, as "a mode of associated living" and a "conjoint communicated experience" (p. 93). In such a world, communication should be considered more than a mere instrument for citizens to transfer knowledge and information. Rather, in a creative democracy, communication would be a symbolic and interactive process of imagining new possibilities and meanings, experimenting with novel institutions and locating or constructing sources of solidarity within a larger community. As Omar Swartz, Katia Campbell, and Christina Pestana suggest, "creative democracy, like the experience of communication itself, is an experiment in the human potential, enlarging our ability to imagine and nurture new expressions of our common humanity and to recognize the primacy of our individual selves -- a sense of both/and, in the sense that as individuals, we are both *apart* from the world in our unique individualities and, simultaneously, inescapably and essentially *a part* of it" (2009, p. 14).

Communication, as I discuss in this chapter, can be conceived in terms of two competing models: one, as a mere means or tool (i.e., *communication-as-mere-*

means) or two, as a way in which persons interact, individually and collectively, with their environment through non-linguistic signs and linguistic symbols (i.e., *communication-as-symbolic-interaction*). To demonstrate how communication facilitates creative democracy, I identify in this chapter a contemporary policy dispute in which the opposing sides embrace, whether implicitly or explicitly, one of these two communicative models and then attempt to resolve the tension through a process of creative reconstruction. My task is important because the dualism between the two types of communication is at the center of most contemporary policy debates concerning how we should value alternative forms of communication (or communicative technologies) as social goods, and a new, more nuanced perspective is necessary to help advance these debates.

One such debate has emerged in the last fifteen years over the question of whether overexposure to electronic media contributes to youth and adult illiteracy. The importance of this question is obvious, given the prevalence of such media in society. Among many literacy experts, educators and policy-makers, there is growing concern that prolonged exposure to these media, particularly the Internet, weakens reading and writing skills -- whether the ability to read a highway sign and write a simple note to the capacity to read a novel and write a formal essay. Being literate is understood as one of those essential tools for the transfer of knowledge, a view that is consonant with the model of communication-as-a-mere-means. Reflecting this concern, the National Endowments for the Arts conducted an extensive survey in order to measure the literacy levels of adults and children throughout the United States. Based on a demographically representative sample, the report shows a correlation between regular use of electronic media and a steep decline in reading non-electronic texts (Bradshaw 2004, p. 1). The survey findings are captured in a single proposition, that literary "reading in America is not only declining among all groups, but the rate of decline has accelerated, especially among the young" (p.1). Some literacy specialists contest the NEA survey's key assumption that the concept of literacy can be restricted to reading and writing in a non-electronic environment. They claim that online reading not only enriches early reading experiences, but also prepares youth for later employment in internet age jobs (for example, in the fields of computer programming, website design, and online marketing). Thus, communication conceived as symbolic interaction enriches individual and collective experience. Teacher and author Clay Shirky articulates this position, noting that what "the Internet has actually done is not to decimate literary reading . . . [but to bring] back reading and writing as a normal activity for a huge group of people" (quoted in Juskalian, 2008, p. 4). Other literary experts concur, observing that literacy "pedagogy now must account for the burgeoning variety of text forms associated with information and multimedia technologies" (The New London Group, 1996, p. 1). Nevertheless, critics of online literacy question the value of reading in an online environment. They cite evidence that greater web activity does not translate into better reading comprehension scores on standardized tests and, in fact, cultivates a disposition to skim, rather than slowly read and carefully comprehend, a text.[1]

What distinguishes the online literacy debate from other contemporary educational policy disputes is the particular way in which the issue is framed. Online literacy is understood almost exclusively through the prism of neurological studies, sociological surveys, and impressionistic evidence concerning how online reading affects basic literacy skills (Barton and Hamilton, 1998; Barton, Hamilton and Ivanic, 2000). Thus, the language of science, social science, and popular commentary serve as what Kenneth Burke (1966) calls a "terministic screen" (pp. 44-5).[2] This scientistic terminology prevents observers and participants from appreciating the debate's historical roots and its broader social-cultural dimensions. In this chapter, I reorient the debate in a more historical and constructive direction, specifically focusing on how we might redesign educational environments and institutions to overcome previously entrenched and obstructive dualisms. In his book *Cultural Literacy: What Every American Needs to Know*, education scholar E.D. Hirsch (1987) reinforces one such dualism in his criticism of John Dewey for advocating *learning-as-doing* rather than *learning-as-reading*. Ever since the publication of his controversial book, Hirsch has been a divisive figure in educational circles. Many educators and educational scholars have long resisted his call to standardize curricula in order to make students literate about Western culture and values.[3] In contrast, Dewey's legacy for educational philosophy has produced a far greater convergence of perspectives. Most educators and scholars agree that the methods recommended by Dewey's educational philosophy integrate students' native interests and reflective processes of inquiry to generate more reflective and considered interests. In contrast, Hirsch claims that Dewey's educational philosophy is anti-bookish and part of a broader progressive educational agenda responsible for a widespread decline in U.S. literacy rates (p. 119).

Although Hirsch wrote long after Dewey's death, his critique still warrants a response. My objective is to reconstruct a Deweyan response that sheds light on the online literacy debate, as well as the tension between communication-as-mere-means and communication-as-symbolic-interaction. I argue that it is possible to bridge the divide between the debate's two sides by reframing the issue, not as an *empirical* question of what scientific methods or impressionistic data indicate genuine improvements in literacy, but as an *aspirational* matter of how to promote a multi-literate and, thus, enriched experience in a thriving Deweyan creative democracy. Framing the controversy in this way allows us to see the issue in a new and more fruitful light, divorced of the narrow and positivistic trappings that have become all-too-common features of the discourse (see Bradshaw, 2004; Carr, 2008; Rich, 2008).

The chapter is organized into five sections. In the first, I articulate the five elements of what Dewey termed "philosophy *as* education." The second section presents the contemporary debate over the value of online media for improving literacy. In the third section, I rehearse Hirsch's critical remarks about Dewey's educational philosophy and its deleterious effects on youth and adult literacy. The fourth section provides a Deweyan response to Hirsch that simultaneously speaks to the online literacy debate and invokes a novel concept in literacy education: new literacies or multi-literacy. In the fifth and final section, I conclude with some thoughts about the broader implications of achieving a multi-literate and creative democracy.

Dewey's Philosophy *as* Education

Dewey offered a vision of philosophy *as* education, rather than a philosophy *of* education (Garrison, 1998). The relevant difference is that, in the case of the latter (or philosophy *of* education), philosophical concepts frame an analysis of pedagogy, as philosophers already analyze other areas of study (e.g., science, math, language, sex and love). In the former (philosophy *as* education), education pervades all philosophical inquiries, for philosophy broadly-construed is, in Dewey's (1912-3/1996c) words, "the general theory of education" (p. 303). Dewey's educational philosophy implies five key elements: (i) habit, (ii) environment, (iii) growth, (iv) imaginative communication and (v) creative democracy -- each of which I will now briefly discuss.

Habit: According to Dewey (1916/1996d), education conceived as integral to philosophy is a "process of forming fundamental dispositions" so that they "take effect in conduct" (p. 338). These dispositions are beliefs and, more generally, habits that together form a person's character. Dewey (1938/1996i) defines a habit as "a way or manner of action, not a particular act or deed" (p. 21). So, a habit is a mode of conduct, not the conduct itself. Values direct choice and action when existing habits prove unhelpful or obstructive to good conduct. Moreover, both values and habits can be evaluated naturalistically, instrumentally, or conventionally. Yet, the ultimate test of a habit's value is whether it directs inquiry in fruitful ways that fund experience with meaning, render new connections, create helpful tools for future inquiries and develop the inquirer's native abilities. James Scott Johnston (2006) makes this point well when he writes that education "is the formal means for the development of the habits and attitudes of inquiry such that growth can occur" (p. 110). The test of a habit's value is identical to the test for the value of education. In other words, what the student "has learned in the way of knowledge and skill [or habit] in one situation becomes an instrument of understanding and dealing effectively with the situations which follow" (Dewey, 1938/1996j, pp. 25-6). So, learning occurs through the accretion of intelligent habits that reflexively guide human action and inquiry, and, thereby, enrich experience.

Environment: For Dewey, the notion of interaction means that living organisms, from sea anemones to human learners, are intimately connected with their environments. Organism-environment interaction gives rise to a basic pattern of adaptive behavior: a state of balance, disruption, adjustment and renewal of equilibrium. According to Tom Burke (1994), the "basic picture, generally speaking, is that of a given organism/environment system performing a wide range of operations as a normal matter of course -- scanning, probing, ingesting, discharging, adapting to, approaching, avoiding, or otherwise moving about and altering things in routine ways, in order to maintain itself" (p. 23). Whether within simple biological systems or complex social ones, environmental disruptions stimulate efforts by organisms to restore equilibrium, to adapt their (functionally-defined) internal and external environments (in a process biologists call "homeostasis"), and to subsequently develop in viable and meaningful ways. While "all organisms are critics in the sense that they interpret signs," Kenneth Burke (1984) writes, what distinguishes humans from other organisms is their capacity to speak, equipped as they are "for going beyond the criticism of experience to a criticism of criticism" (p. 6).

With respect to education, creating an environment that is conducive to learning is incumbent upon the educator. Indeed, Dewey (1916/1996d) states that we educators "design environments" (p. 23). So, mastery of the subject matter taught is not a sufficient condition for being an effective educator. Rather, good pedagogy integrates the subject matter and innovative teaching methods within a learning environment, both appealing to, and disciplining, students' natural impulses. For example, inquiry-based educational methods leverage the teacher's ability to design projects that pique the students' natural curiosity. These same projects should also channel students' native energies by focusing attention on mastering techniques of inquiry and securing reliable outcomes.

Growth. Education for Dewey is a growth catalyst. Growth involves the development of intelligent habits. The ultimate test of a habit's value is whether it directs inquiry in fruitful ways that fund experience with meaning, render new connections, create helpful tools for future inquiries, and develop the inquirer's native abilities. As Dewey (1916/1996d) notes, "Since growth is characteristic of life, education is all one with growing; it has no end beyond itself" (p. 58). Beyond the cultivation of intelligent habits, what exactly does Dewey mean by growth? To answer this, I first examine what Dewey actually wrote and, second, explore an interpretation by a recent commentator. For instance, Dewey writes that "since life means growth, a living creature lives as truly and positively at one stage as at another, with the same intrinsic fullness and the same absolute claims. Hence education means the enterprise of supplying the conditions which ensure growth, or adequacy of life, irrespective of age. (1916/1996d, p. 56). Educative growth occurs when a learner develops her potentialities under propitious circumstances, that is, in circumstances supplied by a thoughtful educator. Teachers design school environments that channel students' native interests into productive channels. As a result, the student inquires, learns and grows.

Does this mean that growth can only occur within the school? Dewey's (1899/1996b) response might seem out of character for a university professor, although it is certainly characteristic of a pragmatist. He notes that the "everyday work of the school shows that children can live in school as out of it, and yet grow daily in wisdom, kindness, and the spirit of obedience -- that learning may, even with little children, lay hold upon the substance of truth that nourishes the spirit, and yet the forms of knowledge be observed and cultivated; and that growth may be genuine and thorough, and yet a delight" (p. 66). Educative growth, then, does not depend on receiving a formal education and, indeed, might need nurturing in a direction *contrary* to formal education. As Kenneth Burke (1935/1989) observed, "adult education in America" trains citizens to become good consumers in a free market economy, having "maximum desire for commodities consumed under expensive conditions . . . [and] picturing the qualities of life in which this commercially stimulated desire is gratified" (p. 269). Without invoking the notion of false consciousness, "Burke saw (as Marx did not) [hegemonic culture] as most effectively carried through at the level of a culture's various verbal and nonverbal languages" (Lentricchia, 1985, p. 24). Of course, the formal school often serves as the point of origin, the carrier of first resort, in efforts by the dominant elite to transmit cultural capital. According to Swartz (2005), "education, as largely experienced in the United States, is often a dangerous form of alienation" (p. 29). Resisting the hegemonic and alienating discourse within American consumerist-capitalist society often demands exposure to counter-hegemonic discourses, informal sources of learning (e.g., associations, protests and independent films), and thus imaginative ways for realizing educative growth.

James Scott Johnston (2006) proposes that the term "growth" has three possible meanings for Dewey: first, it is a biological or "organismic" capacity that humans and other living things have for developing and adapting to their environment; second, growth indicates the emerging evaluative or "judgmental" skills that humans display in solving problems; and, third, it is "experiential" in the sense that humans can learn from experiences and change their behaviors accordingly, thereby cultivating intelligent habits (pp. 106-7). Obviously, these three senses of growth are not mutually exclusive, but overlap considerably, especially when humans grow through learning. Therefore, the learning that takes place both in school and the greater society is a *sine qua non* for realizing Johnston's three dimensions of growth: biological, judgmental, and experiential.

Imaginative Communication: Education also permits learners to become more effective and sympathetic communicators. Communication plays a crucial role in inquiry or problem-solving, as does language, the quintessential means -- or as Dewey (1925/1996e) describes it, the "tool of tools" (pp. 134). Etymologically-speaking, to communicate is to make common. As Dewey (1934/1996h) suggests, communication "is the process of creating participation, of making common what had been isolated and singular; and part of the miracle it achieves is that, in being communicated, the conveyance of meaning gives body and definiteness to the experience of the one who utters as well as to that of those who listen" (pp. 248-9). Dewey's description of communication is continuous with two more contemporary notions: (i) symbolic interactionsim and (ii) the communicative imagination. According Herbert Blumer (1969), symbolic interaction means "the individual is designating different objects to himself, giving them meaning, judging their suitability [as objectives] to his action, and making decisions on the basis of the judgment" (p. 80).[4] Similar to symbolic interactionism, the communicative imagination involves the use of symbols to designate the meanings of objects. Differently, though, it is through imaginative engagement that the communicator achieves "a heightened state of awareness of the influences of communication on their life" (Swartz et al., 2009, p. 54; Engen, 2000; Swartz, 2005, 2006). In other words, communication does not resemble a *mere* instrument, but is instead a way of *enriching* experience, of treating symbols and meanings as human creations and, thus, ends-in-themselves.

Logic is Dewey's term of art for describing the pattern of inquiry common to scientific and ordinary communication. Indeed, logic for Dewey (1938/1996i) signifies the "need for the development of a general theory of language in which form and matter are not separated" (p. 4). Form is nothing less than the techniques of inquiry and analysis; whereas matter is the subject-matter or content for inquiry and analysis. Through language use, form and matter, as well as techniques and subject-matter, can be viewed as reciprocally (or transactionally) related aspects of the same process: the process of meaningful communication. By converting objects in everyday experience into "things with a meaning," communication "whether it be public discourse or that preliminary discourse termed thinking" reconstructs conventional terms into precise instruments for resolving common problems (Dewey, 1925/1996b, p. 132). Likewise, democratic methods encompass the "give-and-take of communication" and collaborative inquiry undertaken by citizens against a rich background of supportive institutions (Dewey, 1927/1996f, p. 332).

Creative Democracy: Democracy as a social ideal demands education for its (even partial) realization; education that generates growth requires (some degree of) democratic engagement. Rather than recommend specific institutional forms, or "political democracy," Dewey (1927/1996f) deploys a set of leading principles (or postulations) that together are termed the "social idea" of democracy (p. 325). As postulations, they are intended to direct subsequent investigations; however, taken alone, they have no direct correspondence with any particular set of institutions. In the essay "Creative Democracy -- The Task Before Us" (1939), Dewey (1996k) orients the democratic reformer toward a lofty, if somewhat vague, goal: namely, the "creation of a freer and more humane experience in which all share and to which all contribute" (p. 230). Likewise, Swartz et al. (2009) define creative democracy, following Dewey, as "a society that continues dynamically to evolve in its ability to be inclusive, fair, and just through the active participation of all its citizens" (p. 12). With respect to democratic education, Dewey rarely recommended particular institutions, curricular designs, or administrative reforms as panaceas for the problems confronting educators.

One exception can be found in third chapter of *The School and Society* (1915) where Dewey proposed a novel design for a school. He envisioned four rooms, each on the corner of a central museum/library and each devoted to an individual area of study (e.g., physical/chemical science, biology, music and art).

Four recitation rooms sit half in the four rooms and half in the central museum/library "where the children bring the experiences, the problems, the questions, the particular facts which they have found, and discuss them so that new light may be thrown upon them, particularly new light from the experience of others, the accumulated wisdom of the world -- symbolized in the library" (Dewey, 1996b, p. 51). Dewey's school design is based on the hypothesis that if we can create public spaces for the purpose of pooling our ideas, sharing our experiences, and discussing matters of common concern, then we can effectively increase opportunities for democratic discussion and learning. Besides designing public spaces, another way to improve the students' learning experiences, enhance their communicative capacities, and pool their intelligence is through technological means. Johnston (2009) finds evidence of this shift toward technology-assisted education in Dewey's landmark 1916 work on education, *Democracy and Education*. In Johnston's words, "There is no need, Dewey thinks, to invent arcane situations and contexts, when the use of technology and method is itself proof of the richness of social interaction" (p. 53). Fifty years after Dewey's death, an educational-technological innovation has generated a firestorm of debate: the expansion of the concepts of literacy and literacy education to encompass competencies for employing new media.

The Online Literacy Debate

In a National Endowment for the Arts' (NEA) press release (Bradshaw, 2004), the author announced the sobering conclusions of their national survey on literacy: "Literary reading is in dramatic decline with fewer than half of American adults now reading literature . . . [and] drops [in rates of literacy] in all groups studied, with the largest rate of decline . . . occurring in the youngest age groups" (p. 10). In addition, the analysis of the survey data shows a strong correlation between the decline in reading rates and increased exposure to electronic media, especially the internet and portable digital devices (such as IPods). Even more distressing for those hoping to remedy the democratic deficit (plummeting levels of civic and electoral participation), the drop in literary reading is correlated with eroding engagement in political and cultural activities. The report ends with a call to "public agencies, cultural organizations, the press, and educators . . . to inspire a nationwide renaissance of literary reading and bring the transformative power of literature into the lives of citizens" (Bradshaw, 2004, p. 12).

The report has attracted the support of a bevy of experts and lay commentators relying on a host of evidence, from survey results to standardized testing data (especially reading comprehension scores) to neurological studies and common-sense impressions (see Rich, 2008; Carr, 2008). Some neuroscientists claim that reading online changes the brain's structure in ways that, different than book reading, can block the development of crucial cognitive skills at an early age (Rich, 2008). In an article in the *Atlantic*, Nicholas Carr (2008) worries that online reading has weakened his "capacity for concentration and contemplation" and, consequently, made it difficult for him to read long books (p. 2). He is not alone. In antiquity, Socrates' interlocutor, Thamus, worried that the development of writing would cause people to lazily record their ideas, rather than commit them to memory, and thus become forgetful (Plato, 2006, 274e-275b). Web technology also endangers the kind of critical thinking that book reading typically generates. In Carr's (2008) words,

> The kind of deep reading that a sequence of printed pages promotes is valuable not just for the knowledge we acquire from the author's words but for the intellectual vibrations those words set off within our minds. In the quiet spaces opened up by the sustained, undistracted reading of a book, or by any other act of contemplation, for that matter, we make our own associations, draw our own inferences and analogies, foster our own ideas. (p. 5)

Much as the ancients feared the displacement of the memorized word by the written word, defenders of book reading in the present age fear that the online word could thoroughly displace the written word. Indeed, the NEA report warns that "at the current rate of loss, literary reading [that is, the reading of novels, short stories, poetry, or drama in any printed format, including the Internet] . . . will virtually disappear in half a century" (Bradshaw, 2004, p. 16).

In response to the NEA survey and its defenders, many literacy experts and Web advocates argue that online reading skills have practical advantages that far outstrip any of their disadvantages (Kress, 2003; McVee, Bailey, and Shanahan, 2008). Children with the ability to easily navigate and identify information on the

Web tend to be more successful in finding digital-age employment. While online reading also involves engagement with text, it is admittedly a *different* kind of experience, more fractured, interactive and conversational than the one-way and serial structure of book reading. If a reader displays signs of low literacy, the Web enables her to glean information more easily and quickly than she would from an inert text.[5] Many advocates of online reading believe that children should be tested not just for their ability to read and comprehend printed texts, but also for their proficiency at finding, reading, and comprehending online materials (Barton and Hamilton, 1998; Barton, Hamilton and Ivanic, 2000; Kress, 2003).

Unfortunately, the narrow framing of this issue has made it difficult, if not impossible, to reach an accord between the two sides. Since appeals to science lend credibility to the different positions, the scientistic discourse that dominates the online literacy controversy has only served to, in Kenneth Burke's (1966) idiom, "deflect" attention away from other relevant dimensions.[6] Turning to consider E. D. Hirsch's critique of Dewey's approach to literacy education is one way of redirecting (or re-deflecting) attention away from the dominant terministic screen. In other words, the reason for this turn is a felt need to explore the online literacy debate in a novel, historical, and even experimental way -- an approach that does not draw exclusively on the positivistic and impressionistic terminology that currently frames the debate.

Hirsch Versus Dewey

Although his best-selling book has attracted comparatively more attention, E.D. Hirsch's original essay "Cultural Literacy" (1983) sheds valuable light on the object of his critique. He argues that American cultural literacy, or children's knowledge of basic facts about their shared history and culture, is in decline mainly because schools have introduced too much subject-matter diversity into the traditional English and history curricula. This drive for diversity was spurred by minority groups concerned that English language and Western culture dominated the content of primary and secondary school courses. However, Hirsch's objective is not to assimilate these groups by way of standardizing the curriculum. Instead, he hopes that this new kind of literacy, what he calls "cultural literacy," will usher in a cultural *lingua franca*: "The big political question is whether we want a broadly literate culture that unites our cultural fragments enough to allow us to write to one another and read what our fellow citizens have written" (p. 167). To confidently claim that our children are literate in the context of U.S. society, Hirsch (1983) insists, literacy education must encompass both substance and technique: "Literacy implies specific contents as well as formal skills" (p. 162). In other words, literacy's meaning is not limited to the basic ability to read and write; it extends to knowledge of culturally-relevant information, such as the date on which the Magna Carta was signed, and command of particular subject-matter integral to one's identity as an American citizen, such as the history of the Civil War and Reconstruction Period.

In the fifth chapter of his book *Cultural Literacy*, Hirsch (1987) locates blame for the decline in cultural literacy in "the fragmentation of the American school curriculum" (p. 116). He describes the fragmentation in the following way:

> The American school curriculum is fragmented both horizontally across subjects and vertically within subjects. For one student in grade nine, social studies may focus on family relations; for another, the focus may be on ancient history. In an American history course in one school, students may focus of industrial America, but in another school, the focus may be on westward expansion. (p. 116)

Rather than standardizing the school curriculum, faculty and administrators diversified or "fragmented" it in order to meet the needs of industry, particularly its desire for workers with suitably specialized training. In Hirsch's words, educators promoted the practical "utility and the direct application of knowledge, with the goal of producing good, productive, and happy citizens" (p. 118).

As for the *causes* of this fragmentation, Hirsch is quite clear. Beginning with a report on the state of secondary education in 1918, two educational philosophies -- namely, Rousseau's "romanticism" (as articulated in *Emile*) and Dewey's "pragmatism" (as articulated in his many writings on education) -- were converted into educational policies and concrete approaches to curricular design. Instead of imposing the discipline of a classical education, whereby students learned to read and write starting with the study of Greek and Latin texts, the progressive educational movement aimed to nurture the student's self-esteem or "positive self-concept" and provide training in the so-called practical arts -- what are termed today, respectively, "child-centered" and "vocational" education.[7] Hirsch (1987) appeals to the distinction between *learning-by-doing* and *learning-by-reading* to support his critique of Dewey's approach to literacy. According to him, "Dewey and his followers agreed . . . with Rousseau and Wordsworth in scorning secondhand, bookish education" (p. 119). In the Laboratory School at the University of Chicago, which Dewey headed from 1896 to 1903, school-age students learned mathematics through cooking and geometry through building construction, rather than through book learning and rote memorization of formulas and equations. However, the purpose of learning-by-doing is not to train students for a vocation, but to direct students' natural curiosity about their environment and channel it in fruitful directions. Learning projects and exploratory inquiries convert native impulses into intelligent habits and stable dispositions.

Surprisingly, Richard Rorty (1999) defended Hirsch's position as democracy-promoting and, thus, decidedly Deweyan. He notes that "Hirsch is dead right in saying that we Americans no longer give our children a secondary education that enables them to function as citizens of a democracy" (p. 118). Conservatives advocate for standardized curricula imparting truth through socialization, while radicals favor individualized curricula promoting academic freedom in faith that "truth will take care of itself" (p. 117). The result, Rorty claims, is that opposing ideological camps have gained command of curricular content at different levels of the educational system: "The right has pretty much kept control of primary and secondary education and the left has gradually got control of non-vocational higher education" (p. 116). Despite associations between Hirsch and educational evangelists on the right, Rorty views the proposals in *Cultural Literacy* not as efforts "to educate for truth" but as "Deweyan hopes for a better educated electorate" (p. 117).

However, Rorty's Deweyan gloss on Hirsch's recommendations could be a case of selective emphasis. In Rorty's favor, Hirsch is not entirely negative in his appraisal of Dewey's impact on literacy education. Hirsch writes that despite "his opposition to book-centered instruction, Dewey assumed that children would become highly literate under his learning-by-doing principles of education" (1987, pp. 120-1). In other words, inquiry-based learning does not eschew all book learning for the sake of educating through engagement in practical projects. Rather, books and other texts do enter the educational process at several junctures, whether in reading a recipe book for the sake of preparing a meal or in scanning an instruction manual in order to design and build a structure. What Rorty conveniently ignores, though, is Hirsch's internal critique of Dewey's pragmatic approach. For Hirsch, pragmatism's method assesses the value of a theory by the *practical* bearing or success of its consequences. Since many Americans display a dismal level of cultural literacy, and a subsection of that population shows signs of poor basic literacy, the Deweyan approach of learning-by-doing, which inspired the dominant policies of progressive educators and administrators over the past fifty years, fails on its own terms.[8] Dewey's disregard for learning-by-reading, Hirsch concludes, has come at an immensely high price: an increasingly illiterate nation.

A Deweyan Response

A response to Hirsch that sheds light on the online literacy debate need not rely on impressionistic evidence, standardized testing data, or neuroscience research, that is, on the dominant terministic screen. To Hirsch's credit, evidence can be found in Dewey's writings that, on its face, militates against book learning. In *Democracy and Education* (1916), Dewey (1996d) writes: "For one has only to call to mind what is sometimes treated in schools as acquisition of knowledge to realize how lacking it is in any fruitful connection with the ongoing experience of the students -- how largely it seems to be believed that the mere appropriation of subject matter which happens to be stored in books constitutes knowledge" (p. 352). At first blush, this quote seems to validate Hirsch's claim that Dewey was anti-bookish. Restored to its proper context, though, it becomes clear that Dewey was criticizing the view that knowledge is "something complete in itself" and thus "something" only to be gleaned from a single source: books (p. 352).

Where else can evidence be found that literacy is a concept inclusive of online reading and writing? Another source is Dewey's own record as an educator, educational theorist, and educational innovator in the Laboratory

School. As a school teacher in Pennsylvania and Vermont (1880-1882), Dewey engaged in the same practical pedagogical activity -- teaching Latin, algebra, and science to school-age children -- that he would years later revolutionize through his writings and experiments.[9] Contrary to Hirsch's claim, the curriculum at the Laboratory School, later to become known as "learning-by-doing," was not anti-bookish or limited to vocational activities. While many student projects began with the manipulation of "fundamental social materials" such as "housing (carpentry), clothing (sewing), [and] food (cooking)," they led to "derived modes of expression, which bring out more distinctly the factors of social communication -- speech, writing, [and] reading" (Dewey, 1895/1996a, pp. 229-30). Literacy mattered for Dewey, as well as the teachers and other curricular designers at the Laboratory School. Dewey (1899/1996b) also shows support for alternative forms of literacy in many of his books and essays on education. Instead of reciting text in redundant and artificial lessons, he advocates for the use of language in context: "The child who has a variety of materials and facts wants to talk about them, and his language becomes more refined and full, because it is controlled and informed by realities. Reading and writing, as well as the oral use of language, may be taught on this basis" (p. 35). As Katherine Camp Mayhew and Anna Camp Edwards (1936) reveal in their account of the Laboratory School curricula, the subject matter taught, including literacy, "was not thought of as something fixed and ready-made in itself, outside the child's experience; nor was the child's experience thought of as hard and fast, but as something fluent, embryonic, vital" (pp. 251-2). In other words, literacy should be construed more widely and dynamically than the traditional ("fixed and ready-made") model of reading books, writing on paper and speaking in person.

Studies have shown that in the developed world, computers have become a mainstay in the lives of children and youth (Buckingham, 2000; Valentine et al., 2000). The identities of children are forged through social networks reflecting the widespread influence of new communicative technologies, such as chats, blogs, twitter sessions, and text messaging. As multimodal means of communication become commonplace, the boundaries between traditional and new media (visual, verbal, aural and text) have blurred (Nixon, 2003). Moreover, young people transgress these boundaries with relative ease, employing multiple media and modes of communication as they participate in global media culture. Leaving behind the traditional foci of literacy education on basic reading and writing competency (e.g., Ong, 1982; Graff, 1987), literacy researchers have begun studying this changing constellation of practices associated with new media and online literacies (Gee, 2000; Luke, 2000; McVee et al., 2008).

The movement for online literacy has emerged in tandem with this novel concept in literacy research. According to its members, children should be exposed to a wide assortment of media and encouraged to develop fluency in utilizing as many technologies as are useful (New London Group, 1996). From a Deweyan perspective, why would it make sense to expand the meaning of "literacy"? Literacy education must augment the child's fund of settled meanings, tailor her skills to a variety of new media in a fast-changing technological environment, and thereby facilitate personal growth. In concrete terms, becoming literate cannot be limited to developing a minimum level of reading and writing ability. If students are to achieve genuine growth through literacy education, then literacy must also encompass the ability to effectively employ new media. In other words, education must cultivate what contemporary literacy scholars, activists and educators call "multi-literacy" or "new literacies" (ibid, p. 5). As a result, the meaning of literacy moves beyond a basic competency (e.g., the ability to read highway signs and follow assembly instructions) to a constructive capacity (e.g., the ability to tweet and blog), a metaphorical key that unlocks the potential for personal and collective growth in an internet age. Swartz, Campbell, and Pestana (2009) claim that, in a creative democracy, "personal growth replaces survival as a base necessity, enabling everyone to contribute constructively to the larger community" (p. 14). Likewise, in a Deweyan democracy, multi-literacy displaces basic literacy, empowering all citizens to have a fuller and more enriching experience of communication itself.

For what reason, then, would we wish to transform our existing democratic society, in which some citizens are illiterate, into a Deweyan democratic society, in which all citizens are multi-literate? The rationale for multi-literacy is simple: If children are expected to become adults who can employ the numerous communicative technologies at their disposal, then they will have to master multiple literacies. In a paper resembling a manifesto, entitled "A Pedagogy of

Multiliteracies," the New London Group (1996) argues that literacy educators must go beyond "'mere literacy' . . . [which is] centered on language only" to a "pedagogy of multiliteracies [which], by contrast, focuses on modes of representation much broader than language alone" (p. 4).[10] In other words, a paradigm shift must occur before the advocates of online literacy can gain an advantage in the debate with traditionalists, from treating communication as a mere means of information transmission to understanding communication as a process of symbolic interaction.

Conclusion

Educating for multi-literacy requires broad-ranging institutional reforms in the schools. "Every institution is," in Dewey's (1893/1996a) words, "an old one modified" (p. 40). As a preparation for modifying existing institutional arrangements, two additional changes are required. First, making the shift toward a multi-literate democracy begs for a change in perspective. The multi-literacy approach rejects the widely-accepted dualism between literacy and technology, understanding the two as transactionally related -- in one scholar's words, as "relations of technologies to texts; discourses; ideologies; and race, class, and gender formations [which] are inseparable from studies of literacy" (Bruce, 1997, p. 308). Second, besides a change in perspective, educating for multi-literacy also demands extensive material and human resources for teaching students to receive, transmit, and communicate their ideas in a wide variety of media (e.g., written, audio-visual and hypertext) (Kist, 2005; Garrison & Dwight, 2003).

To clarify, the argument for multi-literacy is *not* identical to the argument that online literacy -- or any other form of literacy, for that matter -- should displace book literacy. Rather, it is to argue that the pressures of an increasingly diverse and globally connected world make it imperative that children be educated to achieve fluency in a diverse range of media. So, if democracy is to be realized as more than a discrete set of institutions (e.g., the schools, universities, courts, legislatures) -- as what Dewey (1916/1996d) calls "a mode of associated living, of conjoint, communicated experience" (pp. 225-6) and "a way of life" -- then surely this demands the kind of literacy education that would make citizens better adapted to their technologically advanced environments (Dewey, 1996k, p. 226; Ralston, 2008). In the spirit of philosophy *as* education, multi-literacy should provide a set of pedagogical instruments, including specialized curricula and online tests, which empower citizens of a Deweyan democracy to adjust, adapt, and grow in a highly complex environment. Though Dewey (1899/1996b) never endorsed "multi-literacy" (a concept that was introduced more than thirty years after his death), he did argue for the integration of multiple media in the schools. For instance, he noted that in his school "the life of the child becomes the all-controlling aim. All the media necessary to further the growth of the child centre there" (p. 24). Likewise, he acknowledged that the "place of communication in personal doing supplies us with a criterion for estimating the value of informational material in school" (Dewey, 1916/1996d, p. 194). By providing a set of tools, though, multi-literacy is not aligned with the model of communication is a mere means, for these same technologies *qua* pedagogical instruments facilitate symbolic interaction, and thereby enrich individual and collective human experience.

REFERENCES

Barton, D., & Hamilton, M. (1998). *Local literacies: Reading and writing in one community*. London: Routledge.

Barton, D., Hamilton, M., & Ivanic, R. (Eds.). (2000). *Situated literacies: Reading and writing in context*. London: Routledge.

Bauerlin, M. (2008). Online literacy is a lesser kind. *The Chronicle of Higher Education*. (September 19). Retrieved from http://chronicle.com/article/Online-Literacy-Is-a-Lesser/28307

Bloom, A. (1987). *The closing of the American mind: How higher education has failed democracy and impoverished the souls of today's students*. New York: Simon & Schuster.

Blumer, H. (1969). *Symbolic interactionism: Perspective and method*. Englewood Cliffs, NJ: Prentice-Hall.

Bradshaw, T. (2004). *Reading at risk: A survey of literacy reading in America*. (Rep. No. 46). Washington, DC: National Endowment for the Arts.

Bruce, B. C. (1997). Literary technologies: What stance should we take? *Journal of Literacy Research*, *29(2)*, 289-309.

Buckingham, D. (2000). *After the death of childhood: Growing up in the age of electronic media.* Cambridge, UK: Polity Press.

Burke, K. (1966). *Language as symbolic action: Essays on life, language and method.* Berkeley: University of California Press.

---. (1984). *Permanence and change: An anatomy of purpose.* Berkeley: University of California Press. (Original published in 1935)

---. (1989). Revolutionary symbolism in America. In H. W. Simons and T. Melia, (Eds.), *The legacy of Kenneth Burke* (pp. 267-273). Madison: University of Wisconsin Press. (Original published in 1935)

Burke, T. (1994). *Dewey's new logic: A reply to Russell.* Chicago: University of Chicago Press.

Carr, N. (2008). Is Google making us stupid? *Atlantic Mon*thly (July/August). Retrieved from http://www.atlantic.com/doc/print/200807/google.

Denzin, N. K. (1992). *Symbolic interactionism and cultural studies: The politics of interpretation.* Cambridge, MA: Blackwell.

Dewey, J. (1996a). Early works. In L. A. Hickman (Ed.), *The collected works of John Dewey: The electronic edition*, vol. 5. Charlottesville, VA: Intelex Corp.

---. (1996b). Middle works. In L. A. Hickman (Ed.), *The collected works of John Dewey: The electronic edition*, vol. 1. Charlottesville, VA: Intelex Corp.

---. (1996c). Middle works. In L. A. Hickman (Ed.), *The collected works of John Dewey: The electronic edition*, vol. 7. Charlottesville, VA: Intelex Corp.

---. (1996d). Middle works. In L. A. Hickman (Ed.), *The collected works of John Dewey: The electronic edition*, vol. 9. Charlottesville, VA: Intelex Corp.

---. (1996e). Later works. In L. A. Hickman (Ed.), *The collected works of John Dewey: The electronic edition*, vol. 1. Charlottesville, VA: Intelex Corp.

---. (1996f). Later works. In L. A. Hickman (Ed.), *The collected works of John Dewey: The electronic edition*, vol. 2. Charlottesville, VA: Intelex Corp.

---. (1996g). Later works. In L. A. Hickman (Ed.), *The collected works of John Dewey: The electronic edition*, vol. 9. Charlottesville, VA: Intelex Corp.

---. (1996h). Later works. In L. A. Hickman (Ed.), *The collected works of John Dewey: The electronic edition*, vol. 10. Charlottesville, VA: Intelex Corp.

---. (1996i). Later works. In L. A. Hickman (Ed.), *The collected works of John Dewey: The electronic edition*, vol. 12. Charlottesville, VA: Intelex Corp.

---. (1996j). Later works. In L. A. Hickman (Ed.), *The collected works of John Dewey: The electronic edition*, vol. 13. Charlottesville, VA: Intelex Corp.

---. (1996k). Later works. In L. A. Hickman (Ed.), *The collected works of John Dewey: The electronic edition*, vol. 14. Charlottesville, VA: Intelex Corp.

Dwight, J. and Garrison, J. (2003). A manifesto for instructional technology: Hyperpedagogy. *Teachers College Record, 105(5)*, 628-99.

Engen, D. E. (2000). The communicative imagination and its cultivation. *Communication Quarterly, 50(1)*, 41-57.

Garrison, J. W. (1996). A Deweyan theory of democratic listening. *Educational Theory, 46(4)*, 429-451.

---. (1998). John Dewey's philosophy as education. In L. A. Hickman (Ed.), *Reading Dewey: Interpretations for a postmodern generation* (pp. 63-81). Bloomington and Indianapolis: Indiana University Press.

Gee, J. P. (2000). The new literacy studies: Context, intertextuality and discourse. In D. Barton, M. Hamilton, and R. Ivanic (Eds.), *Situated literacies: Reading and writing in context* (pp. 180-96). London: Routledge.

Graff, H. J. (1987). *The legacies of literacy: Continuities and contradiction in western culture and society*. Bloomington, IN: Indiana University Press.

Hull, G., and Schultz, K. (2001). Literacy and learning out of school: A review of theory and research. *Review of Educational Research, 71(4)*, 575–611.

Hendley, B. (1989). Hirsch and Dewey on democracy and education. *Interchange, 20(1)*, 53-60.

Hirsch, E. D., Jr. (1983). Cultural literacy. *The American Scholar, 52(1)*, 159-69.

---. (1987). *Cultural Literacy: What every American needs to know*. Boston: Houghton Mifflin Company.

Hoffman, J. V. (2000). The de-democratization of schools and literacy in America. *The Reading Teacher, 53(8)*, 616-23.

Johnston, J. S. (2006). *Inquiry and education: John Dewey and the quest for democracy*. Albany: State University of New York Press.

---. (2009). *Deweyan inquiry: From education theory to practice*. Albany: State University of New York Press.

Juskalian, R. (2008). Interview with Clay Shirky, part I. *Columbia Journalism Review* (December 19), pp. 1-2. Retrieved from <http://www.cjr.org/overload/ interview_with_clay_shirky_par.php?page=all

Kist, W. (Ed.) (2005). *New literacies in action: Teaching and learning in multiple media.* New York: Teachers College.

Kress, G. (2003). *Literacy in the new media age.* New York: Routledge.

Lentricchia, F. (1983). *Criticism and social change.* Chicago: University of Chicago Press.

Luke, C. (2000). New literacies in teacher education. *Journal of Adolescent & Adult Literacy, 43(5),* 424-35.

Mayhew, K. C. and Edwards, A. C. (1936). *The Dewey school: The laboratory school of the University of Chicago, 1896-1903.* New York: D. Appleton-Century Company.

McVee, M. B., Bailey, N. M., and Shanahan, L. E. (2008). Teachers and teacher educators learning from new literacies and new technologies. *Teaching Education, 19(3),* 197-210.

New London Group. (1996). A pedagogy of multiliteracies: Designing social futures. *Harvard Educational Review, 66(1),* 1-29.

Nixon, H. (2003). New research literacies for contemporary research into literacy and new media? *Reading Research Quarterly, 38(3),* 407-13.

Mackey, M., & Nixon, H. (2003). Media and online literacy studies (New Directions in Research). *Reading Research Quarterly, 38(3),* 388–413.

Ong, W. J. (1982). *Orality and literacy: The technologizing of the world.* New York: Routledge.

Plato. (2006). *Phaedrus* (Jowett translation). Retrieved from http://classics.mit. edu/Plato/ phaedrus.html

Ralston, S. J. (2008). In defense of democracy as a way of life: A reply to Talisse's pluralist objection. *Transactions of the Charles S. Peirce Society, 44(4),* 629-659.

Ravitch, D., and Finn, C. E., Jr. (1987). *What do our 17-year-olds know?: A report on the First National Assessment of History and Literature.* New York: Harper and Row.

Rich, M. (2008). Literacy debate: Online, r u really reading? *The New York Times* (July 27), pp. 1-9.

---. (2009). Fiction reading increases for U.S. adults. *The New York Times* (January 12), pp. 1-2.

Rorty, R. (2000). *Philosophy and social hope.* New York: Penguin.

Ryan, A. (1995). *John Dewey and the high tide of American liberalism.* New York and London: W.W. Norton and Company.

Swartz, O. (1996). Kenneth Burke's theory of form: Rhetoric, art, and cultural analysis. *Southern communication journal, 61(4),* 312-21.

---. (2005). *In defense of partisan criticism: Communication studies, law & social analysis.* New York: Peter Lang.

---. (2006). Reflections of a social justice scholar. In O. Swartz (Ed.), *Social Justice and Communication Scholarship* (pp. 1-19). Mahwah, NJ: Lawrence Erlbaum.

Swartz, O., Campbell, K., and Pestana, C. (2009). *Neo-pragmatism, communication, and the culture of creative democracy.* New York: Peter Lang.

Snyder, I. and Joyce, M. (1998). *Page to screen: Taking literacy into the electronic era.* New York: Routledge.

Valentine, G., Holloway, S., and Bingham, N. (2000). Transforming cyberspace: Children's interventions in the new public sphere. In S. Holloway and G. Valentine (Eds.), *Children's geographies: Playing, living, learning* (pp. 155-173). London: Routledge.

Notes

[1] For a review of this position, see Hull & Schultz (2001) and Bauerlin (2008).

[2] For Burke (1966, pp. 3-5) a terministic screen is a group of symbols that operate as a filter, structuring how they should be made intelligible by other language-users.

[3] Hirsch is not the only scholar to popularize the idea of cultural literacy. Others, including Bloom (1987) and Ravitch & Finn (1987), have lent credibility to the notion that young people must be informed about the history of Western civilization if they are to function as minimally competent citizens.

[4] Although he mentions Dewey in passing, Blumer (1969, p. 78) gives most of the credit for his understanding of objects to another pragmatist, George Herbert Mead. See also Denzin (1992, pp. 5-8).

[5] By referring to text on a page as "inert" I do not mean to comment on the interpretive depth of the text. Surely there is metaphoric movement associated with some level of hermeneutic reader-text engagement. I only mean to invoke the formal properties and presentation of the text as unmoving or unlinked to other text, as opposed to hypertext, which functionally links to other computer text, such that the reader gets the sense of movement while reading. I am indebted to Vincent Colapietro for this point.

[6] According to Burke (1966, pp. 4-5), language does not merely correspond to or "reflect" reality; it also "selects" and "deflects" what the language-user deems is relevant based on his or her ideological commitments.

[7] Although Dewey's educational ideas inspired many members of the progressive educational movement, Dewey did much, as biographers and others commentators attest, to distance himself and his educational philosophy from the movement's simplistic advocacy for child-centered and vocational education. According to Garrison (1998), many "'progressive' educators have erroneously claimed that Dewey demanded a student-centered' education. In his view, however, the act of teaching must coordinate teacher, student, and subject matter. Dewey insisted that the teacher must always connect the subject matter with the student's present needs and abilities, and he thought educational method performed this function" (p. 69). See also Hendley (1989).

[8] It could be objected that Hirsch is equivocating between cultural and basic literacy. However, the two are linked in that, short of living in a society with a deep oral history, basic literacy skills are a threshold requirement for becoming culturally literate.

[9] Unfortunately, there is little record of Dewey's experience as a school teacher, other than anecdotal accounts based on a series of interviews of his former students conducted in the 1950s. According to Ryan (1995), in "Oil City things went smoothly" (p. 58).

[10] Also, see Kress (2003) and Luke (2000). For a case study exploring some of the obstacles to teaching new literacies and teaching teachers to teach new media, see McVee, Bailey, and Shanahan (2008).

CHAPTER 8

Building Bridges Between Tellers and Listeners:
The Role of Digital Storytelling in the Construction of Democratic Frameworks

Margaret Anne Clarke
University of Portsmouth

According to artist and activist Joe Lambert, founder for the Center for Digital Storytelling, "Story is learning, celebrating, healing and remembering. Each part of the life process necessitates it. Failure to make story honor these passages threatens the consciousness of communal identity" (2010, p. 1). It is in this consciousness of communal identity that the democratic nature of the millennium-old cultural practice of digital storytelling resides. The creation of stories and the knowledge they convey and impart to others form bonds of trust in space and through time between communities of tellers and listeners. The purpose of this chapter is to examine the potential of the revival of the storytelling tradition in the digital age for radical democratic thought and practice in the twenty-first century.

Digital storytelling, in its modern form, is a composite of workshop-based, training and collaborative practices enabling the creation of a three-minute narrative, most often recounted in the first person, of an individual citizen's life experiences, based on themes such as community, work, family, love, friendship and personal identity. While the practice is facilitated by multimedia and networked technologies, these are not the center of activity. The practice is aimed at developing people's natural storytelling abilities (Lambert, 2010). As such, the primary aim of digital storytelling is to assert the individual voice of citizens, including those with little or no previous competence in information technology, and to enable them to create an audio recording based on their narrative, which is then enhanced with other multimedia, such as a music soundtrack, digitized photographs, text, and other resources. The term "digital storytelling" has been applied in many contexts, but for the purposes of this chapter, I will restrict myself to the "classic" model of digital storytelling as defined and established by the Center for Digital Storytelling (CDS), the main organization associated with this practice. As defined on its webpage, the CDS views itself as an "international not-for-profit community organization rooted in the craft of personal storytelling. [They] assist youth and adults around the world in using media tools to share, record, and value stories from their lives, in ways that promote artistic expression, health and well-being and justice" (CDS, ¶2).

In the nearly two decades of its existence, the Center has sought to realize its fundamental aim with the wide dissemination of its workshop practices, and further integration of the stories within social activist and civic associations. The establishment of other portals such as Stories for Change (SFC) has brought about the networking and collaboration between these associations on a national scale; at the time of my writing this chapter, the Center, according to its website, has worked with nearly 1,000 organizations around the world and directly trained more than 15,000 people. This work has involved the adaptation of the principles, methods, and practices of the Center in participatory projects of many kinds, including public health and services, educational projects, foster youth, disability, community arts. On an international level, digital storytelling practices have been integrated into work by non-governmental organizations, especially in Africa, to promote training, advocacy and activism for projects involving gender and equality, AIDS, and dislocation caused by civil war.

From its inception by the CDS, digital storytelling has also been explicitly defined by its founders as one of the "identity-based social movements aimed at changing the cultural foundations of society" (Castells, 1997/2004, p. 149). CDS's founder testified that he saw his work in terms of "movement building;" that is, he "wanted to motivate people to change their behavior, to change the distribution of power and relations" (Lambert, 2000, ¶3). The social movements referred to by Lambert aim to effect radical and creative forms of democratic mobilization championing social difference, the politics of identity, and resistance against the homogenizing forces of globalization. In these contexts, information and communications technologies (ICTs) are harnessed in radical ways for two purposes. First, to enable citizens to use the new media for the production and representation of their own experiences. Second, to construct new networks between tellers and listeners. The goal, in other words, is to build new structures linking individuals, organizations and media outlets (i.e., counter networks) which would represent exactly how citizens are experiencing the consequences of national and global governance. The foundation of "movement building," in the context of the work of the CDS, is to give a voice to those excluded from the mainstream media and societal frameworks, and, ultimately, to establish a social movement capable of transforming human relationships for the purpose of broader change in society.

The overarching theme of this chapter is the special association of the digital storytelling movement with democratic renewal, mobilization, and participation. This association is based on two important dimensions of the practice. First, on the potential for creating individual agency and empowerment through the constructivist and expressivist pedagogies which underpin the creation of the stories. Second, on the assertion of individual voice and the lived human experience of those largely excluded from media networks and hegemonic social and political structures. Both dimensions offer the possibility for the transformation from *individual* to *citizen*, because the storyteller is able to represent him or herself as a *social* and, therefore, potentially *political* agent. The subsequent transition from individual citizenship to shared public culture is effected by the subsequent framing and distribution and networking of the stories within dedicated websites (Couldry, 2009, p. 386).

Later in this chapter, I will focus on the specific potential for social transformation: in particular, the role digital storytelling could fulfill, and is fulfilling, within a more general context of the potential expansion of democratic practice and the possibilities created for mobilization, participation, and deliberation through contemporary communications technologies. I will give specific examples of stories illustrating citizen self-representation and the progressive dissemination and integration of these stories within the revival of associational life, new forms of deliberative participation, and emerging concepts such as "micro-democracy," whose foundation is the lived experience of citizens in their encounters with the structures of public governance. These new forms of practice are emerging as a response to the numerous conflicts and challenges to democracy at the turn of the millennium, which have led to what has been termed a "crisis" in democratic frameworks and structures (Blaug and Schwartzmantel, 2004, p. 1).[1]

Such crisis is not a new phenomenon: it was addressed by John Dewey in the aftermath of the dislocation caused by World War I. For Dewey, the crisis in democracy in the early twentieth century was fundamentally also a crisis of *belief*: the mass alienation of the public from the political process and the doubts as to whether, in fact, the public could participate in societies dominated by technologically advanced communications in the hands of corporate elites (Siu, 2002). Alienation and exclusion from the democratic process could only be overcome, according to Dewey, through conscious inquiry, internal growth, and the development of human agency on the part of each individual "to develop through the give-and-take of communication an effective sense of being an individually distinctive member of a community" (Dewey, 1927/1989, p. 154). The "effective sense" which Dewey refers to, however, is not confined to the individual citizen; it can extend to all the modes of human association which comprise society -- whether family, work or the community -- in order to address inequalities of representation, work toward social goals, and to serve the common good.

Dewey's insights are as salient today as they were in the early twentieth century; and, in particular, can be applied to opportunities that now exist for information technologies to play a role as a mediating agent between the institutions of civic society and the perspectives of the citizens who comprise that society. Digital storytelling, "a community practice in a global mediasphere" (Hartley and McWilliam, 2009, p. 3), mediates the individual perspectives of citizens, profoundly informed by the experience of community, history, and nationhood. When amassed and networked though contemporary communications networks, the stories also represent other social dimensions: resistance, empathy, dialogue, interaction, and shared experience. These are all components of the improved communication Dewey saw as the ultimate solution to the fragmentation and alienation afflicting the public sphere and the body politic elected to serve the common good. As he warns, until "the Great

Society is converted into the Great Community, the Public will remain in eclipse. Communication can alone create a Great Community" (Dewey, 1927, p. 142).

The Foundations of Digital Storytelling and Cultural Democracy

Although the structure, methodologies, and processes of digital storytelling were first formally named and defined as a practice in 1993, the practice has deeper cultural and historical roots. According to Lambert, digital storytelling can also be placed within a long tradition of radical cultural democracy in the United States, which was further revived in the 1960s by community-based arts practices expressed in storytelling, folk music, and other forms of popular culture, presented within community theater and multicultural activism. The fundamental aim of such cultural activity was to democratize culture through creative renovation of the artistic disciplines, but this democratization was effected through the participation and involvement of those who were not necessarily professional producers. Storytelling was a "folk tradition" according to Lambert, and was expressed in "the community theater artists connecting with and claiming the folk tradition of 'storytelling'" (Lambert, 2006, p. 22).

This art, in its broadest sense, generated by these communities of practice, frequently addressed social conflicts and political issues of the time; but it was also concerned with broader participatory questions. Partly, the purpose was provide access to art and its production to "all sectors of the population who were underserved by traditional education and vocational training systems" (CDS, "History," ¶2); but also to "to transform oral histories of common people into productions of broad impact and scope" (Lambert, 2006, p. 3). The establishment of the CDS was inspired by the need to further broaden this work, to reinvigorate democratic cultural life, and reconnect it to social and political practice in the contemporary context formed by the networked society.[2] Thus, the multiple dimensions of digital storytelling are also related to changing paradigms which negate the idea of "creation," "creativity," and the "aesthetic" as the exclusive preserve of an elite of artists, authors, or trained professionals endowed with some special, if unexamined, individual talent. This notion divorces artists, the work they create, and the society to which they belong, in an "ideology of property" (Certeau, 1997, pp. 140-142), and, as a concept, is profoundly compromised by neo-liberal ideologies of individual appropriation and ownership. This ideology of property was discussed by Dewey (1934/1980), who pointed out that the development of "art" as a distinctive sphere, de-linked and decompartmentalized from human society and human experience, was in itself a product of the development of capitalism. As Dewey argued, when artistic artifacts of any kind are separated from their "conditions of origin and operation in experience," they "reflect and establish superior cultural status, while their segregation from the common life reflects the fact that they are not part of a native and spontaneous culture" (1934/1980, p. 2).

A perquisite for individuals and communities to reclaim their democratic rights, therefore, must be the restoration of the "continuity between the refined and intensified forms of experience that are works of art and the everyday events, doings, and sufferings that are universally recognized to constitute experience" (Dewey, 1934/1980, p. 2). Creation, within this framework, is related to several things. First, the full coming into consciousness on the part of the participant, "people who believe they are mundane, uninteresting or unmemorable possess beneath this mask a vivid, complex and rich body of stories just waiting to be told" (CDS, "Values and Principles," ¶2). The specific form which the genre takes is thus designed to maximize the potential for the unmasking of personal experience by any participant. This potential is drawn out and released through the pedagogical and collaborative processes of the "story circle workshop" and refined further through the economy and discipline of the "three-minute recorded narrative."[3] This format enables the participant to summarize the most salient features of his or her life experiences, situations, and episodes that we "spontaneously refer to as being 'real experiences'" (Dewey, 1934/1980, p. 20). But these "real" experiences on the part of the participant are also based on "the cultural practices of everyday life . . . [which] is also the ground on which creation everywhere blossoms" (Certeau, 1997, p. 140). These basic elements of culture may be based on much older popular traditions: oral history, family heritage, scrapbooking, folklore, or proverbs, etc., all ultimately rooted in a community practice. Even if half-forgotten by the participant, all these components can be recovered, recreated, and remembered by the practices which digital media enable: the bricolage, assemblage and re-composition of script, voice, sound and image. Such an approach combines the immediacy of the spoken voice, arising of the moment and the immediate situation, with the reflection and interpretation associated with the written text and the illustrative power of the visual image. These dimensions of expression are also the dimensions necessary for integrating the critical imagination of the participant, defined as "meaning, understanding and figuring out the place of the human in the world" (Swartz, Campbell, & Pestana, 2009, p. 34).

The following example from the CDS, "Mixed Race Me" by Yunnie Tsao Snyder (2007), illustrates the digital story as "a transformation of energy into thoughtful action, through assimilation of meanings from the background of past experiences" (Dewey, 1934/1980, p. 63). The story's narrative is described as a "meditation on questions of mixed-race heritage and how the constant dilemma of feeling neither/both affects one's sense of identity and place in the world" (Snyder, 2007, CDS Homepage, "Stories," ¶1). The multimodal flow of images which accompany the narrative are "natural signs" (Bolter, 1996, p. 264) which do not just represent, but evoke. They are drawn from Snyder's childhood and family photograph albums, together with a selection of older sepia-tinted pictures of her ancestors. They also comprise pictures of the environments where she has lived, and iconic pictures depicting wider social activism. The following extract illustrates the participant's identity as flux and transformation, profoundly informed by landscape, family, ancestry and nation:

> This is my ode to mixed-race me, seemingly caught between so many different things. A legacy of Cold Mountain and government cheese, both drenched with American dreams . . . I am middle child of three girls. A sisterhood of Hopi, mestiza, mulatto, half-breed nation . . . through hoodlum shops and boot straps, alcoholics and red envelopes, law books and brush strokes, immigrants and blue collars. Incense, prayers and Dad's tall tales, and oh, those yellow boxes of Werther chocolates sitting among smoke rings. (Snyder, 2007, CDS Homepage, "Stories," ¶1)

Snyder's story represents the assertion of the storyteller's own voice speaking in the present; or, in Dewey's words, "a quickening of what is" (Dewey, 1934/1980, p. 20). This "quickening" represents a moment of peculiar intensity arising from the point where the conversion of past into present evokes an awareness of the potentialities of the future, an infinity of possibilities and future directions. This moment thus carries the self to a full awareness of her agency, that is, her capacity to shape her own environment in relation to interaction and communication with others:

> I need to move forward. I need to move forward towards possibilities, for I also have a dream, too. To rise up, to show up, to keep on not giving up, until things are different for not just me. I have come up, and come to be me, and here I am, to tell the story that has been inherited to me, and that I will inherit on, and I will live up to this legacy that has been blessed to me. (Snyder, 2007, ¶3)

Here, Snyder illustrates the dialogic nature of shared storytelling: the awareness that an individual's own voice acquires meaning and value in relation to the voices of others. Human potential, according to Dewey, can only be fully realized in relation to communication *with others* and the opportunity to share experience. In other words, Dewey suggests that learning to be human involves developing "through the give-and-take of communication an effective sense of being an individually distinctive member of a community; one who understands and appreciates its beliefs, desires and methods, and who contributes to a further conversion of organic powers into human resources and values" (Dewey, 1929, p. 154). Snyder exemplifies this pheneomona when she concludes:

> I am not just the white girl you just want to see, and there is no dragon-lady hidden inside of me. I will let people know that there is no confused one here. Only a purposeful one, to whisper that reminder in your ear, you are more than they think you to be. I am Yunnie Tsao Snyder, and it is through my voice that I will continue to be, and it is through your voice that I will continue to know you, and together, but not in unison, we will speak among one another. (Snyder, 2007, ¶4)

Digital Storytelling as Public Culture: An Affective Practice of the Social

The conclusion to Snyder's narrative also illustrates the way in which the process of digitally remediated storytelling is also capable of rendering the individual voice, based on lived experience, into a culture which can then be publicly shared and related to a collectivity of other voices. Such communication is not the mere transmission of information, but, rather, "an affective practice of the social" (Burgess, 2006, p. 210). The concept of the "affective practice of the social" applies in many different contexts to the stories collected and archived by the CDS and other associations. These stories, while not related under prescriptive conditions, or necessarily oriented to overtly "political" concerns or social issues, can never be entirely neutral in content or intention. They are based on the communication of free agency and choice on the part of the participants: an awareness of their position which is ultimately situated in relation to family, community, social structure, hierarchy, and nation. This sense of autonomy and situatedness must be a precondition for effecting social change in these social structures and hierarchies. In the words of Lambert, we "start with a point of view, because we believe everyone should know that they have one. Even if our efforts are just showing people a way to take responsibility for their own lives, their own stories, as the first step to larger awareness, all our choices are informed with a touch of the subversive" (2009, p. 82). We can see from stories such as "Mixed Race Me" that individual self-awareness through reflection in relation to community, ancestry, and nation is not only self-knowledge, but *contextualized* self-knowledge, capable of being transformed into *social* knowledge, a pre-condition for active citizenship.

More specifically, the personal testimonies from which the greater part of digital stories are composed can be grouped into three aspects which relate them to society, its history, and its concerns; and, from there, to fuller participation in that society. The first is the *empathetic effect* that the stories may have on others. This is brought about by the participatory and collaborative nature of the workshop and story circle, the discussion and sharing which is an integral part of the process of creation. This forms a process of identification which can be extended further with the thematic grouping, sharing, and networking of stories on other platforms and through networked organizations. As the CDS explains, "Sharing stories can lead to positive change. The process of supporting groups of people in making media is just the first step. Personal narratives in digital media can touch viewers deeply, moving them to reflect on their own experiences, modify their behavior treat others with greater compassion, speak out about injustice, and become involved in civic and political life" ("Values and Principles," ¶7).

Second, the stories have a *testimonial capacity*: they bear witness to truths which are not expressed elsewhere or in any more "official" outlet. This converts digital storytelling into a process of resistance which is an inherent characteristic of the process from its genesis to its final distribution on the web or other outlets. The stories, in part, represent an innate struggle on the part of the participants with consciousness, memory, and their relations with others; their networking on media platforms may then enable the challenging of official narratives of events in society which bear little or no resemblance to the participants' own experience. These themes have emerged organically from the original practice of digital storytelling, which, as we have seen, is consciously designed to draw out the experiences of individuals with little or no access to digital affordances or marginalized from accepted social and cultural practices. But these themes have also been adopted by dedicated activists or community groups who, often under the auspices of the CDS, have adopted the practice on behalf of the marginalized or dispossessed, those who have fallen into the "black holes of informational capitalism" (Castells, 1998, p. 162). Such communities rarely have any other outlet for self-expression or representation through global broadcasting or other media networks. The testimony and resistance enabled by storytelling are illustrated in recuperative digital storytelling programs which use the practice as a healing process for groups who have been traumatized by war, domestic violence or abandonment by the community.

Finally, other programs focus on marginalized groups, including youth, in communities underserved by information technology. Two examples of such programs are MASSImpact, a consortium dedicated to disseminating digital media programs involving school curricula, community organizing strategies, and capacity-building activities (MASS Impact Homepage, ¶1) and Third World Majority, a media and resource center established and run by women of color based in the San Francisco Bay area. The aim of Third World Majority is to construct "collective organizational structures in order to challenge top-down, white male-dominated models so prevalent in corporate media" (Benavente, 2008, ¶8). These organizations share the same fundamental aims: to disseminate new media technology as a tool of social empowerment, rather than exclusion, with digital storytelling as a key component. They are dedicated to rectifying unequal representation in the community as a whole, as well as unequal access to community resources. This may take the form of economic exclusion, but it also takes the form of the exclusion of access to information technology on the part of those on the wrong side of the "digital divide," the "shadow public sphere of the "electronically disenfranchised" (Sobchack, 1995, p. 729). Stories created by these groups form "counter-discourses," and, for urban, ethnic, and other communities existing on the margins of society, form part of the struggle against societal amnesia, neglect or ignorance.

Such counter discourses attempt to address on various levels the inequalities within the communities from which they originate. Fundamental here is the basic issue of lack of access together with the lack of skills to use technologies and their platforms for self-expression and advocacy. Indeed, marginalized communities may most frequently experience information technologies and communication systems as an actively malign force -- as an instrument of dominance and surveillance.[4] Digital storytelling provides a means to democratize communication technologies themselves and reclaim them by healing the breach between the human and technology. The stories created by the participants in the programs mentioned above are multimedia artifacts constructed as much from oral tradition, community resources, and found materials as from computers used for purely instrumental purposes, or text literacy, which solely privileges formal written skills. Equally, the composite of discussion, collaborative and workshop practices which precede the creation of the stories revive the Deweyan paradigm of literacy *practices* rather than technocratic literacy *skills*. These literacy practices focus on the "discovery method" in order to foster creativity and imaginative thinking: this method enhances self-expression and the ability to produce content that represents the actual needs and social conditions of the participants. Thus, digital storytelling represents "access," not in the sense of simply making information technologies available, but in enhancing citizens' ability to make use of these devices in order to engage in meaningful social practices and reclaim power through the assertion of voice and the recovery of individual and community histories.

Digital Storytelling, the Public Sphere, and Deliberative Democracy

The need to build an infrastructure capable of providing further mutual support, collaboration, and exchange for all the organizations involved in digital storytelling in different regional contexts has led to the national networked integration of practitioners, their centers, and the creation of media portals to facilitate progressive thematic grouping of stories, their interaction and cross-fertilization. In the process, these portals, and the associations which comprise them, further transform the stories into "public culture" within civil society to be shared and distributed. One example is the establishment of Stories for Change, a federation of associations such as the CDS, in alliance with other organizations who are able to interact with formal structures of governance. This federation, together with others, is oriented to integrating the digital storytelling groups and movements within *civil society*, that is, the sphere consisting of non-governmental organizations, societies, and other forms of association that act as intermediaries between the private economy and the state. SFC, then, is another expression of "citizens acting collectively . . . to exchange information, achieve natural goals, make demands on the state, and hold state officials accountable" (Diamond, 1994, p. 5). Digital Stories become, potentially, an outlet and a means by which political participation on the part of citizens could be increased, in particular for marginalized groups whose voices are not well represented by established political structures. In this section I will examine some of the methods, ideas, and practices developed in order to integrate digital stories and the unique perspectives of the citizens who produce them into decision making systems within the public sphere.

Recent theories concerning the structure of the public sphere have expanded the definition of this concept to include any area of social life in which it is possible for public opinion to be deliberated and formed (Habermas, 1974/2004, p. 350). The expanded public sphere also entails an expanded public discourse, which mobilizes perspectives, arguments, and points of view, what Habermas calls "communicative power" (Habermas, 1994, p. 8). Such power is inspired by the individuals' own sources of motivation, and by their experiences and points of view. Digital stories, once shared and distributed, within the public sphere, foster what Omar Swartz, Katia Campbell, and Christiana Pestana (2009) call "decentered deliberativism" (p. 98), expanding the public sphere still further and fostering a pluralism comprising different perspectives, authentic registers of language, and points of view. These concepts were, again, foreshadowed by Dewey, who, while accepting the need for organized systems in complex societies, posited that these can become richer through the active engagement of citizens in open and free decision-making networks at the local, regional, and global levels. As Dewey noted, "No government by experts in which the masses do not have the chance to inform the experts as to their needs can be anything but an oligarchy managed in the interests of a few" (1927/1989, p. 209).

Yet the ideals of deliberative democracy -- that is, the right of access to knowledge and information, the opportunity for genuine debate and dissent for those affected by governmental policy, let alone any genuine influence over policy-making and political decisions, are still far from reality for the majority of the voting populace (Holton, 2008, p. 182). Two specific problems impede the fulfillment of the vision of theorists such as Jürgen Habermas and John Rawls, both related to the crisis in democratic systems discussed above. To begin with, individualistic and consumerist attitudes, fostered by broadcasting, advertising and other media, have also led to wholesale devaluation of civic and participatory activity, illustrated, for example, in the public disenchantment with political ideologies and the retreat from participation in the traditional political parties. This is also exacerbated by alienation from the specific discourses of law, government, and politics which the citizen must learn if he or she is to participate. Thus, the present use and distribution of contemporary media networks are integral to the crisis in democratic structures. The structure of the public sphere is still concentrated in the hands of elites who are able to harness the media for the purpose of political discourse as "spin" within broadcasting networks in which the only role of the populace is to be courted for votes or represented in demeaning reality TV or chat shows. More recently, new media networks afforded by digital technologies, such as the Internet, promise diverse possibilities for civic engagement within the frameworks of both representative and participatory democracy. Yet, recent evidence has indicated that these opportunities have only been taken advantage of by those sectors of the population already engaged in political mobilization and participation. Findings in the most recent literature demonstrate incontrovertibly that the newer forms of electronic networking have not, in fact, significantly broadened public discourse, and have not fundamentally changed the monopoly of corporate media by powerful economic, structural or political hierarchies (Hindman, 2009, p. 4).

But digital storytelling clearly raises the possibility of cultural resources and the experiential knowledge of citizens to create new dimensions of active discussion, consultation, and debate for citizens within the more heterogeneous public sphere envisaged by Dewey. The exact way in which this could be done is outlined in Lambert's vision of "story catching," a method of harnessing the practice to more overtly political and social aims with the ultimate transformation of political discourses and frameworks:

> [T]o engage us in listening to each other's stories with respect and then perhaps we can sort out new solutions by reframing our diverse connections to the big story . . . as we envision it, story catching will become central to planning and decision-making, the foundation upon which the best choices can be made. (Couldry, 2008, p. 387)

Several fields of application for "story catching," which are also related to new fields of democratic theory and practice, have been developed by non-governmental organizations over the past two decades. One example of the synergy between citizen's narrative and the public sphere envisaged by Lambert is a collaborative venture between Creative Narrations: Multimedia for Community Development, which produces "testimonies that Document, Evaluate and Engage," and the Right Question Project (RQP), which seeks innovative ways to promote "self-advocacy and citizen participation." This participation is a core component of "micro-democracy" as presented by the RQP. *Micro-democracy* is defined as "individuals using essential democratic skills to participate in decisions made in their ordinary encounters with public institutions such as their children's school, the job training program, the welfare office and Medicaid-aided funded health services." These encounters, the site states, "often the end-point of engagement with the public sector can become, instead, the first step up the ladder of democratic action" (RQP, Homepage, ¶1).

A key component of micro-democracy is the creation of digital stories inspired by the encounters of citizens with professionals in institutional spaces which intersect with the formal and associational public sphere: for example, hospitals, schools, and welfare offices. The stories are "the first step up the ladder of democratic action" in fundamental ways. For instance, they enable the perspectives of individual citizens to be presented to professionals and elected representatives, adding to the pool of knowledge and expertise available in the public sphere, and can be disseminated and networked further through media and other public outlets. The stories also enable the citizen-participants to use their own intellectual resources to reflect on the issues which are relevant to their own lives and communities, to foster awareness of the wider contexts which influence or determine their experiences, and to connect those contexts with fundamental questions posed by the structures of power, access to resources and inequalities within society.

One example displayed on the Right Question site is a three-minute narrative entitled "Is Our Baby's Health Important to Government?" created by a young mother, Laura Felix. The story documents in the most direct form the particular ways in which United States' healthcare system impacts particularly hard on women; especially those who hold responsibility for the health of their families and children. Women who have insurance must negotiate an opaque system of regulations, permission, procedures, and barriers designed to hold down costs which restrict even patients with insurance from obtaining medical treatment when most needed. This story relates one mother's direct confrontation with those barriers, and the potentially serious and traumatic effects for herself and her family with an account of her baby's sickness, her specific experiences with the medical services, and her discovery of the lack of insurance access for babies over one year old. The narrative, illustrated with pictures of Laura's family, baby, and insurance card, documents the immediate trauma of her baby's sickness, and from there to Laura's coming to awareness of the link between her personal experience and the in-built deficiencies of public services. The story subsequently reflects on the government's inadequacies in providing health insurance for low-income families, and the inequities built into the system, and finally an appeal to a wider constituency of families like her own. The story concludes:

> Having to think that my son could be very sick next year, I ask myself a lot of questions, like: why do people who have enough money get to have insurance and other people who don't have money get less chances of being insured? Shouldn't we think about our babies when we pick the people who make decisions for our future? Who are the people who make the decisions about who has access and who can't? Have you experienced what it is to struggle with a sick baby and not to have the medicines when they need it? (Felix, 2008, RQP, Homepage, ¶4)

One other core issue facing current political and democratic structures is the attainment of fair representation and social justice for all of the individual and collective identities which comprise a pluralistic modern society. The emergence of new political subjects, and the creation of new forms of identity and new forms of community, has rendered inadequate a conception of justice based exclusively on workers' rights or redistribution of wealth. We have already seen from stories such as "Mixed Race Me" that the "individual," in fact, consists of a *plurality* of identities formed from different encounters with their own personhood, ancestry, and place in society. This concept of individual identity is not a neo-liberal one, and yet cannot be reduced solely to a uniform idea of the "citizen," whose social being is divorced from their race, gender and sexual identity, and who is only able to participate insofar as she or he is initiated into formal and orthodox discourses of the social services, political, and governmental frameworks. Moreover, the identities in contemporary society depicted in corporate broadcasting networks are reduced to highly stereotypical forms. For instance, in "Mixed Race Me," a culture formed of a composite of ethnic, sexual, and gender identities is presented as a positive force, where, in reality, a person who does not fit in with the highly compartmentalized views of society may suffer greatly from intergenerational conflict, neglect, or abuse by both state and society if they do not conform to homogenizing assumptions and discourses concerning identity. This impacts particularly hard on youth, depicted in the media as the grateful recipients of consumerism or as largely white with affluent lifestyles.

The following example is taken from a story represented on the SFC portal, and created as part of the Y.O.U.T.H. Training Project, "Breaking the Silence: LGBTQ Foster Youth Tell Their Stories." The story concerns Nicky, from an Asian family, who suffered physical abuse represented to her as an integral part of religious and cultural tradition. Her queer identity, revealed at the age of thirteen, led to further ostracism in the foster home in which she was placed:

> I told my English teacher about the abuse, and I was quickly sent to the foster care system. I thought I'd finally found a safe haven, but really it was trading one cage for another. Sure, the physical abuse stopped, but the emotional abuse doubled. The other kids in my group called me fag, dyke, homo, freak. Sometimes I would wake up to snickering in the other room, and my body and bed drenched in water. I internalized everything. I was taunted daily and isolated. When I told my staff, they told me to deal with it. It's not like there was a defining tragic moment, it was a constant gnawing away of my self-worth, and just the right to be in the world. (Nicky's Story, 2008, SFC, ¶4)

Nicky's story illustrates the conflicting demands of multicultural societies, within which "traditions" based on religion and received heritage must be respected, and the possible incompatibility of these demands with the politics of sexual identity and personal autonomy which Nicky concludes by espousing and affirming her independence: "At 18, I left the system and flew out of the cage. Now I'm 20, and I see the many challenges I face. I may not have known what my rights were when I was in care, but now I want to make sure all youth know theirs. Tradition no longer binds me" (Nicky's Story, 2008, SFC ¶4).

Nicky's story is symptomatic of broader and conflicting diversities within national society itself. These may frequently represent another obstacle to democratic integration: the pressures caused by diverse interest groups representing issues which may often cause deep divisions within society and which it would be impossible for any constitutional framework of governance to entirely reconcile. Pressure groups often represent deeply felt stances on issues such as abortion, post-civil rights, the legalization of prostitution, and affirmative action. Digital storytelling, by directly representing the impact of the laws concerning these issues on the individuals most immediately affected by them, could further foster constructive dialog between groups holding apparently mutually-exclusive ideas and could be a further conduit for the development of other, more general attributes which should also belong in the broad democratic concept of society (Warschauer, 2004, p. 186).

One example of such an issue is prostitution in the U.S., where contractual sex is still illegal in all states besides Nevada. Associated with human rights violations such as sex tourism and trafficking, prostitution is seen as inherently exploitative and immoral by both conservative and many feminist groups. The story of Maxine Doogan, an organizer with the Erotic Services Providers Union, shares a prostitute's individual perspective in order to defend sex workers' rights to autonomy and self-regulation which could improve the conditions for the sex workers concerned. The following story is illustrated with images which present both contemporary eroticized images of women and archetype of the temptress Eve adorned with a snake, reminding the viewer that the concept of woman's sexuality is informed by a contradictory dualism originating in values rooted in Judeo-Christian morality. The sex worker's voice is urgent and dialogic: she speaks directly to someone who might be one individual but also speaks to the conflicting notions of society as a whole with regard to woman in prostitution:

> You're in a relationship with me, and you don't even know it. You tell me what to wear, you control my money, you pit me and my friends against each other, and when I try to tell you, you don't listen, or, worse yet, you blame me. On one hand, you pretend that, if you ignore me, or abuse me enough, I'll go away and even though you are afraid to be associated with me, you revere me. (Doogan, 2009, SFC, ¶1)

The images portraying the contradictory status of women in society are cross-cut with pictures of Doogan speaking as an advocate for prostitutes' rights, and other images of workers' organization and mobilization. The following extract which accompanies these images illustrates the contradictions involved in liberal democracy's distinction between "personal" and "public" questions. Doogan forcefully contradicts the idea that prostitution, subject to conflicting views of sex as belonging to the personal sphere, does not count as "work" requiring labor rights, still less the right to participate legitimately within the public sphere. This further expands the concept of storytelling as a process of synthesis and interaction which establishes "equivalence" between different struggles for social justice, and negates, for example, the idea of worker's rights pursued at the cost of woman's own interests, or any other interests related to identity or sexuality:

> You're going to try to rescue me. You're going to try to make me work at Macdonald's again . . . . One thing I want you to understand is that we, as workers, need to be in control of anything that has to do with us. Isn't that what most of you want? And some of you certainly have . . . . Don't say you would have acted differently if you had known my story, because you know it now. (Doogan, 2009, SFC, ¶2)

Doogan's story is also emblematic of the argumentation, critical reflection, and dialog inherent in democracy as a process, counteracting both media "spin" and "the pallid and debased level of political debates in contemporary societies that call themselves democratic or 'liberal-democratic'" (Blaug and Schwartzmantel, 2004, p. 6). Moreover, this mode of democratic debate does not attempt the impossible by attempting to eliminate conflict entirely, but, instead, transforms dissent between groups and interests into creative force and practice -- an opportunity for converting personal identity and private interest into an "epistemological tool of public thinking" (Barber, 1984, p. 151).

Digital Storytelling in the Global Mediasphere

As we entered the second decade of the 21st century, global information networks have also opened up possibilities for digital storytelling to be reconfigured and adapted in many different ways on an international scale for participatory purposes. One example is the link of the CDS and other associations in the USA with NGOs in post-apartheid South Africa, where ideals of civil society have had a significant effect on the development of a third sector of NGOs between state and market, and in the development of African ideas of civil society. This has provided an opportunity for the CDS and other institutions to participate in the "global civil society" (Holton, 2008, p. 15) by bringing about a new alliance between non-governmental associations and citizen-led production, and, at the same time, to recover and remediate the "social glue" of shared community experience in the form of citizen-produced

227

stories. These are the building blocks which allow diverse associations to co-operate and share cultural practices and political commitments across national boundaries and across ethnic divisions. According to Lambert:

> The digital storytelling community has described the Internet and new media explosion as a release of a century of pent up frustration at being involved in a one way discourse, electronic media speaks at us but we could not speak back. We want to talk back, not on the terms of the governors of media empires, but on our own terms. (2006, p. xix)

"Speaking back" entails confronting once more the crisis of democracy, which is replicated on a global scale in the form of mass disenfranchisement from the democratic process, monopolized corporate power, and rising levels of poverty in both Western and developing countries (Couldry, 2006, p. 2). Moreover, since much of the world's population is not connected to electronic communication systems of telephone and computing networks, exclusion from the skills, resources, and "knowledge economy" afforded by these networks are greatly exacerbated, widening the gap between those societies and communities with access to the knowledge economy, and those without. This is particularly relevant in the case of the recovery of voices of large but unrepresented numbers of people from their homes in Asia, Africa, and Latin America to the West as either refugees or labor migrants, the subjects of projects such as "Silence Speaks." The narratives of these participants enable a more immediate and intimate knowledge of situations largely depicted in registers which are theoretical and abstract or appropriate to "news" media. They enable us to empathize fully with the pain of people who are either largely invisible within the large part of the labor force or only glimpsed briefly on broadcasting networks as the victims of civil war, dislocation or famine.

One example is the story "Barriers" created by a participant named Waddah, which addresses directly borders, conflict and cross-cultural engagement. The story is an account of a Palestinian immigrant whose early life was irrevocably marked by growing up in an occupied territory. As with the other examples we have looked at, the story is both a micro-political and micro-cultural form: the theme of dislocation, alienation and engagement of the individual is depicted in a narrative that relies on subtle use of imagery and language to engage with wider political themes of the barriers of war, human conflict, and the nation-state:

> Barriers come in many forms. What matters is how you face them. I grew up in a conflict. I woke every morning to the sound of bullets. The smell of the tear gas. The sound of war. Occupations. Curfews. Checkpoints. Evictions. And stolen land. Stolen identity. Resistant. Jailtime. Interrogations. I felt like there was no other world but the one I was in. But God had a plan for me. And an Israeli soldier set it in motion by putting a bullet in my spine when I was seventeen. When I woke up out of being in a coma for seven days, there were new barriers. I couldn't get out of my house because there were sixty steps to climb. The streets and buildings were old and crowded. Accessibility for the disabled was not a priority. (Waddah, 2008, ¶1)

The story continues with Waddah's emigration to the United States. Here, the image of barriers which runs as a unifying thread through his story now symbolize exclusion, not only on ethnic and religious grounds, but for reasons of cultural marginalization and Waddah's status as an immigrant. This exclusion is overcome through Waddah's own exercise of autonomy, single-minded pursuit of education and the will to participate. The metaphor of "barriers to bridges" which concludes the Palestinian's story symbolizes not only Waddah's own transformation from refugee to active citizen, but points towards a vision which transcends local conflict and, again, integrates different struggles against social exclusion, religious and ethnic conflict and closed frontiers of all kinds:

> Some barriers fell, but others arose. Social life, individualism, society and anti-immigrant's policies. All are new challenges, barriers . . . . And after September 11, racial profiling, the Patriot Act, homeland security, and xenophobia made it harder to achieve the so-called American Dream . . . . In 2003, I received my Bachelor of Science in Computer Science. I got my citizenship and now I am working on my Master's in Conflict Resolutions. I have become an advocate for immigrants, refugees and people with disabilities in Oregon and nation-wide. I change barriers to bridges. (Waddah, 2008, ¶3)

Stories such as Waddah's counteract what Nick Couldry (2008, p. 56) terms an "imaginative deficit" which fails to see the interconnected nature of the crisis afflicting economic, political, and social spheres on a national and global level. But the creation of the story and its flow through alternative global media networks also symbolizes the overcoming of barriers between creation and art in all its forms, compartmentalized within a realm of its own and wholly unrelated to life experiences such as Waddah's. As John Dewey pointed out, this barrier between art and experience is itself a product of capitalism and global imperialism, which has brought about "the modern segregation of art and nationalism and militarism" (Dewey, 1934/1980, p. 7). Thus, the story also points toward the potential for intercultural engagement, not solely in the sense of collaboration between professional producers, artists, and authors, but the creation of a new form of culture through the broadening and inclusion of voices which project alternative values capable of transcending conflicts based on ethnic, religious or national divisions.

Conclusion

Throughout this chapter, I have traced some of the themes principally associated with digital storytelling, and, using specific examples, examined the ways in which the practices of digital storytelling embody the concept of communicative democracy as broadly envisaged by John Dewey. This communication is effected by the participation of the public which forms the base on which a democratic society is built. The role of "pluralistic deliberativism" in the public sphere has been developed further in the contemporary era by such thinkers as John Rawls and Jürgen Habermas, and put into specific practice by associations such as the Center for Digital Storytelling and the Right Question Project. Public participation and influence has been a constant and key indicator of democracy from the classical era to contemporary times; but, any prerequisite for this in the contemporary era is the basic principle that an effective voice must be given to every individual, community and constituency that comprises society and nation (Fishkin, 1992, p. 157). The "crisis" in democracy at this juncture in history essentially resides in the fact that this ideal is, as we have seen, problematic and difficult to achieve in the face of the challenges and conflicts facing society -- both national and global -- at the turn of the millennium. Digital storytelling is not a panacea or any kind of complete solution to these challenges and conflicts. The value of digital storytelling lies in the possibilities that it represents. Digital storytelling creates effective voice, constructed from individual citizen-generated perspectives, inspired by concrete and authentic circumstances, and informed by community, and collective heritage.

Transformed into public culture by the associations and organizations which enable the practice, digital storytelling also provides a means of distributing this effective voice through modern technological and communications networks. Such communicative action is also associated with other things, such as the reappropriation of creativity away from the exclusive preserve of elite producers, and resistance to the exclusion of voice, hegemonic corporate interests, and the manipulation of political and public opinion by the mass media. Digital storytelling represents integration and synthesis: the integration of self-expression and interaction with others, the integration of various forms of struggles for social justice. But it also represents the integration of the original distinction made by Dewey between democracy as a social and personal ideal, diffusing throughout modes of human association, with the pre-existing frameworks of democracy as a constitutional system of government comprising elected representatives, offering a constellation of possibilities for the transformation of the "Great Society" into the "Great Community."

REFERENCES

Barber, B. R. (1984). *Strong democracy: Participatory politics for a new age.* Berkeley: University of California Press.

Benavente, J. (2008). Cultural organizing: Third world majority, Raices and M.U.G.A.B.E.E. *Community arts network*, Retrieved from http://www.community arts.net/readingroom/archivefiles/2008/12/cultural_organi_1.php

Blaug, R., and Schwartzmantel, J. (2004). Introduction: Democracy -- Triumph or crisis? In R. Blaug and J. Schwartzmantel (Eds.), *Democracy: A reader* (pp. 1-18). Edinburgh: Edinburgh University Press.

Burgess, J. (2006). Hearing ordinary voices: Cultural studies, vernacular creativity and digital storytelling. *Continuum: Journal of Media and Cultural Studies, 20(2),* 201-214.

Castells, M. (1997). *The rise of the network society.* Oxford: Blackwell.

---. (1998). *End of millennium.* Oxford: Blackwell.

---. (2004). An introduction to the information age. In F. Webster, (Ed.), *The information society reader* (pp. 138-139). New York: Routledge.

Center for Digital Storytelling. About us. Retrieved from http://storycenter..org. about. html

---. History. Retrieved from http://wwww.storycenter.org/history. html

---. Values and principles. Retrieved from http://storycenter.org/principles.html

Certeau, M. (1997). *Culture in the plural.* Minneapolis: University of Minnesota Press.

Couldry, N. (2006). *Listening beyond the echoes: Media, ethics and uncertainty in an uncertain world.* Boulder, CO: Paradigm Publishers.

---. (2008). Digital storytelling, media research and democracy: Conceptual choices and alternative futures. In K. Lundby (Ed.), *Digital storytelling, mediatized stories: Self-representations in new media* (pp. 41-61). New York: Peter Lang.

Creative narrations: Multimedia for community development. Retrieved from http://wwww.creativenarrations.net/

Dewey, J. (1980). *Art as experience.* London: Penguin. (Original published in 1934)

---. (1897). My pedagogic creed. Retrieved from http://www.infed.org/archives /e-text/e-dew-pc-htm

---. (1989). *The public and its problems.* Athens: Ohio University Press. (Original published in 1927)

---. (1958). *Experience and nature.* New York: Dover Publications. (Original published in 1929)

Diamond, L. (1994). Rethinking civil society: Toward democratic consolidation. *Journal of Democracy, 5(3),* 4-17.

Docherty, T. (2006). *Aesthetic democracy.* Stanford: Stanford University Press.

Doogan, M. (2009). Who's your boss? *Stories for Change.* Retrieved from http://stories forchange.net/node/1598

Felix, L. (2008). Is our baby's health important to government? *Right Question Project*. Retrieved from http://rightquestion.org/

Fishkin, J. S. (1992). *The dialogue of justice: Toward a self-reflective society*. New Haven: Yale University Press.

Gilliom, J. (2001). *Overseers of the poor: Surveillance, resistance and the limits of privacy*. Chicago: Chicago University Press.

Habermas, J. (2004). The public sphere. In F. Webster, (Ed.), *The information society reader* (pp. 350-357). New York: Routledge. (Original published in 1974)

---. (1994). Three normative models of democracy. *Constellation, 1(1)*, 1-10.

---. (1996). *Between facts and norms: Contributions to a discourse theory of law and democracy*. Cambridge, MA: MIT Press.

Hartley, J., and McWilliam, K. (2009). Computational power meets human contact. In J. Hartley and K. McWilliam (Eds.), *Story circle: Digital storytelling around the world* (pp. 3-15). New York: Wiley Blackwell.

Holton, R. J. (2008). *Global networks*. New York: Palgrave Macmillan.

Hindman, M. (2009). *The myth of digital democracy*. Princeton: Princeton University Press.

Lambert, J. (2000). Has digital storytelling succeeded as a movement? Some thoughts. *dStoryNews* 2. Retrieved from www.dstory.com/disfo/newsletter_02.html

---. (2006). *Digital storytelling: Capturing lives, creating community*. Berkeley, CA: Digital Diner Press.

---. (2009). Where it all started: The center for digital storytelling in California. In J. Hartley and K. McWilliam (Eds.), *Story circle: Digital storytelling around the world* (pp. 79-90). New York: Wiley Blackwell.

---. (2010). *Digital storytelling cookbook*. Center for Digital Storytelling. Retrieved from http://www.storycenter.org/cookbook.pdf

MASSImpact. Homepage. Retrieved from http://www.massimpact.org/

Mouffe, C. (1988). Radical democracy: Modern or post-modern? In A. Ross (Ed.), *Universal abandon? The politics of postmodernism* (pp. 41-44). Edinburgh: University of Edinburgh Press.

Nicky's story (2008). *Y.O.U.T.H. training project: Breaking the silence: LGBTQ foster youth tell their stories*. Retrieved from http://storiesforchange.net/node/1131

Rawls, J. (1993). *Political liberalism*. New York: Columbia University Press.

Right Question Project (2009). Retrieved from http://rightquestion.org

Silence speaks: Impact on storytellers. Retrieved from http://www.silence speaks.org/impact. html

Siu, D. (2002). Critical philosophy, public problems and the problematic public in John Dewey's political thought. Paper presented at the Annual Society of the American Political Science Association, Boston, MA. Retrieved from http://www.academic.com /meta/p64988index.html

Sobchack, V. (1995). Democratic franchise and the electronic frontier. *Futures, 27(7)*, 725 -734.

Soundararajan, T. (2006) Making community: A conversation with Thenmozhi Soundararajan. In J. Lambert (Ed.), *Digital storytelling: Capturing lives, creating community* (pp. 123-140). Berkeley, CA: Digital Diner Press.

Stone, R. (1996). *The healing art of storytelling*. New York: Hyperion.

Snyder, Y. T. (2007). Mixed race me. *Center for digital storytelling*. Retrieved from http:// www.storycenter.org/stories/index.php?cat=7

Swartz, O., Campbell, K., and Pestana, C. (2009). *Neo-pragmatism, communication and the culture of creative democracy*. New York: Peter Lang.

Waddah. (2008). Barriers. *Progressive communicator's network*. Retrieved from http://pcn.nw.blip.tiv/#1423118

Warschauer, M. (2004). *Technology and social inclusion: Rethinking the digital divide*. Cambridge, MA: The MIT Press.

Notes

1 This crisis takes many forms, but centers on the fragmentation of the body politic caused by the conflicting and diverse interests comprising public life, and the increasing alienation of the public from the representative structures which have been elected to serve them. These specific problems arise against a backdrop of the monopolization of the public sphere by corporate concerns and the dislocation caused by globalization. It is also accepted that corporate monopolization of broadcasting and communication networks is integral to the crisis in democratic frameworks, or, at the very least, has exacerbated the situation.

2 Manuel Castells (1997, 2004) defines the *network society* as an economic and social structure based, in large part, on the use of networked communications technologies and information processing. This profoundly affects patterns of employment, finance and government, all of which are interconnected on an increasingly global scale.

3 Generally, the process of creating a digital story takes three days. The recordings of the stories are preceded by workshops under the supervision of a trainer or facilitator. The workshops comprise an amalgam of pedagogical practices: tutorials, writing exercises, collaborative discussion and scripting, all of which are known as the "story circle" (Hartley and McWilliam, 2009, pp. 3-4). According to Lambert, seven key elements are involved in the process of crafting the experiences, emotions and thoughts of the participants into narrative form. One element is "economy," which is discussed in detail by Lambert (2006, pp. 46-47). Economy of expression and rigorous editing of both script and selection of images is necessary to avoid "meaning overload" which can result from the digital story's multimodal format. Thus digital stories have duration of, generally, three to four minutes.

4 Contemporary network technologies, and, in particular, the Internet have their origins in military and scientific collaboration in the 1960's, related to Cold War concerns. The development of these technologies took place, as Soundararajan (2006, p. 125) points out, simultaneously with the counter-intelligence and repression of civil rights and anti-war groups, native communities, and communities of color. Since the 1960's, the relationship of technology to state-sponsored surveillance networks has broadened with the proliferation of devices such as global positioning satellites, closed-circuit television cameras, and computer data banks which enable greatly increased surveillance capacity. This is used with great effect by the state to monitor marginalized and low-income communities, welfare and social services clients. John Gilliom (2001) documents the highly advanced surveillance system of the welfare bureaucracy on low-income mothers of Appalachian Ohio who, in the day-to-day struggle to care for their families, are subjected to constant monitoring and assessment through a vast network of supercomputers, case workers and fraud agents.

CHAPTER 9

Etiquette as Common Ground: The Relevance of Rules Within Discourse
Communities

Kirstin Ruth Bratt
Penn State University

Moulay Youness Elbousty
Emory University

John Dewey's work in education centers upon the idea of "creative democracy"
as a force that models and nurtures children in their social development.
Creative democracy, as Omar Swartz, Katia Campbell, and Christina Pestana
(2009) have discussed, reinforces the founding ideals of our historical dialogue
as a nation that is constantly evolving in its understanding of what a democratic
nation looks like and can achieve. Democracy, they remind us, is neither static
nor fixed; instead, it is constantly and creatively evolving through social dialogue
and interaction with others. For Dewey, this dialogue evolves most cogently in
schools, for the public school is the workshop of democracy and is an important
"springboard to social progress" (Peters, 1977, p. 112).

Education, Dewey notes, is the cornerstone of our democratic society. At its
best, education serves a social function when the public acknowledges that
students are essential constituents in society and seeks to use educational milieus
to dissolve barriers of class, race, and gender. Those of us whose scholarship
addresses education must be concerned with the ways in which creative
democracy is contextualized in school. When students act within their school
setting, their actions gain meaning in the contextualized sphere of the larger
society. According to Dewey (1897), the "only true education comes through the
stimulation of the child's powers by the demands of the social situations in
which he finds himself. Through these demands he is stimulated to act as a

member of a unity, to emerge from his original narrowness of action and feeling, and to conceive of himself from the standpoint of the welfare of the group to which he belongs" (p. 3). We believe in the importance of making students cognizant of their social relationships and then using these relationships to develop practical and relevant approaches to problem-solving and better relational living.

Dewey argues that "associated living" is the bedrock of a successful democratic society. He explains that education is not a process of acquiring knowledge but, rather, a "process of forming fundamental dispositions, intellectual and emotional, toward man and fellow men" (cited in Tiles, 1992, p. 81). Rosalie M. Romano (2006) concurs with this assessment of the close relationship between democracy and education, stating that Dewey, "Appreciated the close and intimate connections between democracy and education" (p. 503). In our work regarding teacher cohesion, student engagement, and the development of democratic institutions, we have also found that the success of democracy can only be achieved by conscientious efforts directed toward the ideals of collaboration and consensus. As teachers collaborate with one another in organically-created, local communities, we have found that they become empowered to solve problems of local concern and that the commitment to one another and to the students enhances the democratic process. In a small, local community of teachers, voices of dissent and resistance become critically important and well-regarded arbiters of change.

Dewey argues for education as the bedrock of social amelioration and the socialization of the child as the foundation of democratic potential. Through education, social issues can be fixed and societal ills remedied. Jessica Wang (2009) explains that democracy can be modeled and cultivated in a school setting. Indeed, she explains that Dewey was not interested in cultivating young citizens who would be compliant with an institution but, rather, vocal, critical, and thoughtful young participants in democracy. As she notes, "Deweyan democratic education allows everyone to make a contribution in creating a more just and humane world. This requires that we shift the language of rights and responsibilities to that of communication, cooperation, and contribution" (p. 423). Within a democracy, we learn to welcome civil disobedience as a necessary ballast against injustice. As Howard Zinn states, "Without those on bottom acting out their desires for justice, as the government acts out its needs, and those with power and privilege act out theirs, the scales of democracy will be off. That is civil disobedience is not just to be tolerated; if we are to have a truly democratic society, it is a necessity" (1968/2002, p. 25). Similarly, Swartz, et al. explain that Dewey was interested in a creative and dynamic approach to democracy that would be re-interpreted by citizens on an ongoing basis, strengthened by the fact that schools would teach children to think creatively and solve problems. For these authors, a creative democracy is one "that continues dynamically to evolve in its ability to be inclusive, fair, and just through the active participation of all citizens, a society without what [Karl] Marx called a *lumpenproletariate*" (2009, p. 12). The *lumpenproletariate* refers to a surplus population of people considered to be outside of any politically active community, including a nation's homeless, disenfranchised, or imprisoned population.

In this chapter we discuss how people are left out of politically powerful discourse groups and examine two authors from the earlier part of the 20th century who concerned themselves with exclusion and inclusion: John Dewey and Emily Post. In so doing, we interpret Dewey and Post as educators concerned with the democratization of society. As such, each creates a model, or a premise, upon which a creative democracy can be based. However, we also see an antinomy between their purported concepts and the reality of the classroom, which often takes on the hegemonic purpose of creating a compliant populace. The state determines all aspects of public education and its neo-liberal attempts at reform are weakly disguised attempts to gain a firmer grip on the hegemony established in public schooling (see Apple, 2003). We feel it is essential to examine all of these elements within the school context so that students gain a meta-cognitive understanding of the hegemonic forces at large and how they may be counter posed by the creativity of a community at work. We also put forth specific examples of how we might, with our students, co-examine rhetorical and grammatical concepts that uphold hegemony and how we might deconstruct these to support their critical thinking abilities.

As we study the relationships between Post's idea of etiquette and Dewey's idea of teaching, we see and explore connections between the teaching of grammar and the teaching of etiquette, a process that helps us consider etiquette as a type of social grammar through which we can create useful metaphors for the teaching of rhetoric, communication, and composition. In these explorations, we find various conflicting principles: as we find we can use Post's idea of etiquette to teach grammar, we also find that such teaching makes us increasingly uncomfortable about our roles as educators and classroom authorities.

Ambivalence Surrounding Questions of Rhetoric, Etiquette, Privilege, and Power

Our exploration of the relationship between etiquette and grammar demonstrates our ambivalence toward Emily Post and the tensions inherent in the formal teaching of grammar. This close and thorough scrutiny takes place through a variety of lenses. First, we use a narrow lens through which we examine the teaching of grammar as an effort to maintain the social order. Next, we use a wider lens, through which we look specifically at rhetorical choices and their ability to create and maintain hegemony. Finally, we use a mirrored lens, by which we reflect on the rules of specific discourses, defined by James Gee as the "'Identity kit' which comes complete with the appropriate costume and instructions on how to act and talk so as to take on a particular role that others will recognize" (1987, p. 21).

Although her work differs greatly from that of Dewey, Emily Post likewise considered herself an advocate of associated living. Post, a woman from an influential social milieu, was principally interested in the democratization of etiquette. According to her writings on etiquette, the most ordinary person could become well-versed in the social norms of the European courts and, therefore, attain a sort of aristocratic bearing, no matter his or her economic or political standing in the community. For Post, this was one of the most compelling challenges of contemporary life. In one of her most definitive statements, Post argues that the "Best Society is not a fellowship of the wealthy, nor does it seek to exclude those who are not of exalted birth; but it is an association of gentlefolk, of which good form in speech, charm of manner, knowledge of the social amenities, and instinctive consideration for the feelings of others, are the credentials by which society the world over recognizes its chosen members" (1922, p. 3).

Of course, in hindsight, we can see that Post's project was not democratization as much as an effort toward assimilation. To further examine Post's intentions, we can consider how Gee delineates the nature of power and its relation to language. Gee (1987) has defined a particular way of speaking within a particular community, a Discourse, using the capital letter, D, to draw attention to the autonomy of these distinct linguistic communities. In a Discourse, Gee explains, the rules and parameters are ideological, resistant to internal criticism, defined by their relationships to other discourse communities, and concerned with the distribution of power and the centralizing project of the membership. Gee describes discourse communities as concerned with the consolidation of power, a concern we can see if we read carefully between the lines of Emily Post's Etiquette, when she emphasizes the admirable qualities of her own discourse group and encourages their adoption world-wide. For example, Post writes, in 1922, "As a matter of fact, [the] Best Society is not at all like a court with an especial queen or king, nor is it confined to any one place or group, but might better be described as an unlimited brotherhood which spreads over the entire surface of the globe, the members of which are invariably people of cultivation and worldly knowledge, who have not only perfect manners but a perfect manner" (p. 2). This statement clarifies and accentuates the fact her own discourse group is in possession of the highest social credentials and that outsiders must first become conversant with these credentials before they will be admitted.

To develop this point further, we can consider how Frances E. Kendall (2006) explains the maintenance of power in the white community through language. She writes, "One of the areas in which [white people] have the greatest power and privilege is in shaping appropriate language for everyone . . . We use our white privilege to define the parameters of conversation and communication, keeping our culture, manners, and language central" (p. 72). Certainly, we can recognize in Post's project the maintenance of white privilege and power. Furthermore, Kendall writes, "It is essential to remember that we enter into interactions about our blind spots with enormous power and privilege imbalances. Being blinded by our privilege often keeps us from being able to see or to hear clearly, especially if the person with whom we are speaking is different from us" (p. 128). Even in Kendall's "we" is a latent form of hegemony; she has the self-agency to declare the "we" and assume that her audience is white. Nonetheless, her point here is useful. Our conversations with students are often governed by power differentials. Our ability to glimpse or snatch at a truth about the relationship is often shrouded in uncertainty.

On the surface, Emily Post's primary concern seems to be empathy. She reflects at every turn the notion that nobility does not emanate from wealth as much as from a person's ability to anticipate and provide for the emotional needs of others. At least on the surface, it seems that she would easily concur with Chinua Achebe (1989), who writes that a "person who is insensitive to the suffering of his fellows is that way because he lacks the imaginative power to get under the skin of another human being and see the world through eyes other than his own" (p. 149). Yet, as we have seen, Post's underlying message to the implied reader is anything but egalitarian, reinforcing at every turn the social hierarchy of those who have, not resources necessarily, but access to the dominant discourse. For example, her lessons often draw upon metaphors that are most familiar to members of the dominant discourse, including images from commerce and banking, elegant balls and dinners, and luxury travel. For instance, her metaphor for associated living discusses our human interactions as deposits in a bank: "Life, whether social or business, is a bank in which you deposit certain funds of character, intellect and heart; or other funds of egotism, hard-heartedness and unconcern; or deposit -- nothing! And the bank honors your deposit, and no more. In other words, you can draw nothing out but what you have put in" (1922, p. 65). Without consideration for the limitations imposed by poverty, she offers her readers a glimpse toward the future, stating unequivocally that all of our wishes have the potential to come true: "Would you, if you could have your wish granted by a genie, choose to have the populace look upon you askance and in awe, because of your wealth and elegance, or would you wish to be loved, not as a power conferring favors which belong really to the first picture, but as a fellow-being with an understanding heart?" (p. 65). Both possibilities, she assures us, are within our reach.

The goal of Post's reader, then, is to seek worthiness; that is, to fit the profile of the implied reader, manipulating and managing oneself in an effort to find herself within that scope of reference. Of course, this is an impossible feat, due to the fact that Post denies the existence of the other in her effort to claim a wide and general audience for her work. Those who remain outside of Post's implied audience, then, must have landed by their own disgrace and are then unworthy of her gracious welcome. On the other hand, Dewey's invitation to all is sincere: he goes to great lengths to assure his reader that the public school system must accommodate *all* families, as we continually see in his writings. Unlike Post, he deliberately mentions the families of poverty being served alongside wealthy families.

If Emily Post's project is the democratization of etiquette, as she claims, then one must wonder how upward mobility for all could possibly be imagined. Indeed, the *lumpenproletariate* of Marxist theory cannot necessarily gain access to the principles of Post's etiquette or adequate practice in the settings that Post describes. Post pretends to be inclusive, inviting all her readers to become members of this newly-created class of Americans who, despite their economic or family status, can rise to a higher social status on the virtue of their manners and adherence to the rules of etiquette. Yet upward mobility for all requires access to the dominant discourse and practice in its principles; furthermore, upward mobility for all is not mobility if everyone is moving in the same direction. In any case, it seems unlikely that Post could be construed as sincere; rather, the reader must understand that the implied reader of Post is a more focused population than she concedes. Indeed, Post must limit her audience or risk endangering her project. As Deborah Mutnick (1996) explains, "In order to renew belief in the possibility of success, of upward social mobility, as well as justify the systemic need for cheap labor, it would always be necessary to construct an 'other' against whom those more privileged could measure themselves" (p. 104).

Even though Post might respond to this critique by defending her emphasis on polite and sincere listening to others and responding to their needs, still the conversations she expects and defends are firmly rooted in hegemonic discourse. Certainly we can see, in Post, evidence for Kendall's accusation that white privilege is always centralized in an effort to maintain power. In her Etiquette, Emily Post provides various examples of how power is maintained. She concerns herself with the shaping, construction, and maintenance of a centrally-located discourse: a discourse that, while Post promotes it for the general public, is nevertheless located within the American elite classes. Post speaks of this discourse as a hybrid, consisting of a uniquely American sensibility, drawing upon the history and manners of the European courts. Her insistence that this discourse be available to the multitude might be seen, especially by members of her in-group, as a democratizing gesture; however, outsiders would certainly recognize her insistence as an appropriation of power and an attempt to centralize her discourse group and marginalize all others.

Certainly questions might arise as to Post's innocence as a hegemon. Louise Rosenblatt (2005) might have considered her naive yet innocent. She notes that if we "tend to feel that our ways have an inherent rightness and divine sanction, that, too, is an illusion that we share with individuals shaped by other cultures, which seem equally self-justified to them" (p. 52). Yet Ngũgĩ wa Thiong'o would have considered Rosenblatt's apologia not only naive, but also dangerous. Ngũgĩ warns us against being seduced by the seeming innocence of those who are complicit with the colonizing powers, especially those who do not condone or engage in physically violent acts against the colonized. He explains the seductive power of oppression and its relationship to language when he writes that the first mode of captivation "was to suppress the languages of the captive nations. The second [was to elevate] the language of the conqueror. It became the language of the elect" (1994, pp. 31-32).

Also, in terms of hegemonic language, Gayatri Chakravorty Spivak (1996) provides a specific example, in her work on hegemony and language, when she asks of India: "If we were a white country, might our hybrid English have been another English, as different from British as is American? What about the fact that we have flourishing, developing vernaculars? At any rate, the creative level of Indian English was always defined as a deviation" (p. 20). Spivak's question is particularly apt for this discussion because Emily Post makes such naïve assumptions about the greatness of her own discourse group and the rightness of its hegemony that one wonders whether her naïveté is invented or sincere.

Is there a social hierarchy or a democratic principle to etiquette? Truly, Post's message is as ambivalent as our response. Post's goal is at base a democratic one; that is, to treat everyone with dignity and consideration so as to coexist harmoniously and peacefully. Although, in so doing, she emulates the manners of the wealthy: both to draw in the audience and to dignify her topic. She does this because it reflects her belief system: that to be deserving of respect, one must imitate as closely as possible the dominant discourse of hegemony. Post writes, "Etiquette must, if it is to be of more than trifling use, include ethics as well as manners. Certainly what one is, is of far greater importance than what one appears to be" (p. 3)

References to Emily Post on language and etiquette must be placed carefully in their context. Writing in 1922, as the United States grappled with its post-World War I identity on the world stage and in the development of the League of Nations, Emily Post was clearly proud of her country, employing a hegemonic discourse of wealth and privilege, in keeping with pro-war rhetoric, to appeal to the masses. She praises the US as the greatest nation on earth, even as she offers veiled warnings that the country must not fall into disrepute:

> We are studying and cultivating and buying and making, and trying to forget and overcome that terrible marriage of our beautiful Colonial ancestress with the dark-wooded, plush-draped, jig-sawed upstart of vulgarity and ignorance. In another country her type would be lost in his, forever! But in a country that sent a million soldiers across three thousand miles of ocean, in spite of every obstacle and in the twinkling of an eye, why even comment that good taste is pouring over our land as fast as periodicals, books and manufacturers can take it... In our own country, beautiful houses and appointments flourish like field flowers in summer; not merely in the occasional gardens of the very rich, but everywhere... It is no idle boast that the world is at present looking toward America; and whatever we become is bound to lower or raise the standards of life. (p. 619)

Post believed strongly in the divine right of the fittest, and she believed her native country, the United States of America, had earned some claims of divinity. As she describes it, her country, a newly-emerging world power, had been successful in the war and generous with both allies and enemies. This success and generosity created a world stage on which the United States could become a force of change in the world: a force she hoped would reflect not the evil of the Great War, but rather the best of human kindness and goodness.

Not only does Post use war imagery to assert her nation's greatness, but she also uses agricultural, genital, and regal metaphors to reach her readers on a more visceral level. She describes the "best society" as having been sown and cultivated. She refers to those in high social positions as having a "long purse," and she compares "uncivilized" societies with cave-dwellers (p. 1). She explains that jewels and queens should be hidden from the glare of the spotlight, and that those who seek fame through their wealth are often more "jesters" than "queens" (p. 2). These metaphors work to confirm, at least for Post's intended audience, the rectitude and worthiness of the white American upper-class values she espoused. She uses metaphoric language to its best advantage by finding opportunities to admire and even glorify the group she hopes to establish firmly in place as a ruling class.

Emily Post describes etiquette as a set of evolutionary principles governed by the manners of the European courts. Yet the human condition, being dependent upon its social function, has always depended upon civility for its survival. As Nietzsche (2004) writes, our faith in conventions and laws implies a persistent fear of God: "I fear we do not get rid of god because we still believe in grammar" (p. 17). Concerns over rhetoric as it links to etiquette and hospitality can be seen in many formational literatures, from the *Gilgamesh* of the Mesopotamian region to *Sundiata* of Mali to the Homer's *Odyssey*, Cervantes' *Quixote*, Murasaki's *Tale of Genji*, and the Iroquois *Codes of Governance*. Dewey (1997/1938) reiterates the fact that codes of conduct, while they vary from place to place, are universal: "The particular form a convention takes has nothing fixed and absolute about it. But the existence of some form of convention is not itself a convention. It is a uniform attendant of all social relationships. At the very least, it is the oil which prevents or reduces friction" (p. 59). What is unique about Emily Post's version? Certainly its artificial nature, its self-consciousness, and its attention to detail. While most forms of etiquette evolve organically within and according to a particular time and place, Post's etiquette is in fact not organic and is more strict and rigid than most codes because it attempts to adapt a foreign institution, the British court, to a new environment, the American landscape.

Post's assumption that civility might be transported from the external environment, or worse, from a foreign source, is debunked by Hans-Georg Gadamer, who writes, "Learning to speak does not mean learning to use a preexistent tool for designating a world already somehow familiar to us; it means acquiring a familiarity and acquaintance with the world itself and how it confronts us" (1976, p. 63). Post might have done well to adopt a more organic view of hospitality by considering the geographical and political realities of the United States and drawing her examples from the local environment in which she found herself in the early 20th Century, rather than using English country cottages and dinners with Dukes and Earls for her examples. But then she would have belied her true purpose, for she would have had to have been more tuned in to the masses -- the indigenous people of the United States and the centuries of forced and voluntary immigration that created a country very different from Post's beloved England, and her project might have been compromised because her implied audience would have had to change dramatically.

In a manner which would seem unconscionable to Emily Post, a subversive reader of the world might disrupt the social order so carefully described by Post and so seemingly desirable on the surface, at least for Post's implied readers and their followers. Goffman explains that "Unmeant gestures, inopportune intrusions, and faux pas are sources of embarrassment and dissonance which are typically unintended . . . . However there are situations . . . in which an individual acts in such a way as to destroy or seriously threaten the polite appearance of consensus" (1959, p. 210). Such an attitude would be unimaginable to Post, who throughout the etiquette maintains the assumption that all implied readers desire to attain her principles and will apply them if provided access and practice.

Metaphors of Power and Privilege for Novice Rhetoricians

As rhetoricians and communication scholars we wholeheartedly agree to and endorse this assertion of William O'Grady, Johan Archibald, and Janie Rees-Miller (2009) when they write that there is "no such thing as a good grammar or a bad grammar. In fact, all grammars do essentially the same thing: they tell speakers how to form and interpret the words and sentences of their language . . . . There is no such thing as a language that doesn't work for its speakers" (p. 8). With this insight, we began to examine our early experiences with etiquette and its relationship to rhetoric, communication, and democracy. We began to consider the parallels between our demands for, in social situations, "proper" etiquette and, in teaching situations, "proper" grammar. Our debate in the study of rhetoric and composition should no longer be about whether or not to teach explicitly the rules of grammar, but that the rules of grammar must be made transparent for students in much the same way that other hegemonic documents must become transpicuous if a democratic distribution of power and responsibility is a larger social goal. Thus we began to use metaphors from Emily Post's Etiquette to teach grammar as a social etiquette rather than as a series of detached rules and regulations of rhetoric.

For many students, the effort to gain a voice in dominant discourse creates anxiety about how one will be perceived in public. As Judith Butler writes, "If I am trying to give an account of myself, it is always to someone, to one whom I presume to receive my words in some way, although I do not and cannot know always in one way" (2004, p. 67). Post explains that many of the rules of etiquette seem arbitrary to novice practitioners, writing that "many other arbitrary rules for eating food with fork, spoon or fingers, are also stumbling blocks rather than aids to smoothness" (1922, p. 585). Patti Lather, in her discussion of Mikhail Bakhtin and arbitrariness, states, "All thought is not equally arbitrary, Bakhtin argued . . . positionality weighs heavily in what knowledge comes to count as legitimate" (1991, p. 116).

Post can assist us in making the relationship of punctuation to the maintenance of the social order very transparent to our students. As Barthes writes, "The Sentence is hierarchical: it implies subjections, subordinations, internal reactions. Whence its completion: how can a hierarchy remain open?

The Sentence is complete" (1975, p. 50). In general, rules of grammar merely reflect rules of social order. They serve to maintain the hegemony of the powerful, and learning them well can serve either compliance or subversion. Furthermore, we begin to see more explicitly how the very sentence, its form made transparent, becomes a metaphor for the inequitable distribution of power and the false hierarchies that must be constructed for the convenience of the punctuation mark.

On the surface, Post seems to imply that the rules of social order are flexible. She says that a man who wishes to eat with his fingers at home, for example, need only ask for a finger bowl to serve the rules of etiquette, yet even this concession implies a fixed set of pre-determined rules. This manner of thinking about and teaching etiquette has direct parallels to the way that structures of grammar function in writing. Hence, Post's rules are often useful for creating metaphors for grammar instruction. However, once an instructor considers the relationship of etiquette and grammar, s/he is confronted by the fact that such rules of etiquette are inherently hegemonic and elitist. Such an understanding can lead the instructor then to think more deeply and share more frankly with students about the nature of grammar and its relationship to power and democracy.

Post explains some of the difficulties in becoming conversant with the dominant discourse. For non-English speakers, Post states, "English is not beautiful in sound to the foreign ear; it is a series of esses and shushes, lumped with consonants like an iron-wheeled cart bumping over a cobble-stoned street" (1922, p. 611). She goes on to explain that errors in speech and writing become a hindrance when attempting to communicate, stating, "Just as one discordant note makes more impression than all the others that are correctly played in an entire symphony" (p. 604). In these examples, Post illustrates what Dwayne Huebner (1999) explains in his work on discourse: "When language becomes conspicuous as unusable in a given situation, when it becomes obtrusive and gets in the way, or when the 'right' words or language forms are not available to be used, then language shows itself as language -- as words, expressions, and rules for usage" (p. 147). Post's project, then, is to help her implied reader gain comfort with the rules of the dominant discourse. She assures this reader over and over again that gaining access to the discourse is not only possible, but simply a matter of learning and practicing the rules. With adequate training, Post promises, "Americans of the best type go all over the world, fitting in so perfectly with their background that not even the inhabitants notice they are strangers; in other words they achieve the highest accomplishment possible" (p. 604).

Dewey explains that learning rules can be comforting for children, who, by learning the rules, learn to control their own reactions and emotions surrounding accepted modalities. As he notes, "There are certain fairly obvious controlling features of such situations to which I want to call attention. The first is that the rules are a part of the game. They are not outside of it. As long as the game goes on with a reasonable smoothness, the players do not feel that they are submitting to external imposition but that they are playing the game" (1938/1997, pp. 52-53). Similarly, Mina Shaughnessy (1977) posits that novice writers need guidance in understanding the basic codes and principles of rhetoric so that they are aware of the rules of dominant discourse and, thus, able to resist them when they choose to do so.

Dewey explains how an instructor can create lessons in rhetoric that are empty and false or meaningful and relevant, stating, "It is possible, of course, for these social forms to become, as we say, 'mere formalities'" (p. 59). Post explains that the needs of an audience are often unpredictable, but still they must be anticipated; thus, a thoughtful host, or an inviting writer, might anticipate the needs of the audience, whether guest or reader, and might then lead this audience through uncertain moments or conflicts of opinion. To use these ideas in instruction, we consider how Post helps us prioritize the needs of others, and how she simplifies the rules of etiquette so that even a socially awkward person can understand and apply them. The most important quality of the "best society," according to Post, is the ability to use language well, and that means using language appropriately in any given situation. As she explains, "Manners are made up of trivialities of deportment which can be easily learned if one does not happen to know them; manner is personality -- the outward manifestation of one's innate character and attitude toward life" (1922, p. 2).

So we run a risk, by using metaphors from Emily Post to teach grammar, of serving the colonial project to which Emily Post subscribes. Thus, even as we have found Emily Post's *Etiquette* to be a useful source of material for creating metaphors to teach standard punctuation principles, we have also found it a useful source through which to view and critique dominant discourse strategies. This strategy of giving precise definitions followed by expansive examples exemplifies her style as a teacher, and it is this method of teaching that makes her work fluidly transferable to other topics, such as the teaching of grammar. However, it is her insistence on the "correct" and the "acceptable" that makes her ideas so controversial for those of us who want to practice a more liberating pedagogy in writing courses.

Yet these metaphors, rather than serving the project, can also serve to make it transparent. For us, the goal is to explore with students the dominant discourse of the university and its compliance with the social order. Such a demand for order is exemplified in the rhetor's insistence for clear and concise writing, made possible by the rules governing the use of commas, modifiers, sentence structures, and other conventions of modern grammar. Audre Lorde (1999) writes that the oppressor uses various methods to keep masses "occupied with the master's concerns" (p. 113). As writing and communication instructors, it remains our responsibility to remind ourselves and our students of this powerful reality and to concern ourselves with the teaching of grammar and rhetoric in a way that makes the master's concerns pellucid and that uses the master's tools to become interrogators, not only of our internal workings, but also of the external forces that govern us.

The Metaphor as a Device for Teaching Rhetoric, Etiquette, and Privilege

Post introduces complex concepts in an encouraging manner, introducing various puzzles for her readers to analyze and then solve under the careful guidance of a knowledgeable instructor. For example, Post often introduces a certain situation that a person might encounter, such as a dinner invitation to a country cottage, dinner with the queen, and a picnic at the shore with one's close friends; then Post, after describing these widely divergent situations, reduces the expected etiquette into simple principles. For Post, the basic principles for dining with company are always the same: arrive and leave at the most appropriate time, be attentive to the needs of the people around you and grateful to the host, use conversation to charm and delight others, never to offend.

As a teacher of basic principles, Post uses a whole-to-part strategy, beginning with concise and simple definitions; thereinafter, offering specific examples that expand upon, and sometimes complicate, the concept. We see this strategy exemplified when Post writes about how to behave if invited to dinner abroad: "Under ordinary circumstances no knowledge whatsoever beyond the social amenities the world over are necessary. A dinner abroad is exactly the same as one here. You enter a room, you bow, you shake hands, you say, 'How do you do.' You sit at table, you talk of impersonal things, say 'Good-by' and 'Thank you' to your hostess, and you leave" (1922, p. 608). Post follows this rather simple explanation with a catalog of exceptions, expansions, and clarifications. She details more specific expectations, but she always returns to the basic concept, emphasizing that one cannot fail socially if one can maintain the basic principles she sets forth. Post understands the basic reality that Gadamer (1977) presents to us: learning is not just repeating or reproducing but, rather, applying meta-cognitive awareness to the acquisition of knowledge.

Some grammar handbooks could stand to learn from Post's method of whole-to-part teaching. A grammar handbook often lists the basic principles rather than grouping or categorizing them in a way that helps a learner to manage and easily absorb the new information. For example, grammar handbooks often provide somewhere between five and fifteen functions of a comma, giving various details about how to punctuate words, phrases, lists, details, and clauses within a sentence. Even Strunk and White's *Elements of Style* (2008), considered by many rhetoricians to be the most elegant of handbooks on style, delineates the rules governing comma use; following in the tradition of Strunk and White, most grammar handbooks continue to present the rules of the comma as disconnected and separate (Konrad & Adelman, 2000; Shoup & Loberger, 2009; Raimes, 1998). In contrast, Post looks for the simplest explanation of a principle and expounds upon it in subsequent examples. She seeks the simplest path to appropriate behavior, explaining any possible divergences later. In describing the use of the comma, Post might have said that there is really only one function of the comma: to maintain the integrity of the main clause and to subordinate any of its interrupters or contradictors. This would reflect a classic Emily Post style, as numerous examples of simple and clear language resonate throughout the text, always followed by more detailed descriptions and elaborations on the same theme for a more advanced learner or one who requires further explanation.

It is an attribute to Emily Post that we have come to call the comma, affectionately, the "excuse me" mark, and rather than start by offering our students any of the long lists of various comma functions listed in grammar/punctuation guides and internet sites, we begin in Post's style by giving a single, simplified rule to guide them and then allow the more specific details about the comma to follow on a want-to-know or need-to-know basis. In simplest terms, the "excuse me" mark is needed to manage a contradiction or interruption of the main clause, in much the same way that a person of lesser status is expected to offer some apology when interrupting or contradicting a person of higher status. The main clause needs never to excuse itself with a comma, while a subordinate clause must do so if it is interrupting or contradicting the main clause.

Furthermore, the subordinating conjunction, the semi-colon, and the coordinating conjunction are examples of grammatical concepts that can be taught with metaphors according to the rules of etiquette. The rule is simply this: when two equally important figures meet, there must be a separate yet equal maintenance of power between them. Each of the figures must be accorded the same measure of respect. When two main clauses meet, they must be punctuated strongly, so as not to run them together nor allow one to dominate the other. The comma is fine for bridging the gap from one lesser being to a greater, but two people of equal status need stronger punctuation, such as the semi-colon to mark their separate but equal positions. Another option, of course, is to employ a subordinating conjunction that would weaken one of the clauses, making it a dependent clause, and thereby allowing it to be punctuated less strongly, or not at all. In a similar vein John Dawkins (1995) explains the rules of punctuation as quite simple: one must understand that the independent clause is the basis of all punctuation and that all other punctuation marks are meant to create a relationship to this independent clause. Marks exist in a hierarchy and so can either raise or lower the status of added words and phrases, but always in relation to the independent clause.

In the same way that we can learn to subordinate certain phrases or clauses, we also learn to subordinate ourselves to authority. René H. Díaz (2003) argues that teaching grammar systematically encourages students to accept oppression. He postulates that standardized and rigid grammar rules create two layers of society: those who are in control of language and those who are not, and that those who speak "perfect English" are considered to be "at the top of our economic chain" (p. 7). He also quotes James Baldwin who writes, "It goes without saying, then, that language is also a political instrument, means, and proof of power" (2003). Diaz also quotes Dawkins (1995) regarding the relative simplicity of punctuation. Like Post often does, Dawkins reduces a complicated set of seemingly scattered and divergent ideas into a manageable set of principles, claiming that learning punctuation through a systematic procedure is far "easier than learning to use a list of poorly ordered rules" (Dawkins, 1995, p. 546). Similarly, Emily Post does not expect her readers to read her book straight through and memorize every detail; rather, she writes the most simplified expectation first and then catalogues the details on subsequent pages.

Post promotes careful and thoughtful communication, as do other rhetoricians (for instance, Graff & Birkenstein, 2006). Post's contempt for over-dressing and over-doing, and her lessons on hosting a visitor with continual concern for the visitor's needs and comfort can be seen in the rhetorician's concerns as well. As Post writes, "Remember that every word of writing is immutable evidence for or against you, and words which are thoughtlessly put on paper may exist a hundred years hence" (1922, p. 503). Post's admonitions resemble the composition instructor's disdain for wordiness, insistence on audience awareness. Composition instructors expect novice rhetoricians to develop confidence in one's position, anticipate counter-arguments, and establish warrant as a bridge to the reader.

Perhaps not surprisingly, the hegemonic discourse of Emily Post almost mirrors the American style of rhetoric that is typically taught in the American university (see Graff & Birkenstein, 2006; Toulmin, 2003). Rhetoric and composition instructors require a thesis, development of the thesis, and a sense of audience; the assertion, or thesis statement, and its development, must be presented in a logical, ordered, sequential format. Furthermore, the idea of establishing warrant in writing, according to Stephen Toulmin (2003), is to create a bridge of understanding between audience and speaker.

For Post, as for composition instructors, less is more. Post emphasizes, as we often do in our own composition classrooms, rhetorical choices that exemplify one's grace, eloquence, fluency, and precision. As novelist Edith Wharton, writing at the same time as Post and imagining many similar characters as Post, often complains of the vulgarity of the newly-moneyed Americans, so also does Emily Post warn her readers against the vulgarity of those who, newly in possession of wealth and privilege, would flaunt these luxuries in the company of others. As Post explains, to be "over-dressed is always in bad taste" (p. 559) and she sprinkles statements of similar sentiment throughout the text, always encouraging efficiency and simplicity in manners, dress, and habits. Post disdainfully describes the stereotype of the young American girl in Europe as vulgar, garish, giggling, sarcastic, and over-stimulated. She describes this American girl's false sense of intimacy with strangers, especially when she is traveling abroad, and she admonishes all young women against assuming that a stranger who feigns an interest is truly interested in her chatter. In effect, she describes the American girl in Europe as someone who makes poor rhetorical choices.

Edith Wharton's novels often describe a young American girl traveling abroad, and Wharton also includes many "newly moneyed" Americans among her cast of characters. As Post indicates, these newly moneyed are rarely in possession of the rules of dominant discourse, and therefore, make egregious errors, yet she encourages these people to practice correct forms repeatedly, stating, "Many women, . . . handicapped by circumstances, have not only made possible a creditable position for themselves, but have then given their children the inestimable advantage of learning their mother tongue correctly at their mother's knee" (1922, p. 64). Similarly, many students of grammar and rhetoric are new and unfamiliar with the requirements of the essay. Our efforts to train them are also, like Post's, efforts to bridge a gap toward those who are privy to the hegemonic discourse.

Post's stereotype of the vulgar young woman reminds us of one of our own long-held stereotypes: that of the insensitive student writer who does not consider her or his professor a worthy audience for her time and her energy. One young woman we heard on campus recently provided a ready example. Walking along the sidewalk on campus and discussing an essay assignment with her friend, she exclaimed loudly and arrogantly: "Only five pages? Oh that's easy. I can bullshit five pages!" These words are spoken among friends, members of a specific discourse that does not include us, her professors, yet loud enough for any professors walking along the same path to hear. This student discourse demands a flippant attitude, replete with carefully placed casual gestures and calculatedly cool tone. Yet, regardless of the circumstances surrounding the moment, it is plausible that this woman takes for granted the professor's interest in her work, assuming that the professor's position and salary, however paltry, create for her a captive audience who must necessarily be interested in her essays, however poorly constructed or false.

Post, with considerable patience, defends the warrantless young American girl, just as many of us forgive our students for their carelessness, by providing our sincere and heartfelt critique. Post writes that the American girl, however vulgar abroad, is likely a lovely person at home with her family. It is when she finds herself in a strange context that she behaves badly, in spite of her training in good manners. Similarly, writing and other communication instructors often realize that our students feel discomfort as writers, and thus behave strangely. Lucille Parkinson McCarthy (1994) writes, "The contexts for writing may be so different from one classroom to another, the ways of speaking in them so diverse, the social meanings of writing and the interaction patterns so different, that the courses may be for the student writer like so many foreign countries" (p. 151). Understanding the uncertainty and foreignness of our student writers, instructors often respond generously, not so much with forgiveness as with our time and our sincerity, offering our advice and feedback in response to their written work.

Post advocates generosity within carefully established limits. This requires a careful balance of concern for the *community* versus *self-care* that, she claims, does not come naturally to a person but is instead a sign training. She writes, "A really well-bred person is as charming as possible to all, but effusive to none, and shows no difference in manner either to the high or to the lowly when they are of equally formal acquaintance" (1922, p. 67). This sense of the self in relation to the community creates a sense of warrant that is closely related to the idea of warrant in rhetorical situations. Post's version of warrant is related to an individual's ability to seek permission from the other in a social situation. The newly-moneyed, in Post's assessment, have not had access to the discourse of the elite and are unable to communicate with the required elegance and grace. Post's version of warrant, with its focus on rhetorical elegance, is particularly helpful to us in relating the concept of warrant to novice rhetoricians. While the idea may be similar to the crime-show version known by our students: an officer approaches a judge with reasons for a search or arrest and the judge then decides whether the benefit to the public good outweighs the individual's right to privacy, Post's version is more genteel: a rhetorician seeks affirmation by bridging gaps of understanding between rhetor and audience. Post promises her reader that to establish warrant, the rhetor must simply be genuine, sincere, kindly, and intelligent. She writes: "A genuine, sincere, kindly American man -- or woman -- can go anywhere and be welcomed by everyone, provided of course, that he is a man of ability and intellect. One finds him all over the world, neither aping the manners of others nor treading on the sensibilities of those less fortunate than himself" (1922, p. 59). As writing instructors, the idea of bridging gaps between the needs of the individual and the community work best when the author seeks the reader's confidence by demonstrating, through thoughtful and sincere methods of gathering evidence, reasoning logically, and providing examples, that her argument is worth hearing.

Throughout her *Etiquette*, Post's implied reader seems to be the newly-moneyed female in the Post-World War I United States. This newly-moneyed woman seems to be of particular concern to Post. She directs many of her exhortations toward her, emphasizing particularly the need to establish warrant in rhetorical situations, including the need to exercise caution, efficiency, and concern for others. For example, Post argues that a "knowledge of etiquette is of course essential to one's decent behavior, just as clothing is essential to one's decent appearance; and precisely as one wears the latter without being self-conscious of having on shoes and perhaps gloves, one who has good manners is equally unself-conscious in the observance of etiquette, the precepts of which must be so thoroughly absorbed as to make their observance a matter of instinct rather than of conscious obedience" (1922, p. 1). For this newly-moneyed woman, who has long resided outside the dominant discourse and is seeking a way in, Post advocates equality.

The Study of Power Relationships in the Workplace of Democracy

According to Wang (2009), Dewey's work during the 1920s predicted a steady and recognizable trend toward democratic governance, but he did not feel vainglorious about it. Instead, Dewey cautioned against the "conceit" of those "advanced" nation-states for assuming that "they were so near the apex of evolution as to wear the crown of statehood" (p. 409). When we speak of the democratic society, we are implying not only a creative function and force to the people who fully participate in the democratic process, but also a need to carefully guard the democracy against corruption. This democratic engagement requires communication, as Swartz and his co-authors remind us: "Society, particularly if it is understood in terms of creative democracy, implies that communication is an important aspect in the life of all citizens" (2009, p. 43). Education is a key component in achieving democracy, as Dewey makes clear in his many writings on the topic.

While Dewey advocates for few parameters for controlling the behavior of children in opposition to Post whom advocates for many, both, in fact, provide minimal yet useful parameters for the instruction of children. Both attempt to provide meaningful experiences for learners that are meant to be instructive rather than limiting. On the surface, certainly, there are direct contradictions between Dewey's exhortations about the freedom of the child and Post's insistence on company manners. Yet, a closer reading of these contradictions may reveal some common themes related to our contemporary methods of teaching writing, communication, and rhetoric and their relation to democratic structures and the lives of citizens. These contradictions can certainly provide an opportunity for students to examine the hegemony of grammar instruction through lenses that simultaneously compete against and complement one another.

Our discussion of these two divergent authors, Post and Dewey, is based in our most fervent belief that rhetoric, discourse, and literacy are crucial factors determining whether a community and its people simply survive together or whether they form a meaningful social community. As Swartz, et al, write, "Language is an important resource of power for individuals and communities -- power that can be used to institutionalize cruelty, poverty, and hatred, or to emphasize human connectedness and facilitate redescription, transformation, and liberation" (2009, p. 33). We believe that a focus on democracy must include a focus on education, and, as Dewey and Post both exhort us, we must focus on the needs of children to develop within the human family in a manner that promotes and models democracy while also nurturing the child's social intelligence.

John Dewey and Emily Post would easily agree that communication is a necessary element of citizenship. Dewey (1916/1997) postulates that education "in its broadest sense, is the means of this social continuity of life" (p. 2). He argues that education is essential to the existence of human lives. Through education we transmit our customs and beliefs from one generation to another. Thus, education preserves and improves our civilization. Dewey describes manners as rules of a game, a metaphor for the social control that must be part of a community that lives together and respects its individual members. He argues that all societies, going back in history and around the world, have these codes and manners in order to function as social entities: not that the particular forms of such codes and manners are consistent, but that their existence is. Dewey explains that children routinely "at recess or after school play games ... [which] involve rules, and these rules order their conduct . . . . The rules . . . are fairly standardized." Playing-field disagreements usually arise not because there are rules, but because someone violates a rule. Thus, there can be "social control of individuals without the violation of freedom" (Dewey, 1938/1997, pp. 52-54).

We know that John Dewey struggled with similar questions about how the family environment might reinforce or be supported by the school. He strongly recommends that schools restructure their classrooms and promote teaching methods that nurture knowledge-seeking behaviors among children (1899/1990). To undergird his point, he imparts his vision of the ideal home for cultivating young learners. Dewey states that the child should learn through the "social converse and constitution of the family. There are certain points of interest and value to him in the conversation carried on; statements are made, inquiries arise, topics are discussed, and the child continually learns" (Dewey, as cited in Boydston, 1976, pp. 23-24). Philip Jackson calls this cultivation 'learning to learn,' and he explains that the child's world has to expand, providing increasing access to resources for the development of his knowledge base (Jackson, 1998, p. 425). Also concurring with this idea is Jerome Bruner (1996), who writes, "Since schooling is one of life's earliest institutional involvements outside the family, it is not surprising that it plays a critical role in the shaping of Self" (p. 35).

If school is to be a workshop for democracy, it is essential that the school and the family both support democratic principles and, much more importantly, that the nation's children attend these schools together. Unfortunately, in spite of the early ideals of public schooling, public schools are not a place where all children of society come together to learn about democracy; instead, the parents who can afford to do so send their children to private schools. Perhaps we have never fulfilled the ideals of our earliest public educators, who believed they could use the public school as a place to encourage democratic principles, as Richard Rorty (1999) laments:

> The whole point of America was that it was going to be the world's first classless society. It was going to be a place where janitors, executives, professors, nurses, and sales clerks would look each other in the eye, and respect each other as fellow citizens. It was going to be a place where their kids all went to the same schools, and where they got the same treatment from the police and the courts. (p. 33)

As public figures and authors, Post and Dewey share much in common, including their commitment to a democratic society, belief in the power of community, and understanding of how learning occurs through practice, modeling, and motivation. While Post's somewhat half-hearted dedication to equality may certainly be critiqued by post-colonial theory as an assimilationist effort, her dedication toward the ideals of democracy seem sincere. On the other hand, Dewey's idea of democracy is less externally imposed and more organic and community-based than Post's. We can argue that Dewey's commitment is more authentic and closer to an ideal. Yet both authors demonstrate their confidence in the human spirit and its potential to work toward common democratic ideals, albeit through different methods and media. While Emily Post can be accused of an elitism that would likely offend John Dewey, and while Post's concerns for etiquette may be considered by many to be frivolous, we contend that the structural underpinnings of democracy can be seen very clearly through each of these authors and that an understanding of the early 20th century, a time of great change and instability in the world, can be helpful in understanding how our current ideals of democracy and freedom have evolved and might be sustained by our methods of introducing students to rhetorical and grammatical structures of language.

REFERENCES

Achebe, C. (1989). The truth of fiction. In *Hopes and impediments: Selected essays* (pp. 138-153). New York: Anchor.

Apple, M. (2003). *The state and the politics of knowledge*. New York: Routledge.

Barthes, R. (1975). *The pleasures of the text*. R. Miller, trans. New York: Hill and Wang.

Bruner, J. (1996). *The culture of education*. Cambridge, MA: Harvard University Press.

Butler, J. (2004). *Undoing gender*. New York: Routledge.

Dawkins, J. (1995). Teaching punctuation as a rhetorical tool. *College Composition and Communication, 46(4)*, 533-548.

Dewey, J. (1990a). *The school and society*. Chicago: The University of Chicago Press. (Original published in 1900)

---. (1990b). *The child and the curriculum*. Chicago: The University of Chicago Press. (Original published 1902)

---. (1897). My pedagogic creed. Retrieved from http://www. in fed. org/archives/e-texts/e-dew-pc.htm

---. (1997). *Democracy and education*. New York: The Free Press. (Original published in 1916)

---. (1997). *Experience and education*. New York: Touchstone. (Original published in 1938)

---. (1976). *The middle works of John Dewey, 1899-1924, Vol 1, 1899-1901*. In Boydston (Ed.), Edwardsville, Il: Southern Illinois University Press.

Dewey, J. (1991). Creative democracy: The task before us. In J. A. Boydston and R. W. Sleeper (Eds.), *John Dewey: The later works, 1925-1953, 1939-1941, essays, reviews, and miscellany, vol. 14* (pp. 227-233). Carbondale, IL: Southern Illinois University Press. (Original published in 1939)

Diaz, H. R. (2003). On the questionable utility of grammar: A viewpoint. *Lit. lingüíst.* Retrieved from http://redalyc.uaemex.mx/redalyc/pdf/352/35201411.pdf

Elbousty, Y., & Bratt, K. (in press). Team strategies for school improvement: The ongoing development of the professional learning community. *MASCD perspectives*.

Gadamer, H. G. (1976). *Philosophical hermeneutics*. Trans. David E. Linge. Berkeley: U California Press.

Gee, J. (1987). What is literacy? *Teaching and learning. Journal of Natural Inquiry, 2(1)*, 3-11.

Goffman, E. (1959). *The presentation of self in everyday life*. Garden City, NY: Doubleday.

Graff, G., and Birkenstein, C. (2006). *They say, I say: The moves that matter in academic writing*. New York: Norton.

Huebner, D. (1999). *The lure of the transcendent: Collected essays by Dwayne E. Huebner*. Mahwah, NJ: Lawrence Erlbaum.

Jackson, P. (1998). John Dewey's school and society revisited. *Elementary School Journal, 98(5)*, 415-426.

Kendall, F. E. (2006). *Understanding white privilege: Creating pathways to authentic relationships across race*. New York: Routledge.

Konrad, D. C., & Adelman, P. B. (2000). *The grammar handbook*. Good Year Books.

Lather, P. A. (1991). *Getting smart: Feminist research and pedagogy with/in the postmodern.* New York: Routledge.

Lorde, A. (1999). The master's tools will never dismantle the master's house. In C. Lemert (Ed.), *Social theory: The multicultural and classic readings (2nd ed.)* (pp. 446-449). Boulder, CO: Westview Press.

McCarthy, L. (1994). Stranger in strange lands: A college student writing across the curriculum. In C. Bazerman and D. R. Russell (Eds.), *Landmark essays on writing across the curriculum* (pp. 125-155). Davis: Hermagoras.

Mutnick, D. (1996). *Writing in an alien world: Basic writing and the struggle for equality in higher education.* New York: Boynton.

Nietzsche, F. (2004). *Twilight of the idols and Antichrist.* Philosophical Classics. New York: Dover. (Original published in 1889)

O'Grady, W., Archibald, J., Aronoff, M., & Rees-Miller, J. (2009). *Contemporary linguistics: An introduction* (6th ed.). New York: Bedford.

Peters, R. (1977). *John Dewey reconsidered.* London: Routledge.

Post, E. (1922). Etiquette in society, in business, in politics and at home. Retrieved from http://www.bartleby.com/95/.

Raines, A. (1998). *How English works: A grammar handbook with readings.* Cambridge: Cambridge University Press.

Romano, R. (2006). Revisiting education and our present social problems: What would Dewey say today? *Teacher Education and Practice, 19(4),* 502-512.

Rorty, R. (1999). *Philosophy and social hope.* New York: Penguin.

Rosenblatt, L. (2005). *Toward a cultural approach to literature. Making meaning with texts: Selected essays.* Portsmouth, NH: Heinemann.

Shaughnessy, M. P. (1977). *Errors and expectations: A guide for the teacher of basic writing.* New York: Oxford UP.

Shoup, K., & Loberger, G. (2009). *Webster's new world English grammar handbook.* Hoboken, NJ: Wiley.

Spivak, G. C. (1996). Bonding in difference: Interview with Alfred Arteaga. In D. Landry and G. M. MacLean (Eds.), *The Spivak reader: Selected works of Gayatri Chakravorty Spivak* (pp. 15-28). New York: Routledge.

Strunk, W., & White, E. B. (2008). *The elements of style.* New York: Penguin.

Swartz, O., Campbell, K., & Pestana, C. (2009). *Neo-pragmatism, communication, and the culture of creative democracy.* New York: Peter Lang.

Tiles, J. E. (1992). *John Dewey: Critical assessments.* London: Taylor & Francis.

---. (1992). *John Dewey: Political theory and social practice.* London: Taylor and Francis.

Thiong'o, N. W. (1994). *Moving the center: The struggle for cultural freedoms.* Portsmouth, NH: Heinemann.

Toulmin, S. E. (2003). *The uses of argument.* Cambridge: Cambridge UP.

Wang, J. (2009). Reconstructing Deweyan democratic education for a globalizing world. *Educational Theory, 59(4),* 409-425.

Zinn, H. (2002). *Disobedience and democracy: Nine fallacies of law and order.* Cambridge, MA: South End Press. (Original published in 1968)

CHAPTER 10

Discourses that Shape Public Understanding and Use of Electronic Voting
Technology: A Deweyan Perspective

Janet L. Evans
Regis University

Voting is a fundamental communicative practice that even young children
understand and embrace as a means to express structure and understanding.
From counting raised hands or paper ballots to listening for the "ayes" and
"nays," voting as an act of communication is something easily understood and
rightfully conjoined with ideals of democracy and freedom. Yet, although voting
as an ideal is a simple communicative act, the United States voting process itself
is a highly complex subject that is also a deeply embedded cultural practice
revered and mythologized in our culture. By examining some of the
technological underpinnings needed to cast a vote, I help readers of this chapter
broaden their understanding of the unequal relationships and struggles for
control that potentially subverts the American democratic voting process. In so
doing, I expand on John Dewey's vision for "creative democracy" (Dewey,
1939/1993) by heightening awareness of the ways in which discourses about
American citizenship and democracy shape public understanding and use of
electronic voting technology.

Dewey (1939/1993) envisioned an United States democracy anchored in the
fundamentals of human equality and fueled by individual human attitudes, traits,
and dispositions. He noted that "democracy is a personal way of individual life"
(p. 242). For Dewey, democracy is achieved by "a working faith in the
possibilities of human nature" (p. 242). Omar Swartz, Katia Campbell, and
Christina Pestana (2009) expand on this concept, explaining that a creative
democracy is one where "individuals are most effective as citizens when they see
democracy as a personal responsibility and as a way of life, comprehending the

ways in which communication is critical in claiming one's power to direct individual and social change" (p. 43). Citizens claim responsibility and communicate their democratic preferences through the act of voting.

As Dewey himself was aware, the lure of American democracy is intoxicating to its citizenry. Certainly, the dreams of democratic ideals are embedded in our narratives of cherished values, such as freedom of speech and the right to vote. As noted more recently by Andrew Gumbel (2005), "Nobody goes far in American public life without professing to love democracy. It is the closest thing the country has to an established religion; disavow democracy, and you might as well disavow America itself" (p. 27). Ironically, considering the lure of democracy and voting as a means of communicative expression, voter turnout in the United States has often been weak in comparison with other democracies in the world (Piven & Cloward, 2000). As Dewey noted decades ago:

> Skepticism regarding the efficacy of voting is openly expressed, not only in the theories of intellectuals, but in the words of lowbrow masses: "What difference does it make whether I vote or not? Things go on just the same anyway. My vote never changes anything." Those somewhat more reflective add: "It is nothing but a fight between the ins and the outs." (1946, p. 118)

In his reflection on Dewey's political philosophy, Terry Hoy (1998) explains that American democracy was born in the community ritual known as the "town meeting" where more humdrum communal issues about roads and schools were oftem the primary topics of discussion. Hoy recognizes the role of modern technology which has created new associations at the sacrifice of those latter day face-to-face community activities. Lacking that all important face-to-face exchange of ideas can often result in citizen confusion and voter uncertainty. "Widely shared is the view that voting is of little consequence and that the only difference made by an election is 'who gets the jobs, draws the salaries and shakes down the plum tree'" (pp. 102-3).

Beyond issues of voter apathy or uncertainty lie deeper issues that link voter disenfranchisement as a reason for nonvoting. On the surface, many Americans may view our democracy as a model for others, the "gold standard" even. Our leadership with some regularity, asserts that the United States is in the forefront with respect to democratic forms of government. How ironic then, as Piven and Cloward (2000) contend, is the fact that "the United States is the only major democratic nation in which the less-well-off, as well as the young and minorities, are substantially underrepresented in the electorate. Only about half of the eligible population votes in Presidential elections" (p. 3). As explained in the introduction to this chapter, Dewey envisioned democracy as a "way of life." Engaged participation is essential. Yet, there are problems with this engaged participation by every citizen. As Swartz et al (2009) summarize, "civic engagement requires time, a minimum level of education, and material resources -- all things that the poor often do not have in surplus due to their marginalized economic, educational and social status" (p. 99).

Although the results of the historic 2008 election may signal a new turning point in voter diversity and turnout, there are still lingering and troubling issues related to discrimination and citizen rights. In Florida, for example, felons and ex-felons are not allowed to vote. Further, African-American men are imprisoned far in excess of their representative numbers within the Florida population:

> A staggering one in three black Floridian men has a criminal record -- and because Florida is one of just seven states that denies felons the automatic restoration of their voting rights once they have completed their sentences . . . between four hundred thousand and six hundred thousand adults in Florida have lost their suffrage rights because of criminal history. (Gumbel, 2005, p. 47)

Further, Gumbel notes, African Americans have a tendency to support the Democratic candidates by a margin of nine-to-one. This creates a significant imbalance in citizen participation. Once felons have "paid their debt to society," why can they not have their suffrage rights reinstated? Looking at just Florida alone, four to six hundred thousand votes is a large voice of the population to silence. For Dewey, equal participation is not only expected, but vital to individual development. As James Campbell (1995) explains, quoting Dewey, "If one is to be a 'spectator' rather than a 'participant' . . . . that person will assume the attitude of 'a man in a prison cell watching the rain out the window; it is all the same to him'" (p. 180). In the case of Florida ex-felons, they remain in a "prison cell" with respect to their voting rights and the ability to participate in the election process.

The comments of Dewey and other spotlight this key issue with the American voting process: participation or the lack thereof. Voting has long been a site of struggle between different groups, the "ins and outs" (Dewey, 1946, p. 118) trying to control its form and process. The advent of modern technology has merely changed the platform upon which these struggles continue. In this chapter, I argue that the development and use of electronic voting technology forms a symbolic site of struggle between persons attempting to establish the legitimacy and authority of their preferred narratives regarding how that technology should be designed and used.

This politicized struggle over electronic voting technology ignited after the controversial 2000 Presidential election. The infamous "butterfly" ballot design used in the Florida election led to voter confusion about which Presidential candidate was receiving their punched vote. The subsequent recount focused on issues surrounding the ballot design and "dangling chads." "Chad" is a term used to refer to the piece of paper that is incompletely punched out of the paper ballot and still clings to the ballot in one of several ways. A "dangling chad" would be a piece of paper that is dangling by one corner (Jones, 2002, p. 2).

The contentious issues surrounding the 2000 Presidential election have caused "dangling chad" to become a common term and heightened public awareness about electronic voting technology and voter disenfranchisement issues. The spotlight widened to encompass the 2004 Presidential election which was marred by problems with voting machine access, especially in Ohio (a pivotal state in that election) where voters from poorer precincts often had to wait hours to access voting machinery while more elite precincts were able to vote more quickly on that cold, rainy night in November. Further, new electronic voting machinery deployed after the 2000 Presidential election was the center of a swirling controversy of accusations and rebuttals regarding the accuracy of the voting equipment.

Since these fateful elections, the institution of voting and electronic voting technology has been increasingly scrutinized. In light of the problems associated with the 2000 and 2004 Presidential elections, many citizens might express the growing impression, developed by popular media and partisan political discourse, that something is terribly wrong with the voting process, and that technological innovation has only made it more difficult to detect fraud, corruption and failure. As Robert Westbrook (1991) highlights in his discussion of Dewey, regarding government by the people, it may be impossible to determine "whether or not the public possessed the necessary intelligence, for even the most brilliant of citizens faltered in the absence of adequate information on which to base judgments" (p. 312). This chapter is designed to provide "adequate information" to aid the reader in building a better understanding of the complex voting process and the role of electronic voting technology.

Considering these concerns, this chapter explores the questions: How well is electronic voting serving democracy? How could the development and use of electronic voting technology be reconfigured to achieve different goals? What communicative strategies need to be redesigned to achieve these different goals? To situate these questions contextually, I provide a brief explanation of the American voting system followed by the two key sections of this chapter, what I call the "Politics of Technology" and the "Technology of Politics."

The American Voting System

The use of electronic voting technology intersects with policies and practices that determine how election votes from local precincts are tallied to form the contents of a national registry which determines that election's outcome. The process is remarkably convoluted. Douglas W. Jones (2003) has an extensive collection of voting resources, commentary, tutorials and web links that can be used to gain a broad understanding of the American voting process and to help the reader sort through some of these complexities. It is one place to start unraveling this complex process and where I first began my own research into the American voting process.

Jones, a University of Iowa computer science professor who also has lengthy experience examining voting machine encryption processes (Gumbel, 2005), is a member of the National Science Foundation-funded center known as ACCURATE which is an acronym for "A Center for Correct, Usable, Reliable,

Auditable, and Transparent Elections" (ACCURATE, 2009, ¶1). In 2006, I also had the opportunity to visit a special voting exhibition at the Smithsonian. At this exhibit I came face-to-face with the infamous "butterfly" ballot displayed in the actual voting machine. I could easily see the false bottom of an old wooden ballot box and checked out the over-sized and old fashioned lever voting machines. In short, I became enamored by the machinery of voting. A growing understanding of the many examples of voter disenfranchisement cemented my interest in electronic voting technology.

Consider how the rapidly changing technology of our society cannot always keep pace with the instruments of bureaucracy which organize them nor with our own ethical analysis regarding what is the appropriate use of technology in our society and who is best served by that technology. Electronic voting technology is an exemplar of this problem. As Gumbel notes, despite "the technical changes of recent decades, America remains beset by a patchwork of electoral rules and practices that can vary wildly from state to state and from county to county" (2005, p. 8).

The U.S. Constitution provides states with the freedom to set their own election laws, such as those governing special elections. Special elections often shine a bright media spotlight on the state involved. Consider the recent and notable special election of Scott Brown (Republican) as the new senator from Massachusets replacing the late Senator Ted Kennedy (Democrat). This was a highly publicized electoral event. Likewise, Hawaii is receiving some unwanted publicity as it struggles to find funding for a special election to elect a replacement for U.S. Representative Neil Abercrombie. In this situation, there are limited funds in Hawaii's budget and no contracts in place for voting machinery (Gima, 2010). Funds for a special election have been found and requests for an emergency appropriation are underway (Associated Press, 2010, ¶2). This Hawaii special election will likely be a highly publicized event scheduled for May 1, 2010, as "it will be a "winner-takes-all" format, meaning it's an open race without a primary and with no runoff -- the candidate with a plurality of votes wins" which could provide a needed edge for Republicans seeking to overtake a heavily Democratic Congress (Miller, 2009, ¶2).

City or county election officials are tasked not only with registering voters, counting votes, communicating vote tallies to states and on to national levels, but also with selecting voting machinery (for which currently, there is no national standard) and designing ballots (in which much leeway is allowed). Latitude in state and city ballot design is exemplified by the infamous Florida "butterfly" ballot design used in that state's 2000 Presidential election (Wayne and Traugott, n.d., n.p.).

For example, local choice of voting machines is generally open, and may well be determined by the prosperity of the voting precincts or by partisan election officials. During 2004, the Ohio Secretary of State, J. Kenneth Blackwell, who was responsible for distributing the voting equipment to various precincts, was also the co-chair of the Bush-Cheney campaign in Ohio. Later in this chapter I will discuss the congressional report which examined discrepancies with the 2004 Ohio election, but for now consider this one example of voter disenfranchisement.

As Mark Crispin Miller (2005) explains, the setting is Kenyon College in Gambier, Ohio, where two voting machines have been reserved for an estimated 1,300 possible voters. It does not take much imagination to consider the chaos that ensued at that voting precinct. Was this an issue of resources or inadequate information? No, it was not. Election officials were aware of the outpouring of late voter registrations -- a clear signal that voter turnout could be high. Further, in Franklin County, nearly 125 voting machines were left in storage despite analyses which predicted that the county needed more machines for this election. On Presidential election night 2004, voters in some precincts stood in line in the rain for hours. It is not surprising then, that some voters did not vote at all. "In contrast, at nearby Mt. Vernon Nazarene University, which is considered more Republican leaning, there were ample voting machines and no lines" (p. 41).

According to the Election Data Services 2008 Voting Equipment Study (2008) there are an astounding 10,071 government units or entities that share responsibility for national elections. The county of Los Angeles is the largest with 4 million registered voters while there are two towns (one in Maine and one in Minnesota) which only have two registered voters. According to this 2008 study, the election process occurs within 3,117 counties with 183,430 precincts. In addition, there are six New England states that administer elections at the city or township level, adding up to 1,549 additional voting administration sites. Further, in three upper Midwest states a mind-boggling 5,405 local governments are responsible for voting equipment purchases for those three states (p. 6).

The precipitous 2000 Presidential election and dangling chad fiasco in Florida, spurred legislation in the form of the *Help America Vote Act of 2002* (HAVA) which infused $3 billion dollars into the process to help eliminate punch card and lever operated voting machines. The second most popular system of voting in 2008 was *Direct Record Electronic* (DRE) systems available to 32% of registered voters or about 55 million people. The majority, or 56% of registered voters (about 95 million people), would be able to vote using paper ballots that would be optically scanned for counting (Election Data Services, 2008, p. 3).

Contrary to Piven and Cloward's (2000) comments about problems with voter turnout, the 2008 Presidential election showed an increase in reported voters and in diversity, as noted previously. Approximately 131 million people reported voting which represents an increase of 5 million voters since the 2004 election, according to data recently released by the U.S. Census Bureau. Of the 5 million new reported voters, 2 million were black, 2 million were Hispanic, and approximately 600,000 were Asian voters while the change in non-Hispanic white voters was not statistically significant in change (Edwards, 2009, p. 1).

With this brief introduction to some important features of the American voting process, I now develop two strands of thought -- the *politics of technology* and the *technology of politics* -- which highlight the role of discourses about American citizenship and democracy in shaping public understanding and use of electronic voting technology. The technology of politics section will spotlight a few recent voting controversies.

The Politics of Technology

Consider the simple terms themselves: "politics" and "technology." We use these terms all of the time but what do they really mean? Langdon Winner's (1986) evocative definition of politics as "arrangements of power and authority in human associations as well as the activities that take place within these arrangements" (p. 22) well fits the scope of this chapter. This definition suggests key objects and relationships for a critical analysis, including those between people, power, events, institutions, artifacts, associations, practices, and the possibility for change. In the conclusion of this chapter I will explore possibilities for change with regards to electronic voting technology.

Regarding the second term, technology, public understanding has often been limited by definitions of technology that emphasize its "thingness" as a material object with given boundaries, functions, and limitations (Slack & Wise, 2005). Jennifer Daryl Slack and J. MacGregor Wise present several useful definitions that "point to flows, connections, and interpenetrations among the living, the nonliving, producers, users, processes [and] possibilities" (p. 97). Winner (1986) simply calls technologies "forms of life." As he elaborates, the term "technology is "understood to mean all of modern practical artifice" (p. 22). These definitions of technology broaden the traditional definition of "technology" beyond objective and material artifacts to encompass broader social and cultural structures and practices surrounding the human development of tools and systems. Finally, consider Winner's (1986) declaration that artifacts have politics and then one can better appreciate how the potential use of a technology is mediated by the interests and agendas of its audiences and users, i.e., creating a politicization of technology.[1]

Slack and Wise (2005) suggest a "technological cultural" approach to understanding the politics of technology. Specifically, to "raise the question of the politics of technology opens the door to challenge the complex assemblage within which much about technology and culture might be changed, which threatens the institutions and structures of everyday life" (p. 175). Slack and Wise refer to the mediated forms of consequential association that occur among humans, and also in technology development between humans and non-human artifacts, as "a *politics of technology.*" For them, this phrase encompasses "the making and unmaking of . . . connections, the arrangement of actors, and the articulation of possibilities" (p. 174).

Innovative new technologies are frequently heralded as "saviors." Indeed as Winner noted, there is "a long lineage of boosters" trumpeting the "biggest and best" that science has to offer us (1986, p. 20). The only distinction since the 1980's is that bigger is not necessarily better any more. Now, smaller technology, packaged in individually customized forms (frequently manufactured in socially acceptable colors, such as pink for breast cancer supporters) conveys a sense of urgency to citizens to always own the newest technology. Our culture has created the socially accepted label "toys" to signify the purchase of the latest technological device. This is an interesting reflection upon the discourse we use to label new technology -- it is a plaything for consumption and easy disposal, when a newer device comes along. Constantly upgrading technological devices, called "buying new toys," has become a socially acceptable process.

Technology is energized by the mythology of efficiency and progress; it resonates with the mythology of democratic progress as well. Yet, if technology were the fuel of progress, then one might expect the voting public to be re-invigorated using new technology to become better informed about public issues, to use new media to engage in civic groups and to flock to the polls. Sadly, such theories of mobilization appear flawed (Howard, 2003). These myths of efficiency and progress feed on each other, but there is also an underlying irony to this storytelling. Innovative new technologies while touted as helpful to the disenfranchised voter -- say, a bilingual voting machine -- are not necessarily targeted for the disenfranchised minority and poor voter. The harsh reality may be that vulnerable populations appear to become even more vulnerable as new voting technologies are adopted by elite voting precincts.

When the American citizenry develop an unconscious public faith about new technology then they succumb to fundamental communicative fallacies such as the belief that "progress is inevitable," "efficiency is better," and "science is rational." Arnold Pacey (1992) argues that these fallacies serve a political economy: "When people think that the development of technology follows a smooth path of advance predetermined by the logic of science and technique, they are more willing to accept the advice of 'experts' and less likely to expect public participation in decisions about technology policy" (p. 26).

When discussing technological change, it is common to depict the processes as a unilinear, irreversible, chronological progression of increasing technical complexity. As Pacey (1992) notes, this unilinear focus reduces an actual, complex and crowded "freeway" of cause and effect relations between systemic elements into a "one-way road" in which technological change appears inescapable and rational. Subsequently, we accept the "inflexible logic" of this change as an expression of technology's inherent affiliation with society (p. 24). This endless march of innovative new technologies frequently feeds, for example, our stories about increased workplace efficiency and is typically packaged under the label "progress."

Through these communicative fallacies, electronic voting technology is typically viewed as "civilized." Its development and use is entwined with our dominant democratic narratives of our identity as a nation which hides the fact that technological change is often not democratic at all; it is more unilateral or top-down in its deployment by political and economic elites (Slack & Wise, 2005). Yet, "when people are willing to believe that technology drives progress and that technological change is inevitable and good, people are more willing to accept the advice of experts, that is, the technologists who claim to know how technological change is accomplished" (p. 23).

Thus, it should be no surprise that the technological change after the 2000 Presidential election was a dramatic shift to electronic voting machinery, including one popular voting machine called the Diebold Accu-Vote TS described later in this chapter. The advice of experts, such as those at Diebold Corporation, influenced voting precinct administrators flush with HAVA funding.[2] Citizen expectations can literally be "wired" to passively accept this "received view" of technology (Slack & Wise, 2005). When citizens are encouraged to accept rapidly changing technologies, it is easy to see how the contradiction of unilateral technological change can progress to something acceptable (Slack & Wise, 2005, p. 23).

It is important not to lose sight of the important role of communication in explaining how citizens get "wired" to accept technological change. Consider the ground-breaking work of Marvin (1988) who studied the invention of electricity and modern American life. According to Marvin, electronically transformed "communication thus offers a keenly focused view of the process of social adjustment around new technology, which is an occasion for introducing new roles and procedures around unaccustomed artifacts to bring them within the matrix of social knowledge and disposition" (p. 233). In our case, the "unaccustomed artifacts" are electronic voting machinery. Relatedly, James W. Chesebro and Dale A. Bertelsen (1996) elaborate upon the important function of electricity and electronic technology as well, suggesting that critics should look for trends in the way humans "value" new technologies, rate them or appraise their worth. In other words, "Because electricity acts as a central component in the development of new technologies, telecommunications and interactive technologies literally share an 'epistemological zone' where cultural knowledge, values, and identities are shaped and preserved" (p. 136).

In this section, I have discussed the politicization of technology which is marked by the persistence of certain cultural narratives which limit critical insights into the complex inter-relationships of people and technology. Next we turn to the technology of politics section which will spotlight two recent voting controversies.

The Technology of Politics

The intersection of American politics and technology is marked by the persistence of certain cultural narratives which limit critical insights into the complex inter-relationships of people and technology. As I have discussed previously, Americans may hold simplistic, even romantic, narratives of American democracy while other groups of voters have experienced a long history of disenfranchisement and struggle as they seek to exercise their right to vote. From a Deweyan perspective, this disenfranchisement is oppositional to the goals of individuals embracing democracy as a "way of life" (Dewey, 1993). Rather than struggles for control, Dewey envisions a "cooperative undertaking" that gives "differences a chance to show themselves because of the belief that the expression of difference is not only a right of the other persons but is a means of enriching one's own life-experience" (1993, p. 244). Note how well Dewey's vision fits with the ideal of voting -- voting is an expression of differing preferences allowed as an individual right of the citizenry. Unfortunately, that "ideal" is not the "real" state of affairs. Certain voters are still disenfranchised at the polls and technological artifacts surround and shape this condition of voter disenfranchisement. Although, the reader does need to recognize that voters can be disenfranchised in many other ways than via the voting machinery itself, such as problems encountered with voter registration, polling place misinformation, complex ballots and so forth.

As discussed by Pacey (1992), Slack and Wise (2005) in the previous section, new technologies, such as electronic voting equipment, are often presented to the public as *the* answer to their problems with the added boon that machines are not subject to human error. An early example of electronic voting technology is cited by Michael Schudson (1998) who writes that mechanical voting machines were first used in New York in 1892 followed by increasing use by states at the turn of the century. In 1910, the American Voting Machine Company, in a prospectus announcing an issue of capital stock, wrote of its voting machines, "They're almost human in accomplishment and mechanically infallible as to mistakes" (p. 174). This quote exemplifies cultural rhetoric which maintains and promotes electronic voting machines as "a cold piece of machinery" capable of keeping secrets but incapable of committing fraud. The slightly mixed metaphor is that this voting machine is a machine, yet it has human-like qualities minus the error prone ways of a human. In the next section, I more closely examine one specific voting machine that did have some error prone ways.

Diebold Electronic Voting Machine Controversy

Throughout American voting history, there are numerous examples of voting controversy and fraud (Piven & Cloward, 2000; Gumbel, 2005). In this section, I focus upon a recent voting controversy to highlight the communication strategies of technology "experts" -- Diebold Corporation, and their widely-used electronic voting machine: the Diebold AccuVote-TS.[3] In the years following the 2000 Presidential election debacle, Diebold rose to dominance as a voting machine purveyor. At the Diebold Election Systems website, during this period, Diebold declared itself to be "the world's leading voting solutions provider," a company that "provides the financial stability, substantial manufacturing capacity, world-wide service network and proven election expertise needed for your long term election system solution."[4] As the world's leading purveyor of electronic voting technology, Diebold evoked the voice of the "expert."

For example, the phrase "leading voting solutions provider" is an interesting "signifier" (duGay, Hall, Janes, Mackay and Negus, 1997, p. 13). This is a communicative strategy that implies meaning by association. First, Diebold is the self-proclaimed leader, and not just a major contender. Second, online voting technology is called "voting solutions" so that Diebold is represented as a solution to any problems that election officials may encounter with dangling chads or old-fashioned manual voting machines. This is an interesting representation -- a reminder that outdated manual, voting machines with dangling chads did not count every vote properly. The voice of the expert (Diebold) smoothes away any concerns about the new technology, in this case electronic voting technology, and makes the introduction of the new voting machines seem natural and inevitable. The naturalization of voting equipment is done via "signification," that is, creating culture-based significance via the language used.

The *Help Americans Vote Act of 2002* (HAVA) became a windfall for voting machine purveyors, such as Diebold. In the years following HAVA, Diebold received millions of dollars in sales from states given the power (and needed financial support) to purchase new electronic voting technology and remove old voting equipment, such as that which lead to the dangling chad controversy in Florida's 2000 Presidential election.[5] HAVA was a "gravy train" for voting machine purveyors and Diebold jumped on board.

Relevant to understanding this section requires a short foray into the area of paperless balloting, or the material "silence" of the voting machine as signified by the lack of paper. When electronic voting machines were considered faulty, many voters clamored for the perceived safety of a paper ballot or chose to use absentee ballots. An example of this behavior chronicled in the newspaper, *USA Today*, is provided later in this section. A paper ballot constitutes an archival act of communication, and is seen by voters as validation that their vote has been counted. In a way, the desire for a paper ballot has been like a backwards step on the rapid, linear progression of electronic voting technology. Electronic technology has failed us, voters might have said, but I can hold a piece of paper and a piece of paper can be counted by humans. Let us examine how this fascinating reversal in thinking occurred, using our example with the Diebold Corporation Accu-Vote TS voting machine.[6]

In the early deployment of the Accu-Vote machine, paper balloting was not a significant issue. Indeed, the lack of paper ballots could have been seen as a positive contribution toward dealing with the paper ballot dangling chad issue of the 2000 Florida Presidential election. Using the voice of the expert, Diebold used statistics and authoritative testimony to legitimize their role as the leading purveyor of voting equipment while minimizing or not responding to security issues related to the Accu-Vote. For example, in testimony before the Joint Committee on Ballot Security, Diebold Corporation Director of Marketing, Mark Radke, wasted little time in getting to the point that on the March Super Tuesday 2004 Presidential election, Diebold Election Systems had

> *zero security-related problems* at the more than 55,000 Diebold touch-screen voting stations deployed across the country by election officials; over 9 million voters had the opportunity to use *electronic voting solutions*, including the entire State of Georgia ... almost *130,000 visually impaired men and women* had an opportunity to vote without assistance, *310,000 disabled people* could vote more conveniently because the voting booth could accommodate them; *61,000 new American citizens* had the opportunity to vote on a ballot written in their native language; and *562,000 older Americans* were able to vote easily and intuitively. That's a proof of performance that is strong and irrefutable.[7]

This lengthy passage is an excellent example of how Diebold mastered the voice of the expert to shape and mold perceptions about their voting machines as secure and efficient. This rhetoric about technology exploits the language of efficiency and convenience when discussing the design of new technologies. Note how potentially disenfranchised citizens are actually called out in this testimony. This is an illustration of how citizens can be swayed by culturally-based rhetoric as well as becoming "wired" to expect efficiency and convenience with technology.

At the time this testimony was provided, the concerns with Diebold's Accu-Vote election system had not yet arisen. The voter statistics quoted by Radke relate to citizens who are frequently disenfranchised due to their lower social status. Another status implication is that these groups are not sufficiently sophisticated users of previous voting machines because they could not see them, read them, etc. If these marginalized groups can vote, then they can reclaim lost power in the game of "identity politics." This is a common communicative strategy, to highlight important issues, such as voter access, using the voice of the expert technologist as a means to smooth the transition to, and acceptance of, the new technology.

Consider how Diebold uses the term "solution" as a subtle rhetorical reminder of the many problems caused by previous voting machines, such as the punch card system used in the Florida 2000 Presidential election. The Diebold Accu-Vote is the technological solution of choice now. Older machines with dangling chads were the problem, and technology was proposed as the solution by the voice of the expert, Diebold Corporation. This example of technologically deterministic thinking suggests that all technology woes can be supplanted by new technology. "Scarcely a new invention comes along that someone doesn't proclaim it as the salvation of free society" (Winner, 1986). The voice of the expert guides the transition to this new invention and legitimizes the process.

Unfortunately for Diebold, in early 2000, a determined Washington woman named Bev Harris came across the source code for the Diebold election systems software online and began her campaign against Diebold. This campaign was subsequently popularized on Harris' website, *Black Box Voting: Ballot Tampering in the 21st Century* (Black Box Voting, 2009, n.p.). Harris' developed a popular website, *www.blackboxvoting.org*, named after a term for voting machines -- black boxes -- which describes voting equipment where the operations or source code are kept proprietary or released only to select parties, such as election officials. As Gore Vidal (2005) noted, "for the past few years many of us have been warning about the electronic voting machines, first publicized on the Internet by investigator Bev Harris, for which she was much reviled by the officers of such companies as Diebold, Sequoia, ES&S, Triad" (¶19). Activist Harris was among the first to bring the Diebold electronic voting machines problems into the limelight. In 2003, Harris found Diebold's voting machine source code while searching online. "Soon after, researchers at Johns Hopkins University and Rice

University published a damning critique of Diebold's products, based on an analysis of the software" (McMillan, 2006, p. 1).

In addition to Harris' own critique, popular media amplified the discourse surrounding the Diebold electronic voting equipment problem. Shown below is one example which explains not only the machine malfunctions but also the political machinations of then Diebold CEO, Walden O'Dell:

> Faster than you can say "hanging chad," things went wrong. In early 2003, activists found a version of Diebold's secret software on the Internet. The code had so many security flaws that one group would later post a video of a chimpanzee changing votes. Weeks later, Diebold's then-CEO Walden O'Dell famously wrote to fellow Bush supporters in a fundraising letter that he was committed to "help Ohio deliver its electoral votes to the President." It didn't take long for political activists, many of them already suspicious of the new voting technology, to begin diving through the company's dumpsters and picketing its shareholder meetings. (Quoted in Gimbel, 2006, ¶7)

Although Harris was frequently mentioned in media stories, the issues related to electronic vote tampering were not embraced by the media until early 2006, when an enterprising group of technology experts at Princeton University was able to purchase an Accu-Vote TS that had been used in the Georgia 2004 election and revealed some shamefully easy hacking techniques. In the September 2006 *Technology Review*, Princeton University researchers demonstrated several ways that a Diebold electronic voting machine could, with relative ease, be "hacked" (or, accessed and manipulated by unauthorized users). First, the software that operates the machine can be corrupted by generating and inserting malicious codes into the program. Second, the machine's memory card (the type of memory device used on newer voting machines) can be physically exchanged for a different memory card with new software instructions that would then be automatically installed on the Diebold machine. Memory cards are then placed into a machine that tabulates votes.

Hindsight suggests that Diebold Corporation's move into electronic voting technology has been ill-fated. The former Diebold Corporation CEO, Walden O'Dell, was a major contributor to the Bush re-election campaign. His fund raising letter to fellow Republicans promised to deliver the Ohio votes to Bush; an unfortunate choice of words. Later, California election officials grew concerned about the link between CEO O'Dell and his controversial letter and their own concerns about the Diebold voting equipment reliability and security; O'Dell eventually quit Diebold (Associated Press, 2005, n.p.). Equally damning was the headline which blared "Don't trust vulnerable Diebold voting machines, Use absentee ballots" in a *USA Today* article. "What more do people need to hear or to see or to read to convince them Diebold voting machines simply cannot be trusted?" (Kantor, 2006, p. 1).

For Harris, the electronic voting machine battle continues. An August 2009 post to her web site decries,

> By now, almost all voting machine makes and models have been demonstrably compromised, but election officials continue to defend them, news reporters continue to ask the wrong questions, and even public interest groups seem unable to grasp the real reason they get run 'round the hamster wheel every time they present evidence. (Black Box Voting, 2009, n.p.)

This quote and Harris' website, book and activist work are instances of a subordinate player seeking to change the dominant paradigm about electronic voting technology.

What has happened to the Accu-Vote electronic voting machine and Diebold Corporation? Thinking strategically, Diebold decided a few years back to no longer associate their name with voting machinery and created a subsidiary called Premier Election Solutions which offers the Assure Product Suite 1.2.[8] For three years Diebold had been seeking a buyer for their voting machine business which was recently sold to Election Systems & Software. This sale prompted Senator Charles Schumer, Democrat from New York, to write a letter to the Justice Department antitrust department.

> If this acquisition proceeds, one company could control over three-quarters of the U.S. market for voting systems . . . . Given other factors, including high barriers to entering the market, I am deeply concerned that local governments and taxpayers will not be getting a fair deal because too

much market power will be held in too few hands. (Quoted in Zetter, 2009b, n.p.)

According to *Election Data Systems* (2008, n.p.), 348 of 3,117 counties still use the AccuVote-TS machines and 35 counties use the AccuVote-TSX machine. Interestingly, the Accu-Vote machine still exists now as the OSX model and was recently (August, 6, 2009) certified by the *U. S. Election Assistance Commission* (United States Election Assistance Commission, 2009a, n.p.). The EAC began certifying voting machines in 2007 and has certified 3 machines thus far. All of the certified machines are optical scan or DRE machines. The U.S. Election Assistance Commission (EAC) was established by HAVA and is an

> [i]ndependent, bipartisan commission charged with developing guidance to meet HAVA requirements, adopting voluntary voting system guidelines, and serving as a national clearinghouse of information about election administration. EAC also accredits testing laboratories and certifies voting systems, as well as audits the use of HAVA funds. (United States Election Assistance Commission, 2009b, ¶1)

Interestingly, the EAC recently (October 2009) put out a call for 4 technology experts to serve on the Technical Guidelines Development Committee (TGDC), which will develop updated voting system guidelines. Members of this new committee are screened to ascertain that they have no conflicts of interest, but it appears that some members may have conflicts as described by Zetter:

> Linda Lamone, for example, who is on the committee and is also elections administrator for Maryland's State Board of Elections, was chastised by the governor of Maryland as well as her state ethics commission after it was revealed in 2007 that she *appeared in sales literature for Diebold Election Systems* praising the company's equipment -- equipment that experienced large-scale failure the first time the state used it. (2009, ¶12)

With the recent certification of a new version of the Accu-Vote electronic voting machine, watchdogs such as Harris and others have renewed their efforts to follow the next election closely. The struggle continues between the "ins and outs" (Dewey, 1946) as activist Harris fights to keep the public informed about voting machine irregularities while the HAVA U.S. Election Assistance

Commission appears to be offering a more top down, unilateral and limited choice for the next generation of voting machines deployed. The discourse surrounding the Diebold voting machine controversy exemplifies the culturally embedded discourse of voting and the struggle of key players to control the process. In the next section, we will consider a second controversy surrounding voting machine irregularities and voter disenfranchisement that occurred in Ohio during the 2004 Presidential election.

Ohio 2004 Voting Machine Irregularities and Voter Disenfranchisement

Whether a reader agrees with the outcome of the 2000 Presidential election or not, it was evident that the flaws in the Florida voting process needed fixing. Many voting citizens were dumbstruck by the flawed ballots and apparent inequities in the voting system. Yet, defective voting systems are nothing new. Paul Quirk, James H. Kuklinski, and Philip Habel (2002) explain that even before the 2000 election "few citizens had been aware that a substantial portion of votes for major offices were regularly not counted because citizens marked ballots incorrectly or voting equipment recorded them incorrectly" (p. 3). Indeed, in the state of Illinois where Quirk et al (2002) conducted their study, some precincts had higher rates of miscounted votes than others. Despite various proposed reforms, the authors noted that Illinois voting precincts will still have considerable leeway in responding to these issues in determining which voting system to choose. This is another example of the *technology of politics*, in that autonomy may be compromised by local officials serving as agents of national partisan interests.

Uncanny parallels exist between the situation in Ohio during the 2004 Presidential Election and prior elections where voter disenfranchisement has occurred. This argument is developed in the House Judiciary Committee report, "Preserving Democracy: What Went Wrong in Ohio," which resulted from a 5-week investigation by committee member Democrats. Republican committee members declined to participate. Named the "Conyers Report" after its primary author, ranking House Judiciary Committee member John Conyers, Jr. (D-Michigan), this report documents thousands of complaints filed by citizens and others concerning Ohio election issues that ranged from dirty tricks to election fraud. Miller (2005) cites one particularly compelling example of documented pre-election malfeasance in the Conyers Report: "bureaucratic hijinks aimed at disenfranchising Democrats, the most spectacular result of which is 'a wide discrepancy between the availability of voting machines in more minority, Democratic and urban areas as compared to more Republican, suburban and exurban areas'" (p. 41).

One key charge in the Conyers report alleges the attempts to disenfranchise Democratic voters by senior level election officials such as Ohio Secretary of State, J. Kenneth Blackwell, a Republican. (Recall that Blackwell was also the co-chair of the Bush-Cheney campaign in Ohio.) For example, the report's authors note that voting machines were less available in key Ohio minority and Democratic districts than in Republican suburban areas. Not surprisingly, then, voting in these disenfranchised precincts slowed to a snail's pace. So, what did it matter that Democrats had been enormously successful at registering new voters in this district, if those newly registered voters could not get to precincts or find workable voting machines? To situate this voting problem, let us consider a reasonable time estimate for a typical voter to cast his or her vote. Recall the earlier example of Kenyon College: in that case, there were two voting machines available for thirteen hundred voters (Gumbel, 2005). "Assuming each voter took just three minutes to complete his or her ballot, it would still take more than thirty hours to get through everyone. Some Kenyon students said they had to stand in line for ten hours" (Gumbel, p. 291).

If only a few machines are allocated to a given precinct, then clearly long lines develop. This problem of machine access translated to extremely long voter lines in certain districts of Columbus, Ohio in 2004. Here is how Representative Conyers described the situation when the Conyers Report was discussed in Congress in early 2005:

> Members of the House, we are here today not as partisans for one Presidential candidate or another, but because we want to do our duty under the Constitution to protect our democracy. We are here because of the inner-city voter in Franklin County who waited 10 hours in the pouring rain while suburban voters in the same county had no wait

because election officials decided to reallocate voting machines from Columbus to the suburbs. (Congressional Record, 01/06/05, n.p.)

The Conyers Report documented additional election issues which included reporters being barred from polling places due to an aggressive interpretation of loitering laws, voter registration procedures designed to deny voters access to both polling places and registration logs, distribution of inaccurate polling precinct location information and even distribution of fake voter bulletins urging voters to vote on November 3rd when the actual election would have occurred the day before on Tuesday, November 2nd! (Miller, 2005).

These are startling accusations portrayed by the Conyers report. Certainly contemporary party politics have reached an intense form of polarization, characterized by frequent finger-pointing and brash allegations. Yet, issues such as the Ohio voting machine problems and dirty tricks are not limited to one party. Indeed, U.S. correspondent, Andrew Gumbel (2005), posits that cheating in elections is more closely linked to power and opportunity than any given party doctrine.

In the end, the parties belong to one and the same political culture, which has given them shape and been shaped by them in return -- winning is everything -- the only thing. Studying what partisan groups have in common can often be more fruitful, in fact, than focusing on what divides them (Gumbel, 2005 p. xv). For example, one would expect partisan groups to encourage voter turnout, but that may not necessarily be the case.

Consider that voter turnout has fluctuated throughout history. There was a period in American history when voter turnout was at an all time high. "The reliance of nineteenth-century elites on voter mobilization and counter-mobilization drove electoral turnout to heights never achieved since" (Crenson and Ginsberg, 2002, p. 47). As the authors note, voter turnout exceeded the 90th percentile in the Northern states. Ironically, given the availability of modern technology, the level of voter turnout in the new millennium is comparatively embarrassing, especially for Presidential elections. This is an issue not entirely unnoticed by elites, who may actually achieve their goals *as a direct result* of voter apathy. In this situation, voting by every citizen is not a goal. Instead, rules, red tape, and needless legal maneuvering subvert the voting process with the result that many voters lose interest:

> Rather than take issues to the electorate for resolution, today's contending elites attempt to outdo their opponents by litigating, by manipulating administrative procedures, or by the use of mechanisms like privatization, vouchers, or bureaucratic adjudication that remove policy to arenas beyond the reach of their rivals. (Crenson and Ginsberg, 2002, p. 48)

Matthew A. Crenson and Benjamin Ginsberg (2002) carefully note this historical shift from the *voter with agency* to the *voter who merely observes*, i.e., a passive spectator. The observing (although not necessarily observant) voter in this process becomes an audience of the "politically inert" (p. 50). In the U.S., this is an audience of nonvoters that, at the time, numbered an astonishing 60 million. In contrast, Crenson and Ginsberg observe that Western European voting occurs on weekends and without voter registration requirements -- two practices that appear to boost turnout yet are not even considered in the American political process. Crenson and Ginsberg attribute this neglect of voter agency by American political elites as apprehension concerning the consequences of an expanding number of voters. Since one never knows how 60 million eligible voters will vote, some groups may consider it best to exclude certain voters altogether. As they note, elites "have always been wary of popular participation. The critical difference between today's elites and those of the past is not that politicians have overcome their fear of the dark but that they have found the means to avoid the dark altogether" (2002, p. 52).

Speaking from the perspective of a rhetorical theorist, Gerald Hauser (1999) acknowledges the dilemma thusly: "The price of living in a democracy is that the people have a say in decisions made on their behalf. Democracy raises the possibility that informed and reasoned discussion among the governed will shape the politics and policies under which they live" (p. 272). Note how Hauser's consideration of the "possibility" for democracy guided by "informed and reasoned discussion" links to Dewey's (1993) own philosophy regarding the active role of the citizenry in shaping a "creative democracy." Yet, the sad reality today is that many voters are uninformed, misinformed, and/or apathetic. They do not stay on top of key issues and they are prone to expressing narrow self-interests. Miller (2005) also blames the "servile press" for causing Americans -- both liberal and conservative -- to lose faith in the political system to the extent that they are either unaware of, or too dispirited to protest potential fraud in their midst. The situation has not changed much since Dewey's (1946) prescient comments regarding the "ins and outs."

Even sadder is that some of the voting public -- informed or not -- cannot even get to voting machines to cast a vote, as demonstrated by the examples in Ohio during 2004. It is often the poor who cannot "work the system" to understand voting. Others simply grow tired of its demonstrated hypocrisy or complexity. The stage is set for potential fraudulent activity when citizens are so demoralized and disengaged. Thus, we recognize, from Dewey's perspective, that "a fully developed participatory democracy cannot be actualized within a system that excludes effectively entire classes of people from civic engagement" (Swartz et al, 2009, p. 99). In the concluding section, I discuss my initial questions and examine how American citizens can become engaged and educated.

Conclusion

Responding to the 2000 Presidential election controversy in Florida, the *Help America Vote Act of 2002* (HAVA) authorized $3 billion dollars in spending designed to help eliminate punch card and lever operated voting machines. Millions were spent and thousands of new optical scan DRE voting machines were deployed. Considering this massive expenditure, can we conclude that electronic voting is serving democracy well? The answer is a resounding failure in election years 2000 and 2004 with millions of dollars wasted for electronic voting machines that are no longer used nor trusted. While the 2008 Presidential election was not mired in controversy regarding electronic voting equipment, there is clearly a ways to go to resolve many of the issues raised in this chapter.

Unfortunately, what eventually transpired from the influx of HAVA funds was a raft of problems from voting vulnerability to hackers to machine breakdowns. Recall our examples with the Diebold Corporation voting machinery and the Conyers Report. No wonder worried voters and election officials began to cling nostalgically to the presumed security of paper balloting and to abandon the new electronic voting technology. What happened to all of those new voting machines? An August 2008 Associated Press news story explained that thousands of touch screen voting machines "have been shelved because of doubts about vanishing votes and vulnerability to hackers" (n.p.). According to the AP article, it is a multimillion dollar "high tech junkyard." Ohio, the site of voter disenfranchisement in 2004, cannot even sell its $138 million dollar voting system, to recyclers or others, until lawsuits are settled.

On top of voting machine disposal problems lies another irony. Using paper ballots is expensive. "In 2006, using electronic machines, the statewide primary cost her county [San Bernardino county, California] $2.5 million. In 2008, using paper ballots cost $3.4 million" (Associated Press, 2008, n.p.). So, the HAVA funding for new machines did not solve the problem. Indeed the problem appears to have worsened. The results of the HAVA funding influx has been an appalling and extravagant waste of our limited resources.

So, how could the development and use of electronic voting technology be reconfigured to achieve different goals? What communicative strategies need to be redesigned to achieve these different goals? These are questions not easily answered. The American voting process can succumb to local control dominated by officials with partisan interests. Ballots can be confusing, the lack of paper can be a fearful oversight to many and certain ballots are not even counted be they on paper or electronic sources. Further, the voting process is hampered by constantly changing technology and rules that are inconsistently applied across thousands of independent voting precincts.

Furthering the problem are all of the other voices struggling for dominance in the electronic voting arena. This chapter has described a few: Representative Conyers, Ohio Secretary of State Blackwell, voting activist Bev Harris, the investigative team at Princeton University, Diebold Corporation and Premier Election Solutions executives plus the thousands of election officials and election day volunteers. A final key player, HAVA, is already conducting studies of issues related to uniform applications for voter registration and absentee ballots and is commissioning studies of human voting errors and spoiled ballot reduction. All of these players are engaged in the struggle that surrounds electronic voting technology. Lastly, I have not fully addressed a myriad of other voting issues such as usability, consistency of ballot design, registration and disenfranchisement of certain voters, such as prisoners, nor does it introduce problems with the electoral college process or gerrymandering of districts, all of which feed into the American voting process. This is a deeply complex issue.

As Swartz et al note, a "cornerstone of Dewey's theory of democracy is a high level of participation by citizens in public deliberation and decision making" (2009, p. 98). Presently, certain voters are disenfranchised or intimidated, while others are apathetic, disorganized, polarized or fearful. "The prime difficulty, as we have seen, is that of discovering the means by which a scattered, mobile and manifold public may so recognize itself as to define and express its interests" (Dewey, 1946, p. 146). Indeed, how best can such a "scattered public" find their collective voice to express their needs and solutions? For Dewey (1946) and Swartz et. al (2009), democracy should be a routine practice, something which engages the average citizen. In Dewey's words, the strongest point "to be made in behalf of even such rudimentary political forms as democracy has already attained, popular voting, majority rule and so on, is that to some extent they involve a consultation and discussion which uncover social needs and troubles" (Dewey, 1946, p. 206).

In this chapter, I have embarked on a discussion of social needs and troubles related to electronic voting technology. There will always be so-called "experts" and "elites" to guide the average citizen but I recognize that their interests do not lie with commonly-held interests. Further, "the man who wears the shoe knows best that it pinches and where it pinches, even if the expert shoemaker is the best judge of how the trouble is to be remedied" (Dewey, 1946, p. 207). Like that ill-fitting shoe, electronic voting technology may pinch in another way, considering that the term "pinch" is also slang for "steal." Some authors we have quoted in this chapter are convinced that Presidential elections have been stolen. Citizens have an obligation to understand their point of view and to consider their own moral perspective regarding this complex issue. At a fundamental level citizen voters can perform one simple act -- engage in the act of voting itself and communicate their voices and choices in the democratic process. On a larger scale, all of us can benefit from becoming better educated, to consider and then to communicate our interests regarding voting issues and to do this regularly, not just during the periodic election cycles. This last point is central to Dewey's notion of a "creative democracy" (Dewey, 1993).

Recall Westbrook's (1991) discussion of a Deweyan government by the people where he raises the concern "even the most brilliant of citizens faltered in the absence of adequate information on which to base judgments" (p. 312). In addition to the discussions within this chapter, the opportunities to become better educated (and engaged) abound on the Internet. For example, a government-based website at http://www.usa.gov/Citizen/Topics/Voting.shtml explains voting and elections while www.fec.gov/hava/hava.htm is the HAVA website where a person can learn about voting machine certifications. At http://www.verifiedvotingfoundation.org/ there are links by state to numerous citizen committees, task forces, advocacy groups and so forth which are actively engaged in a wide range of voting issues. Professor Jones' website has extensive links and there are frequent posts to Bev Harris' Black Box voting website. The Conde Nast publication *Wired Magazine* is another online resource for news about voting technology. Unfortunately, the American citizenry all too easily can become the unwitting objects, not subjects, in a voting process controlled by dominant political interests. Hopefully this chapter has helped to clarify some of the powerful ways that discourses about electronic voting technology have shaped public understanding and to encourage reader engagement.

By focusing on voting as an act of communication and a deeply embedded cultural practice, this chapter developed two strands of thought -- the *Politics of Technology* and the *Technology of Politics* -- which highlighted the role of discourses about American citizenship and democracy in shaping public understanding and use of electronic voting technology. At the center of this discussion has been the public, the ordinary citizen, "inchoate" as Dewey (1946) once worried and yet pivotal in shaping the discourse which directs the next steps of electronic voting technology development. In the struggle for control of the form and process of this rapidly changing technology, the citizen has a voice to create change as surely as he or she has an opportunity to vote and have that vote counted in the next election.

REFERENCES

ACCURATE: A Center for Correct, Usable, Reliable, Auditable, and Transparent Elections Retrieved from http://accurate-voting.org/faq/

Associated Press. (2005). *CEO quits embattled Diebold.* Retrieved from http://www. wired. com/techbiz/ media/news/2005/12/69823.

Associated Press. (2008). *States throw out costly voting machines: Some hold out hope that the devices will one day be resurrected.* Retrieved from http://www.msnbc msn. com/ id/26296917/ ns/politics/?default.aspx=previewmode&1

Associated Press. (2010). *Hawaii special election money found.* Retrieved from http://www.hawaiinewsnow.com/global/story.asp?s=11823351.

Black Box Voting. (2009). *Officials trot out specious pro-concealed counting arguments.* Retrieved from www.blackboxvoting.org.

Campbell, J. (1995). *Understanding John Dewey.* Chicago: Open Court.

Chesebro, J. & Bertelsen, D. (1996). *Analyzing media: Communication technologies as symbolic and cognitive systems.* New York: Guilford Press.

Crenson, M. & Ginsberg, B. (2002). *Downsizing democracy: How America sidelined its citizens and privatized its public.* Baltimore: Johns Hopkins University Press.

Dewey, J. (1946). *The public and its problems.* Chicago: Gateway Books.

Dewey, J. (1993). Creative democracy: The task before us. In D. Morris & I. Shapiro (Eds.), *The political writings* (pp. 240-245). Indianapolis, IN: Hackett. (Original published 1939)

duGay, P., Hall, S., Janes, L., Mackay, H. and Negus, K. (1997). *Doing cultural studies: The study of the Sony Walkman.* Thousand Oaks, CA: Sage.

Edwards, T. (2009). Voter turnout increases by 5 million in 2008 presidential election, U.S. census bureau reports: Data show significant increases among Hispanic, Black and Young voters. Retrieved from http://www.census.gov/Press-Release/www/ releases/ archives/voting/013995.html

Election Data Services. (2008). *2008 Voting Equipment Study.* Retrieved from www.electiondataservices.com.

Gima, C. (2010). Official wants special election ASAP. *Star Bulletin.* Retrieved from http://www.starbulletin.com/news/20100105_Official_wants_special_election_ASAP.html.

Gimbel, B. (2006). Rage against the machine: Diebold struggles to bounce back from the controversy surrounding its voting machines. *Fortune Magazine*, 154, 9. Retrieved from http://money.cnn.com/magazines/fortune/fortune _archive/2006/11/13/8393084/index.htm.

Gumbel, A. (2005). *Steal this vote: Dirty elections and the rotten history of democracy in America.* New York: Nation Books.

Hauser, G. (1999). *Vernacular voices: The rhetoric of publics and public spheres.* Columbia, SC: University of South Carolina Press.

Howard, P. (2003). Digitizing the social contract: Producing American political culture in the age of new media. *The Communication Review, 6,* 213-245.

Hoy, T. (1998). *The political philosophy of John Dewey: Towards a constructive renewal.* Westport: Praeger.

Jones, D. (2002). Chad -- From waste product to headline. Retrieved from http://www.cs. uiowa.edu/~jones/cards/chad.html

Jones, D. (2003). A brief illustrated history of voting. Retrieved from http://www. cs.uiowa.edu/~jones/voting/

Kantor, A. (2006). Don't trust vulnerable Diebold voting machines, use absentee ballots. *USA Today.* Retrieved from http://www.usatoday.com/tech/ columnist/andrewkantor/2006-09-29-diebold_x.htm

Marvin, C. (1988). *When old technologies were new: Thinking about electric communication in the late nineteenth century.* New York: Oxford University Press.

McMillan, R. (2006). Diebold source code leaked again: Maryland state legislator receives anonymous disks containing code for electronic voting machines. *InfoWorld.com.* Retrieved from http://www.infoworld.com/d/security-central/diebold-source-code-leaked-again-481.

Miller, M. C. (2005). None dare call it stolen: Ohio, the election, and America's servile press. *Harper's Magazine,* pp. 39-46.

Miller, S. J. (2009). Special election rules give GOP hope. Retrieved from http://thehill.com/homenews/campaign/72183-special-election-rules-in-hawaii-give-hope-to-gop.

Pacey, A. (1992). *The culture of technology.* Cambridge: The MIT Press.

Piven, F. & Cloward, R. (2000). *Why Americans still don't vote and why politicians want it that way.* Boston: Beacon Press.

Quirk, P., Kuklinski, J. & Habel, P. (2002). The machinery of democracy: Voting systems and ballot miscounts in Illinois. *Institute of Government Public Affairs Critical Issues Paper.* Chicago: University of Illinois.

Schudson, M. (1998). *The good citizen: A history of American civic life.* New York: The Free Press

Slack, J. & Wise, J. (2005). *Culture & technology: A primer.* New York: Peter Lang.

Stewart, C. III (2005). Residual vote in the 2004 election. Retrieved from the World Wide Web on 03/19/07 at www.vote.caltech.edu/media/documents /vtp_wp2v2.3.pdf.

Swartz, O., Campbell, K. and Pestana, C. (2009). *Neo-pragmatism, communication, and the culture of creative democracy.* New York: Peter Lang.

United States Election Assistance Commission. (2009a). *EAC Certifies Premier Assure 1.2 Voting System.* Retrieved from http://www.eac.gov/News/press/ eac-certifies-premier-assure-1-2-voting-system/base_view

United States Election Assistance Commission. (2009b). *About the EAC.* Retrieved from http://www.eac.gov/about.

Vidal, G. (2005). Something rotten in Ohio. *The Nation.* Retrieved from the World Wide Web on 04/27/07 at http://www.thenation.com/docprint. mhtml?i=20050627&s=vidal.

Wayne, S. & Traugott, M. (n.d.). Information on the means by which votes are tabulated at the local and state level. Retrieved from http;//usinfo.state.gov/ products/ pubs /election 04/nominate.htm

Westbrook, R. (1991). *John Dewey and American democracy.* Ithaca: Cornell University Press.

Winner, L. (1986). *The whale and the reactor: A search for limits in an age of high technology.* Chicago: University of Chicago Press.

Zetter, K. (2009a). Voting tech experts sought by Feds to develop standards. *Wired Magazine.* Retrieved from http://www.wired.com/threatlevel/2009 /09/voting-tech-experts/

---. (2009b). Senate panel to examine sale of Diebold voting machine division. *Wired Magazine.* Retrieved from http;//www.wired.com/threat level/2009/10/ diebold-antitrust-2/.

---. (2009c). Report: Diebold Voting System Has "Delete" Button for Erasing Audit Logs. Retrieved from http://www.wired.com/threatlevel/2009/03/ ca-report-finds/.

Notes

[1] The two examples highlighted in the next section, "The Technology of Politics," will further explain this mediation.

[2] Sadly, Diebold was embroiled in an electronic voting technology controversy discussed in the next section, the "Technology of Politics."

[3] By way of background, Diebold Corporation is a long, well-established corporation, founded in 1859, that manufactured much more than electronic voting technology. Indeed, Diebold was once more well-known for its bank vault security systems and later, its ATM or automated teller machines. From ATM machines, it was a natural progression into the electronic voting machine technology.

[4] This information was retrieved from a Diebold Corporation website that is no longer in existence on the World Wide Web. A later incarnation of the Diebold Corporation website had the URL http://www.dieboldes.com which now will redirect the reader to http://www.premierelections.com/ for their subsidiary company called Premier Election Solutions.

[5] According to HAVA, "the Commission shall make a requirements payment each year in an amount expressed as a percentage equal to the quotient of the voting age population of the State as reported in the most recent decennial census *and* the total voting age population of the United States as reported in the most recent decennial census." (General Responsibilities (Title II, Subtitle A, Part 1 Sections 202,206, 207 & 209)

[6] The early incarnation of the Diebold Corporation electronic voting machine was called the Accu-Vote TS and is now called the Accu-Vote TSX. The Accu-Vote OS is the Diebold Corporation optical scanner voting machine.

[7] Emphasis added. Retrieved from http://www.diebold.com/dieboldes/testimony. pdf./ This World Wide Web URL is no longer available at the Diebold Corporation website; reference also end note 2.

[8] See http://www.premierelections.com/ as well as end notes 2 and 4.

ABOUT THE EDITOR

Omar Swartz (Ph.D., Purdue University, 1995; J.D., Duke University, 2001, *magna cum laude*) is Director of the Master of Social Science program and an Associate Professor in the Department of Communication at the University of Colorado Denver. His primary areas of research and teaching are persuasion, diversity, philosophy of communication, and mass media law and policy. Specifically, his work focuses on the intersections between the U.S. legal system, the history of social injustice and intellectual intolerance in the United States, and the philosophies of Richard Rorty and Michel Foucault. Dr. Swartz is the author of *Persuasion as a Critical Activity* 2nd edition (2009); *The Rule of Law, Property, and the Violation of Human Rights* (2007); *In Defense of Partisan Criticism* (2005); *The View From* On The Road (1999); *Socialism and Communication* (1999); *The Rise of Rhetoric and its Intersections with Contemporary Critical Thought* (1998); and *Conducting Socially Responsible Research* (1997). He is the co-author of *Neo-Pragmatism, Communication, and the Culture of Creative Democracy* (2009). In addition to the above, Dr. Swartz is the editor of *Transformative Communication Studies* (2008) and *Social Justice and Communication Scholarship* (2006) and has authored more than 90 essays, book chapters, and reviews.

ABOUT THE CONTRIBUTORS

Kirstin Ruth Bratt (Ed.D., Northern Arizona University, 2005), is Assistant Professor of Language Arts and Literacy Education at Penn State University. Her research utilizes phenomenological approaches in the study of language acquisition, children's literature, and kinesthetic needs of learners. She prepares prospective teachers to work with bilingual learners. She is currently co-authoring a book on linguistic policies in Morocco and another on the dialectical nature of self and other. Her publications have appeared in the *Journal of Critical Educational Policy Studies*, *Journal of Children's Literature*, *Proceedings of the Northeastern Educational Research Association*, *ALSC Connect*, *Sargasso*, and *MASCD Perspectives*, as well as in the book *Doing Qualitative Research*.

Margaret Anne Clarke (Ph.D., Liverpool University, 1992) is a Senior Lecturer in Portuguese at the University of Portsmouth, UK. Her teaching and research interests focus on the use of multimedia and digital affordances for language learning, and the role of electronic and digital media in cultural and social networks in Brazil and Latin America. Her book chapters have appeared in *Latin American Cyberliterature and Cyberculture*, *Story Circles: Digital Storytelling Around the World*, and *Save As: Digital Memories*.

Musetta Durkee (M.A., New York University, 2007; J.D., University of California, Berkeley, anticipated 2012) was an intern for the Electronic Privacy Information Center and a research associate for the Knight Commission on the Information Needs of Local Communities in a Democracy. Previously, she has presented at conferences on human rights, subjectivity, community, and the arts and has also published in *Performance Research* and *e-mispherica*. She is currently working on a Note regarding rights to anonymous speech online.

Moulay Youness Elbousty (Ph.D. University of Massachusetts, anticipated 2012) is visiting Assistant Professor in the Middle Eastern and South Asian

Studies at Emory University. He has taught English, French, Spanish, and Arabic in various academic settings, including Al Akhawayn University and Daniel Webster College, and he has conducted many workshops in language teaching pedagogy. He has served as plenary speaker, workshop leader, and presenter at national and international conferences. His research interests include applied linguistics, teaching Arabic to non-native speakers, North African studies, and the Alaouite Dynasty in Morocco. He is currently co-authoring a book on linguistic policies in Morocco.

Janet L. Evans (Ph.D., University of Colorado, 2007) is the Chair for Accounting & Finance, College for Professional Studies, School of Management at Regis University. Janet has over 30 years business experience, primarily in the nonprofit sector, where she recently retired as Manager of Budget Operations at the National Center for Atmospheric Research (NCAR). In 2005-6, Janet was the Sullivan Professor for the John J. Sullivan Endowed Chair for Free Enterprise at Regis University, a program which advocates socially responsible business practices. Janet holds a Colorado CPA license and has been part of Regis University affiliate faculty since 1996, teaching accounting, ethics and communication courses.

Cynthia Gayman (Ph.D., Southern Illinois University, Carbondale, 2000) is Associate Professor and Coordinator of the Philosophy Program in the Department of English and Philosophy at Murray State University, in Murray, Kentucky. Her research focuses on American pragmatism, twentieth century European philosophy, and feminist philosophy. Her work has been published in the *Journal of Speculative Philosophy*, *Metaphilosophy*, *Contemporary Pragmatism*, and in the edited collection *The Relevance of Simone Weil: 100 Years Later*.

Annette M. Holba (Ph.D., Duquesne University, 2005) is an Assistant Professor in the Communication and Media Studies Department at Plymouth State University. Her work focuses around the theoretical integration of communication and leisure studies from a constructive hermeneutic approach. Dr. Holba is the author of *Philosophical Leisure: Recuperative Praxis for Human*

Communication and co-editor of *Philosophies of Communication: Implications for Everyday Experience*, and *Media and the Apocalypse*. Her articles have appeared in *Human Communication*, *Review of Communication*, *World Leisure Journal*, and *The New Hampshire Journal of Education*.

Valerie Palmer-Mehta (Ph.D., Wayne State University, 2002) is an Associate Professor in the Department of Communication and Journalism at Oakland University in Rochester, Michigan. Her current research examines the ethic of care, women's forms of resistance, and the negotiation of power in the media and public discourse. Her work has appeared in *Women's Studies in Communication*, *Text and Performance Quarterly*, and *Journal of American Culture*.

Shane Ralston (Ph.D., University of Ottawa, 2007) is an assistant professor of philosophy in the humanities department at Pennsylvania State University-Hazleton. His research focuses on democratic theory, American philosophy, environmental philosophy, and philosophy of education. He has published in *Transactions of the Charles S. Peirce Society*, *Human Studies*, *Education and Culture*, and the *Review of Policy Research*. He is a past recipient of the William James Prize for the best paper in American Philosophy from the American Philosophical Association-Eastern Division.

Scott R. Stroud (Ph.D., Temple University, 2006) is an Assistant Professor of Communication Studies at the University of Texas at Austin. His research focuses on the intersection of pragmatism, rhetoric, and aesthetics. His work in the fields of philosophy and communication has appeared in such journals as *Philosophy & Rhetoric*, *Western Journal of Communication*, *Journal of Speculative Philosophy*, *Contemporary Pragmatism*, and *Transactions of the Charles S. Peirce Society*.

Margaret Rose Torrell (D.A. St. John's University, 2009) is Coordinator of Writing Programs and Associate Professor of English at the State University of New York, College at Old Westbury, where she teaches courses in disability studies, English literature, and Composition. She has forthcoming book chapters and essays on disability studies, masculinity studies, and critical pedagogy.